Revolutionaries They Could Not Break

The fight for the Fourth International in Indochina 1930-1945

By Ngo Van

Published by Index Books (Indexreach Ltd.)
28 Charlotte Street, London W1P 1HJ

Typeset by Sumner Type, London SE22
Printed by Trade Union Printing Services, Newcastle-upon-Tyne

A C.I.P. catalogue record for this book is available from
the British Library

ISBN: 1-871518-07-5

Revolutionaries They Could Not Break

CONTENTS

To Sophie

INTRODUCTION

The heroes of this book, the workers' leaders in Vietnam who fought under the banner of the Fourth International, all came from the same generation. Nineteen of the 21 people featured in pen-portraits by the author (page 122) were born in a single decade, between 1902 and 1912. The one great event which, more than any other, shaped the world in which they grew up was the Russian revolution of 1917, which was widely seen as the first step of a world socialist revolution.

When the workers' organisations, led by the communists, seized power in Russia, the people whose story is told here were approaching the age when they would begin to sense injustice, to seek the reasons for it and the ways to overcome it. Ta thu Thau and Phan van Chanh were both 11 years old; Ho huu Tuong was seven, Tran van Thach 14, Phan van Hum 15. Most of these future revolutionaries came from families which were very well-off by Vietnamese standards — wealthy enough to allow the sons to have a university education, for which they travelled to France, the imperial power which ruled Indochina. There they discovered the ideas which inspired them for the rest of their lives. Most of those lives were to be tragically short because, as this book explains, to be loyal to communist principles in Vietnam in the mid-1940s was to risk assassination at the hands of those who had usurped the name of communism — the Stalinists.

After the Russian revolution, the second event which influenced the political thinking of the Vietnamese revolutionaries was the defeat of the Chinese revolution of 1925-1927. One of the most convincing weapons in the hands of the French Trotskyists who, in the ensuing years, made recruits among the Vietnamese students, was Trotsky's analysis of the Chinese defeat and his critique of the tactics imposed on the Chinese Communist Party by Moscow.

This introduction describes the Russian and Chinese events. Its purpose is to set the scene for the author's narrative, which begins with the formation both of the Stalinist and of the Trotskyist organisations in Vietnam in the late 1920s.

A workers' government had been established in Paris in 1871, and was crushed by the French bourgeois regime after 71 days, but it was in the Russian revolution of November 1917 that, for the first time, the working class took state power and held on to it. Soviets (that is councils) of workers', soldiers', sailors' and peasants' deputies overthrew a bourgeois government paralysed by economic crisis and its participation in the first world war. The initiative for the seizure of power came from the communists, known until 1918 as 'Bolsheviks' (meaning 'majoritarians', that is the majority faction in a split within the Russian Social Democratic and Labour Party).

From the start, the soviet regime fought for survival against overwhelming odds. No sooner had the communists, under duress, signed a separate peace with Germany than they were plunged into a civil war with the restorationist 'white' generals, who were supported by Britain, France, and the US. As Russia's old Tsarist army disintegrated, a new 'red' army was formed out of it to resist the 'whites'. The civil war was accompanied by economic collapse and a serious famine. The communists emerged victorious because they not only expropriated the capitalists' property in the name of the urban working class, but also encouraged the peasants, the vast majority of the population, to expropriate the landlords.

No one was more surprised by, or more hostile to, the revolution than the social-democratic leaders in western Europe. These leaders, from their positions at the head of parties supported by large trades unions and millions of workers' votes, believed in reformist parliamentarism and class collaboration. They had abandoned the revolutionary content of Karl Marx's ideas. When the first world war broke out on 4 August 1914, the German, French, British and other 'socialist' leaders had declared themselves in favour of their 'own' capitalists' war effort, and the Second International, formed in 1889 to unite all socialists, effectively collapsed. Its revolutionary wing — in which the Russian Bolsheviks were the largest and best-organised force — denounced the social-democratic leaders as traitors, told the workers that 'the main enemy is at home' and called on them to 'turn the imperialist war into civil war'.

The reformist leaders thought the Russian revolution had gone quite far enough in February 1917, when the Tsarist empire collapsed and a bourgeois government was formed, soon to be led by Alexandr Kerensky. The Mensheviks ('minoritarians' in the split), part of the right wing of the International, had a majority in the urban soviets. They gave 'critical support' to the Kerensky government and assumed that Russia would now take the road of capitalist development with a parliamentary democracy.

After the February revolution, even many of the Bolsheviks had seen their immediate future role as the extreme left wing of a bourgeois democracy. The Bolshevik perspective had always been for the working class to take the leadership of a revolution that — because its first tasks were those of agrarian reform, abolition of absolutism, etc. — was bourgeois. But the communist leader, Lenin, returning from exile, denied that these tasks — which he summed up in the slogan 'bread, peace, land' — could be carried out by the bourgeoisie. The bourgeois revolution, he insisted against the initial opposition of his own comrades, had to 'grow over' to a workers' revolution. The soviets had to take power. On this he found complete agreement with Trotsky, who, also returning from exile, soon joined the Bolsheviks.

When they took power, therefore, the communists faced not only armed rebellion by the Tsarists and the bourgeoisie, but also the opposition of the social democracy, including its left wing. Karl Kautsky, the leading theoretician of the Second International, claimed Russia was 'not ready' for working-class power. To revolutionary socialists across the world, however, the communists' success was a supreme inspiration. With state power in their hands, they were able to carry out proposals made during the war to found the Third (Communist) International, or Comintern. Its congresses in Moscow brought together revolutionary workers' leaders from all over the world. It had newspapers, theoretical journals, universities, and organisers, all of which gave impetus to the rapid growth of communist organisations everywhere.

Russia had only taken what its leaders considered to be the first step in an international revolution. 'We have created a soviet type of state and by that ushered in a new era in world history . . . nobody can deprive us of this', wrote Lenin, in 1922. 'But we have not finished building even the foundations of socialist economy . . . the joint effort of the workers of several advanced countries are needed for the victory of socialism.' (Collected Works, Vol. 33, p. 206). But the revolutionary wave which swept Europe immediately after the war soon ebbed. The German workers' insurrection in January 1919 was defeated; so was the soviet government formed briefly in Hungary in 1919. The crowds who had gathered in the streets of Moscow awaiting the news were dismayed. Even more serious was the defeat of the 1923 workers' rising in Germany, which was attributable to the vacillation of the Communist Party and of some leaders of the Comintern who advised it. This reinforced the isolation of the Russian revolution, which in turn strengthened conservative forces inside the country.

As early as 1918-1920 the Russian working class which had made the revolution was almost broken up trying to defend it. Many of the great factories where the soviets had been based were closed; large numbers of the most politically-conscious workers died in the civil war; others were forced back to the countryside by famine. By the end of 1920 there was little trace left of the soviets; collaboration between the communists and other workers' parties had broken down and many of the latter were banned. Plummeting industrial and agricultural production forced a retreat: in March 1921, to restore lost production and restart trade, the New Economic Policy was adopted, allowing a limited amount of capitalist business and, in turn, strengthening the naturally right-wing small businessmen and farmers. Well before Lenin's death in January 1924, the communists in government were overwhelmed by an army of administrators who brought with them all the habits learned under tsarism.

These conservative forces found their expression in the Communist Party itself, in the bureaucratic tendency headed by Joseph Stalin. It retreated from revolutionary internationalism (hiding behind the anti-Marxist 'theory' of 'building socialism in one country'), tolerated Great Russian chauvinism and adopted a conservative economic policy. Its methods were to suppress what remained of democracy in the soviets and then in the Communist Party itself. The Left Opposition to this bureaucracy, formed in 1923, was soon headed by Trotsky, leader of the 1917 revolution and founder of the Red Army.

After Lenin's death in 1924, the Comintern was increasingly dominated by Stalin's policy of building 'socialism in one country', that is, not building it anywhere else. The struggle in other countries was subordinated to the requirements of the bureaucracy in the Soviet Union. The communist parties elsewhere in the world became its tools. The first great catastrophe for which Stalin's line was responsible was the defeat of the Chinese revolution of 1925-1927.

The growth of capitalism in China had stimulated a bourgeois nationalist movement, the Guomindang led by Sun Yat Sen, which sought to unify the country against the northern landowner-warlords and against Japanese imperialism. The workers' movement also grew, strongly influenced by the Chinese Communist Party, formed in 1920 with the aim of 'the dictatorship of workers and peasants, the abolition of private property and the gradual attainment of communist society' (see Brandt et al., 1952, p. 65). Just as the Bolsheviks in Russia had seen their role as fighting for the political independence of the working class in the bourgeois revolution, so the Chinese communists saw it as their task as to participate in the bourgeois democratic revolution under their own working-class banner, opposing themselves to the national bourgeois party.

The Comintern bureaucracy, however, turned its back on this perspective, and instead sought a political alliance with Sun Yat Sen. Behind this lay the belief in Moscow that the best, rapidly-achievable, result, which would bring military and diplomatic gains for the Soviet Union, was a Guomindang victory. Guided by these opportunist considerations, and turning its back on working-class internationalism, the Comintern, from late 1922, put increasing pressure on the Chinese communists to abandon their own separate organisation and join the Guomindang.

In May 1925, the shooting of strikers in Shanghai by British troops provoked a revolutionary upsurge. The Comintern, increasingly under the control of the Stalin faction, laid down a line to the Chinese communists which essentially subordinated them to the Guomindang, whose leaders were paraded as guests of honour in Moscow. The Guomindang, led by Chiang Kai-shek since Sun's death in 1925, was itself very clear that the working-class movement and the Chinese communists were its main enemies. In March 1926 the first 'fruits' of the Comintern's pro-Guomindang policy were realised in Canton where the Guomindang staged a coup, massacring workers and communists.

The Chinese workers' movement continued to grow. Unknown to the Chinese communists, Trotsky fought almost single-handedly in the Comintern against Stalin's policy, putting forward proposals for the development of the independent workers' movement, the formation of soviets, and the call for a workers' and peasants' government. These policies were rejected, amidst growing hysteria against the Opposition. Comintern advisers in China instructed the communists to subordinate the workers' movement to the Guomindang; they refused even to publish a resolution of the Chinese communists calling for a break with the Guomindang. In April 1927 came a second massacre of communists and workers, in Shanghai.

Now the Comintern switched its support from Chiang Kai-shek to the 'left' Guomindang of Wang Ching-wei, which formed a government in Hunan. As landless peasants came into violent conflict with Wang, the communists called on them to place faith in his government. In August 1927 Wang repaid the communists, as Chiang had, with a new massacre.

This third bloody defeat ended the greatest ever mass revolutionary movement in east Asia. What few forces remained of the Chinese communist party were in December 1927 plunged, on Stalin's instructions, into a series of suicidal adventures in which thousands more died. These culminated in the 'Canton commune' in which a few hundred communists — badly prepared, poorly armed and unsupported by the workers — were quickly routed by the nationalist military.

The Chinese Communist Party was effectively destroyed in the working-class centres. It was resurrected by Mao Zedong in 1931 in Kiangsi, not as a working-class party, but as the commanding stratum of the peasant 'red army'. Of this party, which the Vietnamese Stalinist leader Ho Chi Minh took as a model, Trotsky wrote: 'The party actually tore itself away from its class.' (See 'Peasant War in China and the Proletariat', in Trotsky 1976, p. 522).

It was in the midst of China's betrayed revolution that the Thanh nien, forerunner of the Indochinese Communist Party, was formed by Ho Chi Minh (see Chapter 2). It was Trotsky's writings on China, sent from his exile in Kazakhstan to the sixth Congress of the Comintern in 1928, that were pored over by the Vietnamese students won to the Trotskyist Opposition in Paris (see Chapter 3).

Trotsky characterised the policy imposed by Moscow on the Chinese communists in 1925-1927 as essentially 'Menshevik'. In Russia the Mensheviks had argued that, since the revolution was bourgeois, it could fulfil only certain limited tasks (a bourgeois democratic political system, agrarian reform, etc.). The working class initially could be no more than the left wing of the bourgeois revolution; only at a later stage could it expropriate the bourgeoisie and strive towards socialism. On China, Stalin — who appeared to carry the authority of Bolshevism — reasoned in essentially the same way. The revolution was to have two 'stages': at the first, bourgeois stage, the role of the working class was to ensure the victory of the national capitalist party. Only when the bourgeois revolution had run its course would specifically working-class, socialists tasks be on the agenda.

In Russia in 1917, the Bolsheviks had rejected the Menshevik logic that the bourgeois character of the revolution meant that the bourgeoisie had to lead it. They insisted that, in the epoch opened up in 1914 by the end of capitalism's historically progressive development, the working class was the most capable, consistent force in the democratic revolution. In March 1917, when the Russian bourgeoisie came to power, it was unable to carry out even the tasks of its 'own' revolution. Its links with the international bourgeoisie and its fear of the workers prevented it from conceding even 'bread, peace, land'. The bourgeois revolution had to be superseded by the working-class revolution.

Stalin claimed that in China the leading class was the national bourgeoisie and insisted that the working class should be politically subordinate to it. He argued, as the Mensheviks had, that the bourgeois nature of the revolution meant that the national bourgeoisie had a progressive role. The result was that the national bourgeoisie, effectively with Moscow's support, crushed the working class — the one force which, Trotsky insisted, was capable of carrying forward the struggle for democratic demands such as agrarian reform.

Trotsky's theory of 'permanent revolution', set out after the 1905 revolution in Russia, was now updated in line with his conclusions from the Chinese experience. In the imperialist epoch, the national bourgeoisie in the underdeveloped countries, tied to the historically declining world capitalist system, could not carry through the tasks of the democratic revolution. 'The complete and genuine solution of [these tasks of] democracy and national emancipation is conceivable only through the dictatorship of the proletariat as the leader of the subjugated nation, above all of its peasant masses' (Trotsky 1962, p. 152). To carry through these tasks, the working class must 'make deep inroads into the rights of bourgeois property. The democratic revolution grows over directly into the socialist revolution . . .' (p. 154). The taking of power by the working class can only be the start of the revolutionary process; and the taking of power in one country is only the first step towards a socialist revolution that 'begins on the national arena, unfolds on the international arena and is completed on the world arena' (p. 155). The Trotskyists of the 1930s saw the development of this theory as the essential, and precious, gain from the bloody Chinese defeat.

Revolutionaries They Could Not Break is the first comprehensive account of the Vietnamese Trotskyists' activity to be published in English. It is important for everyone, young and old, who wants to fight injustice and oppression. It is a contribution to the recovery of history through the fog of Stalinist falsification — a fog that has already been partly swept away by the events of 1989-1991 in the former Soviet Union and eastern Europe.

In the case of the Vietnamese workers' movement, the fog of falsification is that much thicker because of the crisis of the Fourth International, which Trotsky founded in 1938. This is the final point with which this Introduction will now deal.

Readers will see below (chapter 6) how Trotsky and his supporters had, until 1933, regarded themselves as a faction of the Communist International. In that year, the leaders of the German workers' movement effectively capitulated to Hitler, a catastrophe for which the Trotskyists considered Stalin's policy mainly responsible. When the Comintern reaffirmed, after the event, the correctness of its line in Germany, the Trotskyists declared that a new, Fourth, International was needed. Trotsky's supporters in Vietnam, as everywhere else, considered themselves representatives of this International, which was to have its founding conference in Paris in 1938.

After the second world war there was a lengthy discussion inside the Fourth International about the changes that had taken place in eastern Europe and China. In 1950-1951, some of its leaders, including its then secretary Michel Pablo, and Ernest Mandel, concluded that the Stalinists were succesfully carrying through much of the Trotskyist programme; that the class struggle in the next period would be expressed in a struggle between the imperialist and Stalinist 'camps'; that Trotsky's policy of building a new International should, in many countries, be replaced with 'entryism of a special type' into the Communist Parties, with the perspective of 'pushing them to the left'. Pablo emphasised that, in Vietnam and China above all, the Trotskyists should give the Stalinist parties 'critical support' and attempt to join them. When tried out in Vietnam, this policy was politically suicidal, and actually led to the death of some Trotskyists in Stalinist-controlled areas.

The Pablo-Mandel line implicitly questioned the very purpose for which the Fourth International had been founded: to resolve 'the crisis of working-class leadership' by a successful struggle against, above all, the Stalinists. In 1953 this line led to a split in the International as the Socialist Workers Party of the US and other important sections rejected it. By the 1960s, when Ho chi Minh's regime was at war with the US, Pablo had renounced the Fourth International all together. But the groups led by Mandel were among those glorifying Ho as the leader of a 'socialist revolution'. They centred their activity on collaborating with the Stalinists in the anti-war movement in Europe and the US, and abandoned any effort to re-establish the Fourth International in Vietnam. For years, the surviving group of Trotskyists in Saigon was left with virtually no contact with its European counterparts.

This policy also involved, in effect, helping the Stalinists to bury the real history of the Vietnamese Trotskyists. The Stalinist slanders against the Vietnamese Trotskyists (that 'they ignored the peasantry', 'they collaborated with the Japanese', etc.) were not only left unanswered by many so-called 'Trotskyists', but were sometimes actually repeated by them. Young Trotskyists curious enough to ask what had happened to the Vietnamese movement were told it had been 'marginalised by history'.

Revolutionaries They Could Not Break shows that the Trotskyists were not 'marginalised', but persecuted by the Stalinists for defending the political independence of the working class and refusing to collaborate with French imperialism. They did not fail in their efforts to give leadership to the workers. If they failed in anything it was in their realisation of the murderous lengths to which the Stalinists would go to stop them.

The text of this book first appeared in French, in 1990 and 1991, in *Cahiers Leon Trotsky*, Nos. 40 and 46. Thanks are due to Harry Ratner, who translated the text into English. It has since been edited and revised by the author.

Simon Pirani
July 1994

EXPLANATORY NOTES

The three countries of Vietnam

The events described in this book took place in Indochina under French domination. The present Vietnam was made up of three countries, or 'Ky', whose inhabitants were known as the 'Annamite race': Tonkin or Bac ky (the north), capital Hanoi; Annam or Trung ky (the centre), capital Hue; Cochinchina or Nam ky (the south), capital Saigon.

About 60 ethnic minorities, who have scarcely any written history, live in the mountains and forests of the three 'countries': these include the Tho in the north, the Cham in the centre and the Khmers of the south.

Tonkin and Annam were protectorates from 1883 and Cochinchina was a colony from 1861. In 1887, the French formed the Indochinese Union, comprising the three countries of Vietnam and Cambodia. Laos was incorporated into Indochina six years later. Following the tradition of the Chinese rulers, the French colonisers called the indigenous population 'Annamites' (An Nam means 'pacified south'). The Tonkinese and Annamites were 'French-protected people', the Cochinchinese were 'French subjects'. During the 1930s in France the first internationalists among the Vietnamese students refused to call themselves Annamite and called themselves Indochinese. We use the word 'Annamite' instead of 'Vietnamese' in all pre-1945 documents.

Abbreviations

AOM   The French Archives Nationales, Section Outre Mer
BDIC   Bibliothèque de Documentation Internationale Contemporaine, at Nanterre University, Paris
CHEAM   Centre des Hautes Études sur l'Afrique et l'Asie modernes
PCI   Indochinese Communist Party
VNQDD Vietnam quoc dan dang (National Party of Vietnam)

Quoc ngu

Quoc ngu, the national language, is the Annamite language. It was romanised in the seventeenth century by the missionaries to help their evangelical work. No accents have been used on Vietnamese names in the text. Vietnamese readers may use the quoc ngu index (page 223).

Vietnam under the French

Red River

Ha giang

Lao cay

Cao bang

TONKIN

CHINA

Bac kan

Tuyen quang

Lang son

Yen bay

Phu tho

Thai nguyen

Dien bien phu

Vinh yen

Bac ninh

Mong cai

HANOI

Hai duong

Hon gay

Hoa binh

Hadong

Haiphong

Nam dinh

Thai binh

GULF

Ninh binh

OF

Thanh hoa

TONKIN

HAINAN
(CHINA)

NGHE AN

Nam dan

Vinh

Ha tinh

QUANG BINH

LUANG PRABANG

Dong hoi

VIENTIANE

L
A
O
S

Quang tri

Thuan an

HUE

Tourane

Hoi an

QUANG NAM

Mekong River

QUANG NGAI

Quang Ngai

ANNAM

C
H
I
N
A

S
I
A
M

BINH DINH

Qui nhon

PHU YEN

Tuy hoa

S
E
A

KHANH HOA

C
A
M
B
O
D
I
A

Da lat

Nha trang

COCHINCHINA

Tay ninh

Bienhoa

BINH THUAN

Thu dau mot

Giadinh

PHNOM PENH

Chau doc

Plaine des

SAIGON

Phan thiet

Joncs

Ha tien

Sa dec

Cholon

Long xuyen

Go cong

Baria

GULF

Vinh long

Ben tre

Cap Saint-Jacques

OF

Can tho

Tra vinh

SIAM

Soc trang

Bac lieu

0   150   300

Camau

km

Poulo Condore
prison island

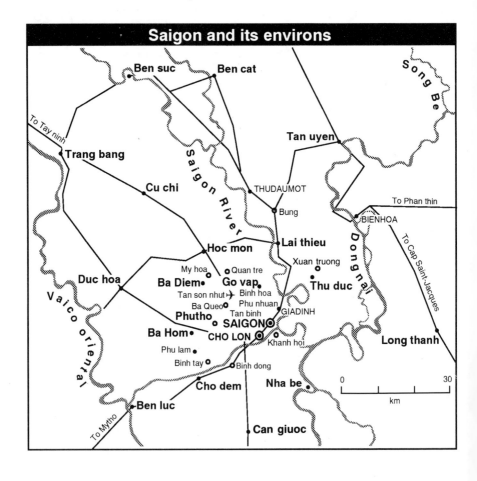

Saigon and its environs

Song Be

To Tay ninh

Ben suc Ben cat

Trang bang

Saigon River

Cu chi

Tan uyen

THUDAUMOT

Bung

To Phan thin

BIENHOA

Dongnai

Lai thieu

Hoc mon

Xuan truong

To Cap Saint-Jacques

My hoa Quan tre

Ba Diem Go vap

Thu duc

Duc hoa

Tan son nhut Binh hoa

Ba Queo Phu nhuan

Tan binh

Phutho

SAIGON

GIADINH

Ba Hom

CHO LON

Khanh hoi

Long thanh

Phu lam

Binh tay Binh dong

0 30

km

Cho dem

Nha be

Ben luc

To Mytho

Can giuoc

Vaico oriental

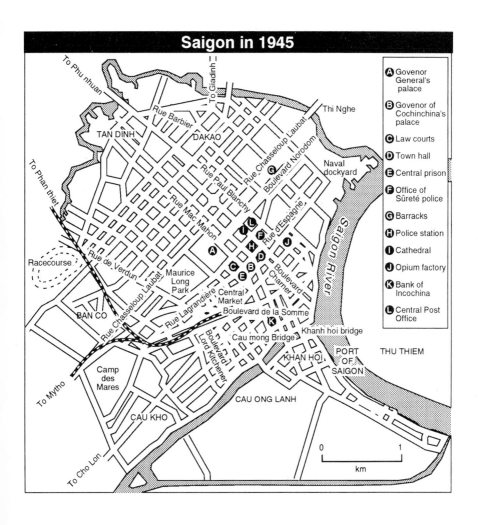

Saigon in 1945

A Govenor General's palace

B Govenor of Cochinchina's palace

C Law courts

D Town hall

E Central prison

F Office of Sûreté police

G Barracks

H Police station

I Cathedral

J Opium factory

K Bank of Incochina

L Central Post Office

To Phu nhuan

To Gladinh

Thi Nghe

Rue Barbier

TAN DINH

DAKAO

Rue Chasseloup Laubat

Boulevard Norodom

Naval dockyard

To Phan thiet

Rue Paul Blanchy

Rue Mac Mahon

Rue d'Espagne

Saigon River

Racecourse

Rue de Verdun

A

L I
F
H
C D J
E B
Boulevard Charner

Maurice Long Park

Rue Lagrandiere

Central Market

Boulevard de la Somme

K

Khanh hoi bridge

BAN CO

Rue Chasseloup Laubat

Cau mong Bridge

Khan hoi bridge

PORT OF SAIGON

THU THIEM

Boulevard Lord Kitchener

KHAN HOI

To Mytho

Camp des Mares

CAU ONG LANH

CAU KHO

To Cho Lon

0   1
km

1

HOW OUR HISTORY IS TOLD

History is often the history told by the victors. Among the historians who have dealt with Vietnam, more than one, his mind clouded by the fumes of the epoch, has taken the side of the victors.

'I only believe history told by witnesses who had their throats cut', said Pascal. These words were quoted — what cynicism! — by Jean Chesneaux who, 20 years after the Moscow trials and on the eve of Khrushchev's secret report on Stalin's crimes, was still writing, in *Contributions to the History of the Vietnamese Nation*:

> In 1937-1938, the Trotskyist leaders such as Ta thu Thau, who . . . violently criticised the programme of democratic reform which the Indochinese Communist Party had persuaded moderate Vietnamese and anti-fascist colonial elements to accept, and who refused to see the Japanese danger as the most menacing, broke with the communists. They hoped thereby to weaken the national unity which the communists had inspired. But they no longer had the relative influence they had previously enjoyed when the popular movement was in its infancy.
>
> Reduced to a small sect, having wandered off the high road which pressure of public sentiment had momentarily forced them to take, they soon completely degenerated, going as far as to become direct agents of Japan in 1944-1945. (Chesneaux, 1955, p. 220.)

Double error or double slander? The 1937 split was the work of the Stalinists who started the shameful slander about 'the Trotskyist agents of Japan'. Before the truth could put on its boots, the lie travelled round the world. Twelve years later, the American historian Joseph Buttinger uncritically repeated Chesneaux's allegation:

> Ta thu Thau, whom Chesneaux accuses of being a Japanese agent during

1944-1945, was eliminated by the Vietminh in 1946. (Buttinger, 1967, p. 566.)

An 'intellectual blood stain'. (Lautréamont, p. 341.) Was the slander washed clean when, in 1987, Chesneaux, challenged by a reader, finally withdrew it? Then, he wrote:

Obviously the phrase about the Vietnamese Trotskyists agents of Japan (Contribution, p.220) was marked by the Stalinist climate of the French Communist Party in 1952-1953. I willingly agree to withdraw it. (*Chroniques Vietnamiennes*, Paris, July 1987.)

As for the bureaucracy of the Vietnamese Communist Party it droned on, in 1983, keeping alive the old clichés:

After the Japanese coup d'état against the French [in Vietnam in March 1945], a certain number [of Trotskyists] became agents of French imperialism; others publicly became spies for Japanese fascism. Ta thu Thau, leader of the Fourth International in Vietnam, collaborated with the Tan Vietnam group, a pro-Japanese organisation sponsored by the Japanese to try to seize power before the Vietminh. (*Tap chi cong san*, no. 2, Hanoi, 1983, p 59.)

The same refrain is taken up by the Stalinist 'Resistance Veterans' of the South:

After the Japanese coup . . . the Trotskyists raised the pro-Japanese banner even higher. (Ha huy Giap, 1987.)

It is almost half a century since the lives of the young Indochinese Trotskyists were cut short. Their voices have been definitively stilled. While in the USSR light is beginning to filter through on to the witch-hunts of the 1930s, the Vietnamese Stalinists' lying continues.

The aim of this book is to help make known the facts as they were, in what is today called Vietnam.

2

THE BIRTH OF COMMUNISM IN INDOCHINA

Indochinese Communism[1] emerged from nationalism — the nationalism which, in the 1920s, took hold of radical youth from the 'less cultivated classes' born in the first decade of the twentieth century.

At the end of 1925 these youth demonstrated, both in Tonkin and Annam, demanding a pardon for the nationalist leader Phan boi Chau. In 1926, they flung themselves into the school strikes against the jailing and sentencing of Nguyen an Ninh, founder of *La Cloche fêlée* (*The Cracked Clock*). They rallied at the funeral of Phan chau Trinh.

These three names — Phan boi Chau, Nguyen an Ninh and Phan chau Trinh — were symbols of the revolt against colonial domination for the more progressive youth, who were soon to emigrate and come into contact with Marxist-Leninist ideology. Between 1925 and 1928, four underground political groups were born: the Thanh nien cach mang dong chi hoi, or Thanh nien for short (Association of Comrades of Revolutionary Youth), formed in Canton in July 1925; the Tan Viet cach mang dang, or Tan Viet for short (Revolutionary Party of the New Viet), formed in Annam in July 1925; the Viet nam quoc dan dang or VNQDD (National Party of Vietnam), formed in Tonkin in December 1927; and the Hoi kin Nguyen an Ninh (the Nguyen an Ninh secret society), formed in Cochinchina in 1928. These groups were the heirs of the movements led by the mandarins and the intelligentsia of the old school, of armed revolts, military plots, conspiracies and terrorism. Their common aim was to drive the French out of Indochina.

The Thanh nien, nationalist embryo of the PCI

The first of these movements, the Thanh nien, was the forerunner of the Parti Communiste Indochinois or PCI (Indochinese Communist

Party), which was succeeded in turn by the Vietnamese Communist Party which holds power today.

The founders of the Thanh nien were members of the Comintern (Communist International), and the reasons for its formation are to be found in a change of policy made in Moscow from 1923 onwards.[2]

After the defeat of the German revolution in that year, Moscow went on a 'quest for ready-made revolutionary forces outside the proletariat, whence came . . . the friendship above classes with the Guomindang' ('What Now', 12 July 1928; Trotsky 1974a, p. 192).

According to the Stalinist theory of 'not skipping stages', Moscow advocated a policy of adaptation to the national bourgeoisies of the colonial and semi-colonial countries.

The Third International, soon to be won over to the theory of building 'socialism in one country', became an instrument of Russian diplomacy, assigning to the Communist Parties the role of 'frontier guards' of the USSR. In 1923-1927, under Moscow's orders, the Chinese Communist Party became an appendage of the Guomindang, allied to the USSR against Western and Japanese imperialism in the Far East.

The Comintern, at its Fifth Congress in 1924, put forward the idea of building bipartite worker-peasant parties in the Oriental colonial and semi-colonial countries, in imitation of the Chinese CP. This idea had been formulated by Joseph Stalin in his *Problems of Leninism*. The task of these parties would be to achieve a nationalist revolution, neither bourgeois nor proletarian, against imperialist domination.

With this in view, Nguyen ai Quoc (Nguyen the Patriot), the future Ho chi Minh, set out to organise — but from a 'sanctuary' abroad — a proto-Bolshevik nationalist movement. He had been delegated to China by the Comintern in December 1924, as secretary to Mikhail Borodin, the Comintern representative who was then acting as adviser to Sun Yat-sen, the Chinese nationalist leader.

In Canton — out of reach of the French Sûreté and with the blessing of the local powers — Nguyen ai Quoc contacted several émigré compatriots, confused former supporters of the defeated Phan boi Chau.

With them, he set up the Thanh nien (Association of Comrades of the Revolutionary Youth). He reported to the Comintern of 12 February 1925:

At present I am not an Annamite, but a Chinaman. My name is Ly Thuy and not Nguyen ai Quoc . . . We have set up a secret group of nine members, of whom two have been sent to Indochina. Three have left for the front and one is on a military mission (as aide to the Guomindang). Five members of the group are ready to be admitted into the [Chinese] Communist Party and two have been accepted into the [Chinese] Communist Youth. (Trung Chinh, 1970, pp. 5-21; and Huynh kim Khanh, 1982, p. 66.)

In June of that year, he began publishing a duplicated bulletin in quoc ngu, *Thanh nien* (*Youth*). It had a dual orientation, consisting both of racial passion and of the political line of the Third International. On 12 September he issued the following inflammatory appeal:

Brothers of the same race, let us love one another! We are 20 million human beings of yellow skin and red blood, all descendants of the noble Hung Vuong [a legendary king]. Our civilisation has been shining for over 4,000 years. What heroes our country has produced! . . . We have spread as far as Champa and Cambodia and our glory has resounded throughout the Far East. (*Thanh nien*, 12 September 1925.)

The Thanh nien welcomed recruits from Vietnam and trained them. Political education consisted of an initiation into the new language of revolution, the history of the Chinese and Russian revolutions, the glorification of the Bolsheviks, who 'help the oppressed peoples regain their liberty', the history of working-class movements of Europe and America, and of anti-imperialist struggles in Asia and Africa. It condemned the 'impotent' anarchists, the socialists of the Second International ('bound to the imperialists'), the monarchists of Prince Cuong De and the terrorists of Phan boi Chau.

'All that remains to us, dear compatriots, is to join the only energetic and effective party, the Communist Party (*Thanh nien*, 22 August 1926) and follow the road of the Communist International (*Duong Kach Menh* (The Revolutionary Path), 1927). This will lead to a popular govern-ment with elected worker, peasant and military representatives at its head; it will apply the principles of the New Economic Policy to develop the economy of the country in collaboration with the possessing classes.'[3]

Practical activity was studied in minutest detail. First, underground work, the organisation of a meeting (khai hoi), recruitment and the organisation of cells. Then semi-clandestine activities, with leaflets and strikes. Finally open activity, with the seizure of power 'when the party will have members in all strata of society'.

His training completed, the candidate was admitted as a comrade in the Thanh nien only after a solemn initiation before the tomb of Pham hong Thai. This 'national hero' had been killed on 19 June 1924 after his attempt to assassinate the French Governor General of Indochina, Merlin, on a visit to Canton. The candidate accepted the sentence of death at the hands of his comrades in the event of any 'serious error'.

The 'comrades from Canton', having become more or less professional revolutionaries, returned home to win recruits, primarily, from their own cultured middle-class milieu — teachers and students, clerical employees, minor officials and rural notables — who were sent in their turn to Canton for training.

Nguyen ai Quoc arranged for their admission to the Whampoa (Huangpu) Military School, set up by Moscow for the Guomindang. They were intended to set up self-defence groups and provide the leadership of armed insurrections for the seizure of power.

Quoc fluctuated between a nationalism laced with racism and proletarian internationalism. Printed on page two of his *Thanh nien* were the hammer and sickle and the *Communist Manifesto*'s appeal, 'Workers of the World Unite!'. He even disavowed the word 'motherland', which was

> invented by the politicians in order to subordinate the people to the law and force the proletarians to defend by arms the assets of the owners and the interests of the capitalists. (*Thanh nien*, 20 December 1926.)

Two contradictory tendencies thus developed within the Thanh nien, one for communism, the other for Sun Yat-sen's 'Three Principles'.[4]

There were two other agitational papers which came into Vietnam from Canton: the *Bao cong nong* (*Workers' and Peasants' Journal*) and the *Linh kach menh* (*Revolutionary Sharpshooter*) which from the beginning of 1927 called on conscript soldiers to refuse to fire on their compatriots in the event of unrest.

A revolutionary network with iron discipline was being set up on the fringes of the apparatus of colonial domination. It was a highly organised underground network, a rival power in embryo. The Tong bo (directing committee) with its headquarters in Canton was its brain and supreme tribunal. It appointed a Ky bo (country committee) in each of Vietnam's three countries (Tonkin, Annam and Cochinchina). The Ky bo appointed a Tinh bo (provincial committee) for each province.

These controlled the Huyen bo or Quan bo (divisional committees), which in turn presided over the district committees, which ruled the Chi bo (cells) and To (nests) in the villages. They were the basic units of the whole pyramid, which also included Thanh bo (town committees, made up of street and factory cells).

What greatly helped the Thanh nien to take root in Vietnam itself was the nationalist passion which in 1925 gripped the school students of Tonkin and Annam after the trial and conviction of the defeated terrorist Phan boi Chau, and in 1926 took hold of the youth of Cochinchina after the conviction of the anarcho-romantic Nguyen an Ninh.

The Thanh nien was spared during the tragedy of the Chinese revolution in 1927.[5] The Tong bo (directing committee) lived in apprehension of the bloody outcome of the Chinese Communist Party's subordination to the bourgeois Guomindang — ordered by Moscow and in operation by May 1926. But the Thanh nien was reassured by General Li Jishen. All this time the Chinese workers and coolies were being massacred in April by Chiang Kai-shek in Shanghai, by Li Jishen and Zhang Fakui in Canton, and then by both together in April, October and December, and again at Wuhan in July, by the same soldiers of the Guomindang.

Moscow had obstinately refused to arm the Chinese Communist Party; Russian arms were supplied exclusively to the Guomindang. And Stalin was still declaring on 21 April 1927 that events 'had completely confirmed the correctness of the Comintern's line'. Trotsky had fought against this line: how could the bourgeoisie in its conflict with imperialism not seek to crush the workers and peasants who were fighting for themselves?

Let us dwell awhile on the last act of this tragedy.

The Canton Commune: prelude to the 'Third Period'[6]

In November 1927, Moscow ordered the communists of Canton to start an insurrection with the slogan 'All power to the soviets of delegates of the workers, the peasants and the poor'. The designated date was 13 December, the day the 15th Congress of the Communist Party of the Soviet Union was due to open. Maybe a success would help silence Trotsky and the Left Opposition. The balance of forces was catastrophic: Canton's revolutionary committee could rely only on 200 former cadets of Whampoa, influenced by the Chinese CP, and on some

500 workers with a derisory supply of arms (about 50 rifles, 30 or so revolvers and 200 grenades).

The plot having been leaked, the insurrection was brought forward by two days. During the night of 10-11 December the cadets shot their officers and, together with pickets of armed workers, attacked the Guomindang detachments scattered throughout the town. Aided by the element of surprise, the insurgents held most of the city after a day of bitter street fighting.

The Canton Commune was proclaimed. It freed a thousand political prisoners who joined the insurrectionary forces; it decreed the confiscation of the possessions of the big bourgeoisie and the banks, the transformation of the houses of the rich into workers' dormitories, the nationalisation of the land and the establishment of soviet power in the villages. But the working-class population had not taken part in the uprising. Within three days the insurgents had fallen under the bullets of Li Jishen's and Zhang Fakui's troops (temporarily united for this task), and aided by a bombardment from the British, Japanese and Chinese gunboats.

Here is the Thanh nien's triumphalist account, given — without a trace of political analysis — while corpses were still piling up in the ruins of the city:

> On 11 December, the workers, peasants and Red soldiers of Canton, following in the footsteps of the Paris Commune, took up arms, overthrew the nationalist government and set up a soviet regime.[7] This first great victory of the working class is the most striking event in the revolutionary history of the Far East.
>
> . . . Unfortunately, three days after their victory, the communists suffered a serious setback and had to abandon power. . . . The losses suffered by the communists are as follows: killed 10,000, shot, 2,500; Russians assassinated, 18. An incalculable number of women, children and foreign revolutionaries also died during those bloody days. (*Thanh nien*, 17 December 1927.)

Leaving the leadership of the Thanh nien in the hands of Ho tung Mau, Hong Son and Lam duc Thu — his contemporaries, and former supporters of Phan boi Chau — Nguyen ai Quoc left Canton on the day after the April repression, and was safely in Moscow from the summer onwards.

In May 1928, the Thanh nien held a provisional national congress in Hong Kong. The directing committee nominated its representatives on the country committees; for Cochinchina it chose Le van Phat, alias My, supplanting the original delegate, Ton duc Thang. Some months after returning to Saigon, My met his death at the hands of his own comrades.

The crime at 5 rue Barbier[8]

During the night of 9-10 December 1928, a crime reminiscent of a bygone age was perpetrated in the heart of the Thanh nien's Cochinchina section. The death penalty stipulated by the organisation's statutes for 'serious error' was pronounced against My for 'his approaches to our sister Thi Nhut'. He had not 'disregarded his personal feelings so as to devote himself entirely to the revolution'! Three young comrades, 28, 24 and 23 years old, were to carry out the sentence decided by a 'revolutionary tribunal' constituted by Ton duc Thang, senior member of the Country Committee.

The real reasons (bruised vanity, sexual rivalry?) for a sentence out of all proportion to the 'error' have remained hidden.

On 15 July 1930 the Saigon Assizes condemned the three executioners to death; the teacher Ton duc Thang, future successor to Ho chi Minh, to 20 years penal servitude; and Pham van Dong, Ho chi Minh's future prime minister, to ten years. The Thanh nien's Cochinchina section was completely destroyed, with 25 more of its members being sentenced to a total of 100 years' imprisonment. On 22 May 1931, in the middle of the retreat of the peasant movement and of the White terror,[9] the heads of three young revolutionaries were chopped off after their last cry of 'Down with French imperialism!' They were: Tran Truong, from Mytho, metal worker at the arsenal; Nguyen van Thinh, born at Vinh, a tailor; Ngo Thiem, an accountant, from Nghe an.

The official biographers and historians prefer not to recall a crime which could tarnish the image of the 'hero of the Black Sea', Ton duc Thang, so named in memory of the mutiny of April 1919 on a French warship when he, an Indochinese native, was chosen by the French crew to hoist the red flag.

The Comintern's 'left' turn

Speaking of the defeat of the Chinese proletarian revolution at the Sixth Congress of the Comintern in July 1928, Nikolai Bukharin, Stalin's right-hand man, finally recognised that class collaboration with the bourgeoisie had been its essential cause, 'from which flowed the lack of independence of [our] party [which] sometimes acted as an obstacle to the agrarian revolution and the workers' movement'. In line with this view, the Comintern made a complete about-turn in the colonial and semi-colonial countries: it decreed an end to the blocs with nationalist parties, the creation of communist parties independent of the bourgeoisie, the adoption of a class-against-class policy and the proletarianisation of the communist parties. The colonial 'masses' and their movements were to develop under the leadership of the 'metropolitan proletariats'.

The 'winning of the streets' and the 'direct struggle for power' were now the order of the day, according to the strategy of the 'Third Period' — so designated by Vyacheslav Molotov — which was to witness the disintegration of the capitalist world. (The First Period, from 1918 to the defeat of the German workers' revolution of 1923, having been characterised by the profound economic crisis of capitalism in the era of imperialism and the rising revolutionary wave in Europe; the Second, from the Fifth Comintern Congress in 1924 to the Sixth Congress in 1928, by the temporary stabilisation of the capitalist world with the proletariat on the defensive.)

This about-turn by the Comintern was to speed up the metamorphosis of the Thanh nien into a Communist Party — but the false appraisal of the period would give rise to disastrous adventurism in the three Annamite countries. The Third Period of 'errors', as Trotsky called it, was beginning.

The impetus towards 'proletarianisation' in the Thanh nien was first felt in Tonkin, where there already existed an important industrial proletarian concentration in the mines and textile mills, while in the south of Vietnam a rural proletariat existed on the rubber, coffee and tea plantations.

The Thanh nien had taken root since 1925 mainly among poor peasants in the provinces of Haiduong, Thaibinh, Bacninh (Tonkin), Nghe an and Hatinh (Northern Annam) and in the rice-growing west of Cochinchina. Now it was necessary to cultivate another soil. In September 1928, Ngo gia Tu, of the Tonkinese section, assembled his comrades to work out a plan of proletarianisation: the activists now plunged into the 'coalmining hell' of Maokhe, Uongbi and Campha, into the textile mills of Namdinh, the cement works of Haiphong, and the railway workshops of Truong thi (Annam). They reached as far as the plantations in the south, and Michelin in Phurieng, where the coolie-slaves[10] had spontaneously reacted to endless brutalities by killing overseers, as often Annamite as French.

The transformation of the Thanh nien from a party of 'unity of all Annamites for national liberation' into a class struggle party was about to take place quite naturally, but not without upheaval. From 1 to 9 May 1929, the Thanh nien held a National Congress in Hongkong attended by 17 delegates, who came from China, the three Annamite countries and Siam (now Thailand). The Tonkin delegates, Ngo gia Tu, Tran van Cung (Quoc Anh) and Nguyen Tuan (Kim Ton) argued for the immediate transformation of the Association into a Bolshevik Party; repudiated by the Tong bo (directing committee), the 'undisciplined' delegates walked out, were expelled and proceeded immediately to the building of a communist party.

The Thanh nien was approaching the end of its life. It closed its Congress with the adoption of a Programme-Manifesto, 'Proletarians unite!', consonant with the resolutions of the Sixth Congress of the Comintern, while still refusing to call itself the Communist Party.

The Tong bo (directing committee) justified its refusal in this way:

> Beforehand, we had envisaged only a national revolution so that the revolutionaries might remain united for the emancipation of the Annamite people; four-fifths of the party members, recruited from intellectuals and petty bourgeois, monopolised the leading posts; we did not know how to organise factory cells, our members knew nothing of 'democratic centralism'; we were not ready for the formation of a Bolshevik party. (*Thanh nien*, 23 September 1929.)

The birth of the Parti Communiste Indochinois (PCI)

Almost a year passed between the break-up of the Thanh nien and the creation, in several stages, of a unified party in Vietnam.

In June 1929 the Tonkin section assembled its Town Committees (Hanoi, Haiphong) and Provincial Committees (Namdinh, Thaibinh and Bacninh) and constituted itself as the Parti Communiste Indochinoise or Dong duong cong san dang (Indochinese Communist Party). This party redoubled its propaganda among the workers and peasants as far as Cochinchina, where Ngo gia Tu won the support of the very active Dao hung Long, who was to join the emerging Left Opposition in 1931. It circulated its press in the three countries, the *Bua liem* (*Hammer and Sickle*) in Tonkin, the *Bon se vich* (*Bolshevik*) in Annam and the *Co cong san* (*Communist Flag*) in Cochinchina.

Faced with the growth of the PCI, the activists of the Thanh nien in the south in their turn adopted the title of Communist Party in August 1929, calling theirs the An Nam cong san dang (Annamite Communist Party). Its organs, apart from the theoretical journal *Bon se vich*, were two agitational papers, the *Cong nong binh* (*Workers, Peasants and Soldiers*) and the *Hoc sinh* (*Pupils*).

To these two communist groups rallied most of the former supporters of the Hoi kin Nguyen an Ninh (Nguyen an Ninh Secret Society), which was broken up in 1929 after the man who inspired it, Nguyen an Ninh, was sentenced to three years in prison. He had been tried with 115 co-defendants, peasants and rural *notables*.[11]

A second, more important, regrouping took place inside the Tan Viet. This party, established in North Annam, had gathered some young nationalist intellectuals around the elderly writer Le Huan and other 'ex-convicts of Poulo Condore'; it wanted to co-operate closely, as 'the party of the interior', with the Thanh nien, the 'external party'. It was to disappear from the political scene, to the advantage of the Thanh nien and then of the Communist Party. Its demise was caused first by the haemorrhage of its young members who, from 1926 on, it sent to Canton to be trained and who were often won over to the 'external party', and second by the severe persecution of 1929 (265 arrests in Annam, including that of Le Huan who died in prison).

In October 1929, in response to demands for recognition of the Thanh nien and the two new-born Communist Parties, Moscow ordered them to fuse. This they did in Hongkong on 3 February 1930 under the direction of Nguyen ai Quoc, who arrived from Siam as the delegate of the Comintern. Nine delegates (Quoc, four from Thanh nien, two from the PCI and two from the Annamite Communist Party) proclaimed the formation of the Vietnam cong san dang (Communist Party of Vietnam). The word 'Vietnam', already part of the title of the nationalist Vietnam quoc dan dang (VNQDD), or National Party of Vietnam, was deliberately chosen for its emotional impact on the petty-bourgeois intelligentsia. Nguyen ai Quoc was reluctant to allow the nationalist party the monopoly of any initiative, despite any political compromise this might entail. In October, on Moscow's orders, the Communist Party of Vietnam took over the name PCI, previously that of the rebellious Tonkinese section.

The PCI took over the organisational structure of the Thanh nien with nominal changes (its central committee was named the Trung uong instead of Tong bo; country committees were named Xu uy instead of Xu bo). The party was from the start well implanted among the peasants and it rapidly extended its influence in the towns. In March 1930 the Sûreté estimated its strength in the south at 53 full members and 47 candidate members working in 22 cells. Eleven of these cells were in Saigon, five in Cholon, five in the provinces of Sadec, Cantho and Vinh long and two in Mytho. In addition there were ten red trade unions with some 234 workers of the Saigon-Cholon region and four peasant unions with about 465 members. (See 'Lettre du Gouverneur general au ministre des Colonies', AOM, Slotfom, III 48.)

Three months later the PCI launched, from north to south, the organised struggle of the peasant masses.

Even if during the 'Third Period' it sometimes criticised its founder, Nguyen ai Quoc, for his 'remnants of nationalism' and his 'opportunist theories' (*Bon se vich*, 5 December 1934), the PCI was unshakeable in its submission to the zigzags of the Stalinist line, which led in 1930-1931 to the bloody defeat of the peasant movement.

Six years later, after the Stalin-Laval pact, there came for the PCI the abandonment of the class struggle and of the fight against imperialism — and, in unity with the French Communist Party, support for a Popular Front for the maintenance of the integrity of the French Empire. Then, after the Hitler-Stalin pact, came the 1940 slaughter in Cochinchina, confusion . . . and a fanatical anti-Trotskyism, on a par with the obscurantism of religious fanaticism, which would lead directly to the assassinations of our comrades in 1945.

3

NATIONALISM AND TROTSKYISM AMONG THE ÉMIGRÉ STUDENTS IN FRANCE 1926-1929

From January 1926 *Viet Nam Hon* (*The Annamite Soul*), 'free forum of the Annamite students and workers', was published in France with the same orientation as *La Cloche fêlée* (see page 3). It was edited by Nguyen the Truyen, a friend of Nguyen an Ninh, and was the organ of the Phuc Viet (Annamite Independence Party). Supported by the Ligue Francaise Contre l'Oppression Coloniale et l'Imperialisme (French League against Colonial Oppression and Imperialism), it soon recruited over 200 Annamite students, furniture trade workers, waiters, cooks and seafarers.

This party wanted to be legal, and sought 'methods for regaining the independence of the people of Vietnam'; it condemned the collaboration practised by the Constitutionalist Party ('a victim of pirates should not collaborate with them'); it was in favour of unity 'overriding social distinctions, such as philosophical, political and religious differences'; it aimed at 'defending fellow-countrymen oppressed by the feudalists and capitalists'. The paper was banned several times and reappeared under the title *Phuc Quoc*, and then in French as *L'Ame annamite*, *La Nation annamite* and *La Résurrection*. It campaigned against the terror in Indochina, the plunder of the land, the coolies' miserable conditions (on the Michelin rubber plantations) and the corporal punishments inflicted on women as well as men.

Phan van Chanh, Huynh van Phuong and Ta thu Thau collaborated with Nguyen the Truyen and it was to them that he entrusted the leadership of the Annamite Independence Party when he returned home in January 1928.

In April the French Communist Party, which had until then supported the Annamite Independence Party, set up an Annamite Communist group, the Lao Nong (Worker and Peasant), which tried to infiltrate it. The Lao Nong was led by Nguyen van Tao, an illegal immigrant since his expulsion from Chasseloup-Laubat College. He published a paper, also named *Lao Nong*, which spoke in a clear class language: 'When the revolution triumphs the workers' and peasants' party will take power'. As a delegate of the French Communist Party to the Sixth Congress of the Comintern in 1928, Tao defended the Congress policy of creating in Indochina a Communist Party independent of the nationalist movements.

As well as infiltrating the Annamite Independence Party, the Stalinists slandered it. *L'Humanité* accused it of abstaining from the struggle against Taittinger's Jeunesses Patriotes (Patriotic Youth).[1] Answering the slander, Ta thu Thau attacked the 'paid hacks of the French Communist Party's Colonial Commission' who tried to transform militants into 'robots carrying out their ukases':

> From our indescribable slavery, we cry out to all the oppressed of the colonies: unite against European imperialism, white or red!

In March 1929 the Annamite Independence Party was forcibly dissolved (it had never been authorised), for having attempted to 'undermine the integrity of the national territory'. At the Seine tribunal Thau flung the accusation back in the face of the accusers: was it not France that had undermined the integrity of Annam?

Together with some of his comrades, Thau was about to abandon his 'youthful folly', nationalism, and join the Trotskyist Left Opposition. He was 23. The Annamite Independence Party had had its day.

The Indochinese Left Opposition in France and the massacre at Yen Bay

In 1929 the Dong duong cong san doi lap ta phai (Indochinese Left Opposition) was launched in Paris. It developed from the contacts made by Ta thu Thau and his friends with Alfred Rosmer and the International Left Opposition. In France these Annamite students discovered far more than their predecessors had — a modern culture, the philosophy of Rousseau and Montesquieu, the 'natural and inalienable rights of man and the citizen', the constitutional form of European nations, a political freedom.[2] They also discovered a new 'liberating idea' which opened their eyes to international horizons: a critique of the already counter-revolutionary direction taken by the Russian Revolution and its consequences for the revolutionary movement in Indochina.

The Annamite Independence Party had been dissolved in March. The Group of Indochinese Emigrés assembled around Ta thu Thau, Huynh van Phuong and Phan van Chanh included not only the veterans 'in whom the patriotic chord no longer vibrated' but also new comrades, opposed to the collaborationist line of the Constitutionalists or suspicious of the Stalinists of Nguyen van Tao's Lao Nong group.

Of the four clandestine nationalist parties of Annam, two were destroyed by the repression in 1929. A third, the VNQDD, was soon to meet the same fate.

On 9-10 February 1930, Tonkinese soldiers at the French military base at Yen Bay staged a mutiny/insurrection at the instigation of the VNQDD. After the rising was suppressed, the VNQDD was dealt mortal blows: 2,000 arrests, 1,086 indictments, 80 death sentences, 383 deportations, 106 sentences of hard labour and 105 of terms in prison. In France, this repression united the Annamite émigrés of all political tendencies in a common indignation and common demonstrations: in the university towns, in the ports and at the May Day rallies. Many were arrested for shouting slogans, distributing leaflets and fixing stickers on walls, like the one signed by Ta thu Thau:

> Proletarians and oppressed peoples, stop the imperialist crimes. Colonial assassins, liberate our comrades condemned to death at Yen Bay!

On 17 May, the Communist League (the French group of the International Left Opposition), and the Group of Indochinese Emigrés issued a ringing declaration, calling on workers to attend a protest meeting at the Bellevilloise. It urged everyone to face their responsibilities when the cases of the 39 condemned to death at Yen Bay arrived in Paris for review.

On 22 May, a Committee of Struggle constituted by the Lao Nong and the Group of Indochinese Emigrés rallied a hundred or so Annamite students and workers of all tendencies in front of the Elysée, demanding the release of those condemned to death.

> The police, surprised by this unexpected and imposing demonstration, waited for reinforcements before intervening. Workers on neighbouring building sites expressed their sympathy with the demonstrators . . .

Twelve of our comrades were arrested. (*La Vérité (The Truth)*, Paris, 30 May 1930.)

Further arrests followed; at the Mur des Fédérés, the memorial to the Paris Communards,[3] on 25 May — and even at comrades' homes. Altogether there were about 40 arrests; 19 of those detained were taken to Marseilles and put in the hold of the *Athos II*, which was sailing to Indochina. Among them were Ta thu Thau, Huynh van Phuong and Phan van Chanh; members of the Lao Nong; members of the Federal Union of Students, which was under Stalinist influence, and of the General Association of Indochinese Students, which was under the influence of Tran van Thach (who became a Trotskyist in 1937).

On 28 May, the Communist League took over the organisation of the meeting at the Bellevilloise, the call for which had been issued on 17 May by the arrested Annamites. The meeting was held under the auspices of the Emigrés group.

Despite all the protests, 13 heads fell as dawn broke at Yen Bay on 17 June 1930. Louis Roubaud, who was present at the executions, described this legal crime in his book *Vietnam!*[4].

On the eve of being guillotined, one of the founders of the VNQDD, Nguyen thai Hoc, who was 26 years old, took upon himself the responsibility for the insurrection in a letter to the French deputies:

In 1927 I organised the Annamite nationalist party, with the intention of chasing the French out of the country and setting up a truly democratic Annamite republican government . . . If the French want to continue to occupy Indochina peacefully they must abandon all brutal and inhuman methods . . . give back to the Annamites elementary individual rights, freedom of movement, freedom of education, freedom of association and of the press; they must no longer allow the extortions carried out by officials . . . give the people education, develop native commerce and industry. . . .

Your enemy, the revolutionary Thai Hoc

The only one of the four clandestine nationalist parties to survive this terrible year was the Thanh nien, set up in 1925 in Canton by Nguyen ai Quoc under the aegis of Moscow; a 'party in exile', its leadership had not risked destruction and it expanded by absorbing fugitives from the other nationalist organisations.

It was reorganised in 1930 as the Indochinese Communist Party (PCI), and recognised in 1931 as a section of the Comintern on which it depended both politically and materially. On 24 June this PCI, new-born but already secreting Stalinist poison, greeted the return to Saigon of our comrades expelled from France — Thau, Chanh and Phuong — with thousands of leaflets denouncing them as counter-revolutionaries.

'What to do after Yen Bay?'

From April 1930 onwards the two organs of the Communist League, *La Lutte de Classes* (*The Class Struggle*) and *La Vérité* (*The Truth*), opened their columns to the Indochinese Trotskyists. In the former, Huynh van Phuong published 'An Assessment of Indochina and the Annamite Bourgeoisie'. In it, he savaged the ideological mercantilism of the bourgeoisie represented by the Constitutionalist Party, which used the revolutionary pressure of the masses in order to win for itself concessions essential to its development. In *La Vérité*, from April to June, Ta thu Thau published an analysis of revolutionary perspectives as they appeared after Yen Bay.

In his review of the 'revolutionary' anti-imperialist movements, Ta thu Thau emphasised their 'reactionary essence' from the start of the (French) conquest up to about 1900. Mandarins and educated people loyal to the reigning Vietnamese dynasty carried out assassinations, guerrilla warfare and military plots against French domination and penetration, 'their basic motivation being opposition to the new life-styles and methods of production'.

He argued that from 1900, the anti-imperialist movements were driven by a liberal nationalism, and 'though different in their social content and organisation, have in common demands of a bourgeois character: economic freedoms and independence'.

He saw the Yen Bay uprising as 'the work of the left faction of this nationalism, attracting students influenced by the Chinese revolution and supporters of Sun Yat-senism (a synthesis of democracy, national-ism and socialism), a faction which has opted for the violent overthrow of imperialism'. While declaring the Left Opposition's 'solidarity with the 52 condemned to death', he affirmed its 'revolutionary right to criticise': Yen Bay was 'a barely organised revolt, localised, lacking contact with the civilian population and ideologically inadequate'.

He concluded that a Marxist understanding, which neither the Communist International nor its French section had provided, was necessary; nationalism, 'subjectivist politics', which had served both 'nominal' communism and the VNQDD as a 'theoretical base' and as a substitute for 'revolutionary class consciousness', could lead only to defeat. 'Only revolution based on the organisation of the proletarian and peasant masses is capable of liberating the colonies.' All that the Stalinist bureaucracy had achieved was a grouping around 'Stalinist slogans . . . without any serious discussion. It is up to the Opposition to create a conscious vanguard in the colonies.'

The colonialist penetration had created a capitalist class society in Indochina, he wrote.

> In their general outline the relationships of the social classes are as follows:
>
> On one side, a new proletariat (in the mines, large enterprises — dredging, public works, electricity, cement, distilleries, transport — all new industries) harshly exploited and having as yet no political experience. A peasantry, exploited and dispossessed by the great landed estates and the concessions of land to the large companies and to the Catholic Mission, and making up three-quarters of the Indochinese population. Side by side with the industrial proletariat there is an astonishingly rapid growth of a waged working class in the rice and rubber plantations . . .
>
> On the other side, a European and Chinese bourgeoisie dragging behind it the native bourgeoisie and domesticating a part of the petty bourgeoisie thanks to a relatively large military and administrative apparatus.
>
> In between these two camps there exist the intermediate classes (rural petty bourgeoisie, lower civil servants, intellectuals) which are still numerous, the process of class differentiation having not yet come to an end.
>
> The world, though still divided politically into nations, tends to form an economic whole . . . the world bourgeois revolution develops in parallel with capitalist expansion itself . . . Democracy has sufficiently unmasked itself for there to be no longer room for a democratic revolution. There remains now the proletarian socialist revolution . . . The question of independence must be merged with that of the proletarian revolution. The choice, 'independence or slavery', now poses itself in another more concrete form: 'socialism or nationalism'. (Ta thu Thau, 1930.)

In this text we see the fundamental opposition between the theory of 'bourgeois-democratic revolution' put forward by the Indochinese Communist Party and that of the permanent revolution.

The first is defined by the Comintern as the initial stage of the Indochinese revolution, as a historical stage of national liberation, which would establish a 'workers' and peasants' democratic dictatorship' to carry out land reform (expropriation of the 'feudal' land owners); the bourgeoisie, left in possession of their property — the development of capitalism under the control of the workers' and peasants' government — will co-operate in the industrialisation of the country, thus contributing to the numerical and cultural growth of the proletariat; when the relationship of forces becomes favourable to the workers the next, socialist, stage, will commence under the dictatorship of the proletariat.

The second theory, based on the class struggle, predicts the carrying out of the democratic tasks (national liberation, land reform) by the dictatorship of the proletariat, supported by the peasantry, which will transform the democratic revolution, in the course of its development, into a socialist revolution.

This revolution cannot be achieved within national boundaries but becomes permanent by spreading internationally until the triumph of the new society over the whole planet.

The declaration of the Indochinese Oppositionists

Phan van Hum and Ho huu Tuong, who had travelled respectively from Toulouse and Lyons to participate in the Paris demonstrations against the death sentences at Yen Bay, had escaped the police. Having fled to Brussels they issued a duplicated sheet, the *Tien quan* (*The Vanguard*), in order to clarify the problems of the Indochinese revolution in preparation for an eventual Congress of Revolutionary Annamite Emigrés (Annam cach mang xuat duong dai hoi). In it they expressed the same ideas as had Ta thu Thau in *La Vérité*; they underlined the danger both of remaining tied to 'old school' Sun Yatsenism, and of believing, as did others of the 'new school', that they had assimilated the teachings of Marx and Lenin after a few months' stay in Moscow. Rosmer, having met our two comrades, invited them to expound their ideas freely in *La Vérité*, even if they did not adopt the platform of the Left Opposition.

On the night of 13-14 July 1930, Hum and Tuong, accompanied by the French Trotskyists Pierre Naville and Raymond Molinier, were able to go back across the frontier and return to Paris. Together with La van Rot (Léon) and Nguyen van Nhi (both from the provinces), Tran van Si (Ernest) and Nguyen van Linh (René), they revived the

Emigré group which became the Indochinese group of the Communist League (Opposition). It was joined by the student Nguyen van Nam (Antony) and tthe seaman radio-operator Nguyen van Cu (Capitaine), among many others.

Pierre Frank, another leader of the French Trotskyist party, organised some discussions with the Vietnamese oppositionists in the woods around Paris; they also met at Ernest's at 65 rue Monsieur-le-Prince. In August the Group made its position clear by publishing the Declaration of Indochinese Oppositionists,[5] which affirmed loyalty to the Comintern ('the Comintern is our international organisation . . . the Comintern, however grave its errors, is the only revolutionary organisation of the proletariat') — and, simultaneously, set out the differences that separated the Group from the Communist International and the Indochinese Communist Party. Notwithstanding these differences, it called for the defence of the USSR.

The thesis on colonialism of the Second Congress of the Communist International had been 'trampled underfoot' by the Comintern's leadership under Stalin, said the Declaration.

After the 'bloc of four classes', the continuing entryism of the Chinese CP into the Guomindang, and the opposition to the creation of soviets during the development of the Chinese revolution, came the raising — during the period of counter-revolution — of the slogan of soviets, and the Canton putsch. It was this policy which lost the Chinese revolution of 1927; it hinders the formation of Communist parties in the Far East . . . the Opposition is working to correct the positions of the Communist International . . .

The Communist movement in Indochina . . . did not know the glorious period of the first four Congresses of the Communist International led by Lenin and Trotsky, but it did know the period of the disintegration of the International through the policies of Stalin. . . . This policy supports the thesis of the 'national bourgeois democratic revolution first' . . . The leadership of the Communist International also supports the centrist policy of the creation of a bipartite party of workers and peasants . . . and accords the peasantry a revolutionary capacity which it does not have . . .

Nationalism, which at all times has been a reactionary ideology, can only forge new chains for the working class . . . Only the working class, allied with the small peasants, can overturn imperialism and the bourgeoisie . . .

Moreover the Communist International commits a grave error by dividing its programme into stages, without basing itself on the process of revolutionary struggle in the colonies: 1. national emancipation and national unity; 2. conquest of democratic liberties; 3. socialist revolution. Life is not going to follow this decision of the International; it is more complex. The Indochinese workers themselves demand that these three aims be pursued together. Our slogan is: overturning of the bourgeoisie and the conquest of democratic freedoms by means of the dictatorship of the proletariat.

We oppose the idea of a bipartite party, said the authors of the Declaration. 'At present, when a single unified party, the Indochinese Communist Party, has just been formed by the fusion of the various revolutionary parties of Indochina — three communist parties and three nationalist parties — our task is to clarify this party ideologically and to urge it along the road to true communism.' This, they concluded, meant a struggle against, among other things, 'the nationalist and terrorist tendencies in the Indochinese CP' and 'Stalinist bureaucracy and empiricism which weaken the working class.'

Trotsky wrote to his new supporters on 18 September 1930. While apologising for not being concrete enough himself, since he knew little of the social situation and political history of Indochina, he advised them to be even more so themselves; for example not to forget the agrarian question when they spoke of democratic freedoms, and to consider in more detail the question of nationalism, which was not always reactionary. ('On the Declaration by the Indochinese Oppositionists' in Trotsky, 1973, p. 29.)

4

THE PEASANT MOVEMENT OF 1930-1931

In the countryside, against a background of crisis and general misery, aggravated by floods, droughts and bad harvests, the Indochinese Communist Party (PCI) mobilised tens of thousands of poor and landless peasants, day-labourers, in an open struggle against the colonial power. They raised the slogans 'da dao de quoc quan lang dia chu, chia dat cho dan cay ngheo' ('Down with imperialism. Down with the mandarins, *notables*[1] and landowners. The land to the peasants!'.) It could not, and did not try to, launch an accompanying movement in the towns. This produced a serious setback which led to numerous massacres of peasants and was a heavy blow to the cadres of the party in 1930-1932.

The demonstrations began on 1 May 1930. In their hundreds and thousands, the peasants marched in disciplined columns on the county towns to demand the reduction of the personal tax, this crushing poll tax which they never managed to raise; a moratorium on payments (which were due that month) the abolition of forced labour; the equitable redistribution of common land and the reduction of land rents.

The demonstrations in Cochinchina, peaceful at first, were soon dispersed by rifle and revolver shots. They turned into jacqueries. Hundreds of peasants fell under fire at Cho moi, Duc hoa, Hoc mon, Ba hom, Ben luc and Cho dem.

But neither gunshots, arrests nor tortures halted these processions of misery through 13 of Cochinchina's 20 provinces, on which marched women, children and old people, waving banners and red flags emblazoned with the hammer and sickle. Terror was unleashed in the villages, where the *notables* traced suspects and delivered them to the Sûreté — and the peasants responded. They cut the throats of these police informers; they sacked the communal buildings and burnt the registers and archives in the provinces of Giadinh, Cholon and Bentre. New military posts were established on the border of the Plaine des Joncs, in the 18 thon vuon trau (18 hamlets with betel plantations), at Hoc mon, Ba Diem and Duc hoa — areas reputed to be rebellious ever since the arrival of the French.

At the beginning of 1931, a state of collective responsibility was declared at Cao lanh, Sadec, where 2,311 peasants were made to endorse, either by signature or by thumb print, a 'statement of submission' which committed them to respect French sovereignty without reserve; to cease opposing the established social order; to guarantee public order in the village; not to hide any one sought by the judiciary and deliver them up, whether or not they were their immediate chiefs or companions.

The movement peaked in September-October 1930 and then ebbed. It received no working-class support. We cannot count as such the strike of 1 May by 250 coolies at the electric power station of Choquan, Cholon; that, in October, of 600 workers of the East-Asiatic company and of 80 coolies at the Phuoc hoa plantation; nor that in December of 150 coolies at the Phu rieng plantation. The movement declined and only manifested itself sporadically until February 1931.

Some militants spontaneously spoke up in the streets of Saigon, gathering small crowds. On 8 February 1931 police inspector Legrand tried to arrest one of these 'agitators' at the exit from a football match, and was struck down by a self-defence group. It was the anniversary of the Yen Bay insurrection. The youth, Hui (Ly tu Trong), would be guillotined for this the following November.

The principal leaders of the Indochinese Communist Party fell one by one into the clutches of the police in 1930-1931. Ngo gia Tu, one of the its founders, was deported to Poulo Condore and perished while trying to escape. Tran Phu, the party's general secretary, who had returned from Moscow in April 1930, died under torture at the hands of the Sûreté on 6 September 1931.

The Nghe Tinh Soviets

In Annam the peasant movement swept through the poorest provinces, Nghe an and Ha tinh, then spread to Quang ngai, Binh dinh and Nha trang. The peasants, following the path their forebears trod in 1908, marched for the reduction of the personal tax and against forced labour ... perennial demands of the poor. But this time they were organised and led by the literate youth, 'Canton and Moscow returnees'.

Despite increasingly deadly repression, the demonstrations multi-plied. In September they took on an insurrectional character.

From August 1930 onwards the demonstrators attacked the sub-prefectures of Nam dan, Do luong, Thanh chuong (Nghe an), Can loc, Ky anh and Huong son (Ha tinh). They freed prisoners, destroyed alcoholic drink shops, cut telegraph wires; some Catholic churches were set on fire, railway stations were sacked; hated mandarins and *notables* killed. The provincial committee of the Communist Party threw the 'radicalised masses' into the seizure of power, following the directives of the Sixth Congress of the Comintern (the 'Third Period' policy).

In September the peasant unions at Thanh chuong, Nghi loc and Nam dan in the Nghe an province formed into soviets. Protected by their self-defence groups, they took over the administrative tasks abandoned by the *notables* and militias. They did not take over the landed estates but limited themselves to redistributing the common lands monopolised by the *notables*, to confiscating and redistributing the reserves of paddy, organising collective agricultural labour, abo-lishing taxes and imposing rent reductions on the landlords. They undertook literacy classes and political education. The soviets spread in Ha tinh, at Can loc, Thach ha, Huong son . . . despite repression which consisted of aerial bombardments, massacres of villagers and the burning of villages by the native Guards and the Foreign Legion. It was a repetition, on a vaster scale, of the bombings and military operations against the VNQDD at Co am in February 1930.

In April-May 1931 most of the leaders of the soviets fell at the hands of the enemy. Nguyen duc Canh, one of the founder members of the PCI, was captured and beheaded. The movement gradually subsided. The population was tried not only by the repression but by the threat of famine. The harvests of the fifth and tenth months of 1930 had been lost, due to drought, and people lived on corn, potatoes and millet imported from other provinces.

At the end of May 1931 the massacre by the Foreign Legion of 468 inhabitants of the village of Yen phuc, Nghe an, in revenge for the killing by insurgents on 29 May of Sergeant Perrier, created such a furore that, in a decree on 2 June, the Governor General, René Robin, ordered a Commission of Inquiry. A hearing on what became known as 'the scandal of Vinh' followed, on 12 June 1933, which culminated in the acquittal of the three accused. At this hearing, before the Criminal Court of Hanoi, Commandant Lambert of the Foreign Legion passed the responsibility for the massacres back to Robin; he stated that

Governor Robin had verbally instructed that as few prisoners as possible be taken. This verbal order is corroborated by the secret telegram of 8 October 1930, No. 280 RS of the 'Résident supérieur':

Ré[sident] Supér[ieur] Annam and Co mat [secret Court counsel] to all Residents and provincial mandarins, Annam: . . . all demonstrations will be dispersed in the same manner (by armed force); all *notables* and all notabilities possessing real influence in the villages will be held responsible in their persons and their goods for disorders . . . in their villages . . . ; all communist agitators must be considered outside the law and must . . . be immediately rendered harmless by any means without having recourse to preliminary investigations or regular arrest . . . . ('Report of the Commission of Inquiry into the events in North Annam', 6 June 1931, Overseas Section of the French National Archives, AOM NF C332.)

The military, freed of all restraint, together with aerial bombardments, had killed some 10,000 natives, against the loss of only two French lives, those of Inspector Legrand and Sergeant Perrier. 'Legionnaries enter the homes, take whatever they want, rape the women and girls . . . Men and youths are arrested and shot in cold blood, without trial'. ('Letter from an old settler of North Annam', quoted in Viollis, 1935, p. 158.)

Viollis tells how, on 12 September 1930, only six bombs dropped by plane on demonstrators at Hung nguyen, three kilometres from Vinh, killed over 200 people. According to the protest of the Saigon lawyer, Charles Cancellieri, correspondent of International Red Aid, nearly 500 demonstrators were killed in Annam on the bloody day of 1 May 1931 (*La Dépêche d'Indochine*, 18 June 1931). According to official figures 1,760 bodies were counted up till June 1931 in the three provinces of Vinh, Nghe an and Ha tinh.

This is the official tally of sentences pronounced from 1930 to January 1933, according to the Reply of the Minister for the Colonies to Deputy Henri Guernut in the French parliament:

By Criminal Commissions	1,094
By native tribunals, Tonkin and Annam	5,083
French tribunals, Cochinchina	720
Number of Annamites sentenced	6,987

Of these 164 were condemned to death (88 were executed: 38 in Tonkin, 46 in Annam and 4 in Cochinchina). Still held in Tonkin were 1,091, in Annam 1,879; and 2,810 were conditionally set free. (*La*

Dépêche d'Indochine, 2 February 1933.) But the toll would get heavier still. Further trials followed in May and September 1933 in Saigon.

The trial of 122 members of the Indochinese Communist Party

In the trial of PCI members in May 1933 in Saigon, three of the accused were absent: one, accused of having killed an informer, had already been guillotined in March after a hasty trial; two others had died under torture during the preliminary investigations.

'The trial concerned six quite unrelated incidents which, contrary to all judicial rules, had been amalgamated in order to put together a whole batch of communists', one of the defence lawyers wrote to André Viollis. 'This procedure nevertheless had the advantage of discrediting the Communist Party and portraying its members as a bunch of miscreants.' The hearings were pushed through at great speed.

> In this matter, as in all matters to do with 'communists' [wrote the lawyer], the preliminary questioning is done by the Sûreté (this is legally an abuse of authority). The accused are kept in custody for several months and sometimes, as in this instance, for two or three years.
>
> In line with an altogether Asian refinement, unmentionable tortures are inflicted on them. Several came up for the hearings crippled for life. One of them exhibited his arm, broken while subject to the strappado torture. [This form of torture involved the victim's hands being tied across his back and secured to a pulley; he was then hoisted from the ground and let down half way with a jerk.] Electric shocks are even used, not to mention crushed fingers and pins pushed under the nails. These are merely the normal procedures. Thus are confessions obtained.
>
> Once these confessions are recorded, the accused is brought before the examining magistrate so that he may confirm them. The accused is warned, for good measure, that if he retracts his confession he will again be tortured, to death if necessary. (Viollis, p. 185, 1935.)

In the space of five days, 109 militants of the PCI were tried, accused of 'forming a secret society, plotting against the security of the state and criminal association'. The verdict was delivered at 4.30 in the morning of Sunday 7 May. Eight death sentences, and 900 years of hard labour and prison for 101 condemned people, of whom one was 89 years old!

The French Governor General of Indochina, Pierre Pasquier, wrote to the Minister for the Colonies recommending clemency: 'I myself was very much moved when I learnt of the severity of the sentences.'

The Amnesty Committee set up in France by Francis Jourdain — to which Marius Moutet, André Viollis and Louis Roubaud belonged — intervened with the Minister for the Colonies and organised information and protest meetings with our comrades, notably Phan van Hum.

On 11 May, four young Frenchmen belonging to the Communist League, the French Trotskyist organisation, organised a publicity stunt aimed at breaking through the press silence and snatching from death the eight condemned of Saigon. Around 4 p.m. they went to the General Office for Indochina in Rue Boétie, where an exhibition of oriental art was being held. They smashed the windows and precious objects and provoked a huge scandal. Atlan and Lastérade were arrested, Craipeau and Rosenthal got away. The following day's papers, reporting this impudent demonstration, said that its target was the Saigon verdict — 'odious' according to the French socialist paper *Le Populaire*; 'just' said *Le Figaro*. 'Stop the new crime of French imperialism against the condemned of Saigon!' said the appeal of the Communist League to the Paris workers, which was reported in *Le Populaire*.

On 16 May an Amnesty Committee meeting at the Salle des Sociétés Savantes attracted 1,200 people.

The death sentences were commuted.

5

THE INDOCHINESE LEFT OPPOSITION

Shaken by the peasant movement and by the repression of 1930-1931, Vietnam had sunk into an atmosphere of police terror; the very word 'communism' ('cong san') aroused fear.

Our three comrades expelled from France, Ta thu Thau, Huynh van Phuong and Phan van Chanh, had been put under police surveillance as soon as they arrived in Saigon. They started by looking for means of subsistence. Ho huu Tuong renewed contact with them in Saigon at the beginning of 1931 and together they looked towards the formation, in secret, of an Indochinese section of the International Left Opposition.

The tragic fate of the Nghe Tinh peasants threw the ranks of the Indochinese Communist Party (PCI) into disarray. The central committee criticised the Annam country committee for having launched a 'premature insurrection' ('bao dong non'). Militants in Nghe an, in opposition to the provincial committee, formed an independent group, Vung hong (Red Clarity).

In Cochinchina, Dao hung Long, then the PCI's special representative in West Cochinchina, set up another group at Ca mau, the Lien minh cong san doan (Communist League), which distributed the paper *Vang hong* (*Red Clarity*) in the Baclieu region. It criticised the party for its adventurism in Nghe Tinh and its terrorism in the south, where the movement had degenerated into a jacquerie.

Dao hung Long, who had come into contact with Ho huu Tuong in May 1931, expressed support for the theses of the International Left Opposition. The Moscow leadership was heading for disaster. Its policy had, in 1927, resulted in the Shanghai workers being crushed by the Guomindang, to whom Moscow had subordinated the Chinese Communist Party; it had led to the putsch and massacre of the Canton workers in December that year. The Nghe Tinh putsch had only been a repetition. The PCI had not concentrated its efforts on the workers; by according to the peasantry a revolutionary potential it did not possess it could not become the vanguard of the proletariat which — however young and feeble now — was destined to hold in its hands the nerve centres of the system of economic exploitation and colonial domination.

Dao hung Long turned the Saigon group's activities towards the workers and coolies. With Ho huu Tuong he published a theoretical journal, *Thang muoi (October)*, of which there were eight issues between August 1931 and March 1932, and an agitational paper *Cong san (The Communist)*. Having been put in touch with Ngo van Xuyet, who was employed at Descours et Cabaud, he organised together with him a 'friendly society'. The word cong hoi (trade union) smelled of communism and scared people — coolies, drivers and employees.

In November 1931, the Ta doi Lap (Indochinese Left Opposition) was launched by Ta thu Thau, Phan van Chanh, Dao hung Long, Huynh van Phuong and Ho huu Tuong, with *Thang muoi* as its theoretical organ. Basic Marxist writings — the *Communist Manifesto*, the *ABC of Communism* by Bukharin and Preobrazhensky, Engels' *Socialism: Utopian and Scientific*, about 15 titles in all — were published in Annamite (quoc ngu) by the Ta doi lap tung thu (Left Opposition Publications).

Disagreements surfaced at the preparatory conference of April 1932. Should the Opposition's policies be fought for within the Communist Party or in a separate Trotskyist organisation? Despite the absence of an immediate decision, the Left Opposition nevertheless continued its activity. In co-operation with the Dong duong cong san (Indochinese Communism) group, Ta thu Thau published the bi-monthly agitational *Vo san (The Proletarian)*. The first number appeared on 1 May 1932, at the same time as the pamphlet *Organising a Factory Cell* and other publications.

All these publications were stencilled and duplicated, all revolutionary activity being strictly clandestine and there being only a handful of Trotskyist militants.

Their movement, barely created, was temporarily broken up by repression. The 'printing presses' of *Vo san* and of Left Opposition Publications were discovered and, on 6 August 1932 and the following days, 65 comrades and sympathisers were arrested by the Sûreté, 30 in Saigon, the others in Giadinh, Baclieu, Soctrang and Baria provinces. Dao hung Long and Ho huu Tuong were not taken until 24 October and 11 November.

Due to lack of evidence, Phan hieu Kinh was released in August and

Vo buu Binh and Huynh van Phuong in December. Ta thu Thau, arrested in August, was released on bail after six months and later given a two-year suspended sentence.

After nine months in custody awaiting trial, 16 of the 21 militants of the Left Opposition were tried in Saigon on 1 May 1933, and sentenced for 'belonging to a secret society and subversive activities' (Article 91 of the modified Penal Code). Phan van Chanh was given a four-year suspended sentence; Nguyen van Minh (alias Hoang), Tran van Xuan and Nguyen van Hoang were given eight and four months respectively; Nguyen van Thuong and Pham van Dong got five and four years. Several had residence bans (enforced residence in a specified area) imposed for 20 and ten years for possessing firearms. Nguyen huu Hoa, Le van Ho, Nguyen van Be, Pham van Lua and Vo thi Bang (alias Nguyen thi My, who died less than a year later as a result of torture) were, respectively, sentenced to 18 months, one year, 15, six and four months. Ho huu Tuong, Dao hung Long, Nguyen van Dai, Tran hai Thoai and Nguyen hue Minh were respectively given three-year suspended, one-year, ten, six and three-month sentences. Tran thi Muoi, Dao hung Long's woman companion, was acquitted.

Ta thu Thau has described the conditions under which his comrades were held in detention at the Sûreté where torture, formerly only occasional, was used regularly from 1930 onwards after the PCI came on the scene, its aim being to extort 'spontaneous confessions'. His pamphlet, *Three months with the Sûreté at rue Catinat*, was handed to the workers' commission of inquiry headed by Gabriel Péri in 1934. In it the following cases are detailed: that of comrade Nguyen van Hoang, who, unable to withstand his torture, hanged himself in his cell, and was cut down still alive and kept naked in irons for more than two months; that of the woman comrade Nguyen thi My, who was carried out from the interrogation on a stretcher and admitted, the next day, to the Choquan hospital; that of Pham van Dong who plunged a file into his own throat when the Sûreté searched his home and found his home-made revolver, and who died at Poulo Condore; those of Nguyen van Thuong and Nguyen van Be, who were taken every two hours to the torture chamber.

I was prostrated every time my comrades were tortured [wrote Ta thu Thau]. I suffered more each time they were taken towards the spiral staircase. I asked myself whether they would stand up to the torture sufficiently to keep our secrets and avoid the arrests of the comrades still at liberty. (*Tranh dau*, 9 February 1939, written in quoc ngu.)

The Indochinese Group of the Communist League (Opposition) in France

The Indochinese Group of the Communist League, which had remained in France, tried to carry out the anti-imperialist struggle side-by-side with the Stalinists. On 19 April 1931, Tran van Si joined a Committee set up in Paris on the initiative of Nguyen van Tao to oppose the Colonial Exhibition. The latter was repatriated on 27 April before the opening of the Exhibition.

In June, Nguyen van Linh and his friends planned a demonstration near the Angkor Temple; its aims were to protest against further deportations of Annamites, to demand the release of political prisoners and the recall of Governor General Pasquier, 'guilty of the merciless repression of the Indochinese revolts'.

After the peasant movement in Annam and Cochinchina had been totally crushed, the group in September 1931 addressed a long 'Letter to the Comrades of the Indochinese Communist Party', which was being torn apart by the repression. It repeated and amplified the criticisms it had made in the previous year of the Stalinist theory of the national bourgeois-democratic revolution, of the nationalist ideology of a struggle for independence devoid of class content, and of the theory of the bipartite worker-and-peasant party for colonial countries.

> Our party still allows intellectuals, peasants and artisans to predominate in its ranks. We must try to make our party a real organised vanguard of the proletariat, by constant efforts to recruit the best workers from the mines, factories and plantations. We identify ourselves with the International Left Opposition because the errors from which we wish to protect our party are nothing but particular aspects of the centrist politics imposed on the International by the Stalinist leadership . . . Its theory of socialism in one country endangers proletarian internationalism and undermines the consolidation of the gains made in the USSR. (*La Lutte des Classes* (*The Class Struggle*) No. 34-35.)

'Our party'! The illusion persisted, of being accepted in the PCI as a reforming faction.

The reaction of the Annamite Stalinists in Paris was sharp:

> Fellow workers and revolutionary students, you must regard the disciples of Trotsky as dishonest counter-revolutionaries! They are the vanguard

of the bourgeois counter-revolutionaries (Stalin). (*Vo san*, 15 February 1932.)

In July 1932, the *Cahiers du bolchevisme* (*Bolshevik Notebooks*), organ of the French Communist Party, also reacted, in an article by Hoang the Cong, against the critical spirit — which, in the turmoil caused by defeat, seemed to permeate the ranks of the PCI youth. He described them as 'opportunists' of 'ill-fated leanings', pushed 'inevitably towards Trotskyism'; he reminded them of their duty of ideological obedience:

> [The 'opportunists'] do not want to understand that the Nha que [peasants, country people, with a derogatory meaning like 'bumpkin'] are subject to a truly feudal exploitation . . . Their second error . . . is to deny the necessity of the bourgeois-democratic stage in the revolution. (*Cahiers du bolchevisme*, July 1932.)

In February 1932, the Paris group of Indochinese Oppositionists, at the time about 40 students, started a roneotyped bulletin, the *Dong duong ta phai cong san* (*Indochinese Communist Left Opposition*) which subsequently became *Duoc vo san* (*Torch of the Proletariat*). It insistently drew attention back 'to the errors of the centrists (Stalinists), their insufficient propaganda in the industrial centres, the mining regions of Hongay and the rubber plantations of Cochinchina'. Already on 28 August 1932 it was criticising the disastrous Stalinist theory of 'social fascism' which was to render impossible an anti-Hitler front of the German Communist Party with the workers of the Social Democratic Party.[1]

In August 1932, the Opposition group distributed among Vietnamese émigrés a leaflet in quoc ngu calling on them to protest at the arrests of the Trotskyists in Saigon and castigating the silence of *L'Humanité* on the subject.

The group sent Nguyen van Linh as a delegate to the Amsterdam Congress Against Imperialist War (August 1932), six months before Hitler's triumph.[2] Linh could not, as an exploited colonial, be refused the floor. He reproached the centrists for mixing the red flag with the flags of pacifism and bourgeois nationalism; war could not be avoided without destroying the regime which caused it; the 'struggle against war' was, in Trotsky's words, only a sham if one did not make the main task the struggle against the powers and the classes which held all the productive forces; and the so-called 'building of socialism in one country' created a mortal inertia in the proletariat. The proletariat of the colonies could only base its hopes on unity with the world proletariat.

Our comrades were active also in the Committee for the Defence and Amnesty of the Indochinese and Colonised Peoples, organised by Francis Jourdain in March 1933. They belonged to the Indochinese Mutual Aid and Cultural Association and to the Sociological Study Circle where they met some militants expelled from the Colonial Section of the French Communist Party, including Hoang quang Giu, Nguyen van Tu, Vu van Tan and Bui Dong, who sympathised with them.

Faced with the impossibility of activity within the PCI, this 'amalgam of revolutionary nationalism and Stalinist centrism', the Indochinese group explained to the International Secretariat of the Left Opposition (letter of 2 October 1933) its intention of building a new Indochinese communist party — like the German comrades who were moving towards the building of a new German communist party after Hitler's victory.[3]

6

TROTSKYISTS AND STALINISTS IN
SAIGON 1933-1937

The birth of the La Lutte group in Saigon

In the midst of the suppression of the clandestine Stalinist and
Trotskyist movements in 1931-1933, some militants known to the
authorities but still at liberty — Nguyen van Tao (a Stalinist), Ta thu
Thau, Phan van Chanh, Huynh van Phuong and Ho huu Tuong
(Trotskyists), Trinh hung Ngau (an 'anarchist'), and Le van Thu and
Tran van Thach (pro-Trotskyist nationalists) — grouped around the
senior figure of the nationalist Nguyen an Ninh. They put up a list of
candidates for the Saigon municipal elections of 30 April and 7 May
1933[1]. This 'workers' panel', standing against that of the Constitutionalists, consisted of five workers, headed by Tao and Thach, and including
the apprentice typographer Nguyen van So, a future Trotskyist. Its
platform consisted of workers' immediate demands (the right to strike,
the eight-hour day) and universal suffrage. Since a paper in the
Annamite language would have needed authorisation, they published
a paper in French, *La Lutte* (*Struggle*), from which the group took its
name.

On the very day that Saigon awoke to the shocking news of the death
sentences on eight communists — 7 May 1933 — Tao and Thach were
elected. For the first time two 'communists' were going to sit on the
Saigon Municipal Council as spokespeople for the coolies, workers and
other defenceless groups. On 12 August the elections of both Tao and
Thach were declared invalid!

The *La Lutte* group dissolved itself after the elections, *La Lutte*
ceasing publication after its fifth issue. Ninh and the Trotskyists
collaborated in the literary review *Dong Nai*, published by Phan van
Hum, and in the well-known journal *Phu nu tan van* (*Women's News*),

which brought a new way of thinking and a new view of the world to the radical youth. In these sombre times, talks on dialectics by Thau and Hum at the House of Mutual Education of Cochinchina inspired a number of educated youths, employees and some workers. To spread Marxist ideas, Thau translated Politzer's *Principes de philosophie* into quoc ngu.

The 'legal' militants were brought together for a second time for the workers' commission of inquiry.[2] On 18 February 1934 this commission, led by Gabriel Péri, a French Communist Party parliamentary deputy, contacted not only Ninh but also Stalinists, Trotskyists and nationalists while conducting inquiries in the factories and villages. Péri promised Ninh the support of the French Communist Party, and financial aid from the Comintern, for the reconstitution of the revolutionary movement in the south and the renewed publication of *La Lutte*.

Ninh insisted that the collaboration of the Trotskyists be accepted, vouching for their revolutionary worth and their competence, without which it would be difficult to publish a paper in French. Stalinists and Trotskyists reached agreement to prepare for the coming elections on the basis of a common fight against the immediate enemy, the colonial administration and its auxiliary, the Constitutionalist Party. They would restrict themselves to a paper for the defence of the workers and peasants without broaching the questions of Stalinism or Trotskyism, while propagating classical Marxist ideas, a shared theoretical foundation. The articles would be unsigned (no personal publicity).

The group, thus reconstituted, restarted the weekly *La Lutte* from October 1934, and soon began elaborating a programme common to its three tendencies. It put up six candidates, three Stalinists and three Trotskyists, for the elections of 3 and 17 March 1935 to the Conseil Colonial (Colonial Council) — a powerless consultative assembly but a possible platform for agitation. The group demanded a general political amnesty, a parliament elected by universal suffrage, freedom for trade unions, wage rises, the distribution of the rice-fields and common lands among the day-labourers, the distribution to the needy of 300,000 hectares of abandoned rice-fields and of excess stocks of rice belonging to the landowners, the redistribution of the large estates among the poor peasants and the immediate abolition of the personal (poll) tax.

As public meetings were banned, the *La Lutte* group distributed thousands of leaflets and organised meetings with less than 20 participants, which were legal. None of the candidates was elected (the poll was subject to veto) but they obtained 17 per cent of the votes to the detriment of the Constitutionalists.

Two months later, the Saigon municipal elections of 6 and 12 May confirmed *La Lutte*'s growing impact on the petty-bourgeois and ordinary people of the city. One Trotskyist, Thau, one sympathiser, Thach, and two Stalinists, Tao and Duong bach Mai, were elected, as against only one Constitutionalist. The forceful speeches of the four 'communists' in the Municipal Council made a great impact and aroused lively popular sympathy as well as raising morale. Those in power found it difficult to tolerate the revolutionary use made of this platform; the four were arrested on 28 December 1935, after their homes and the offices of *La Lutte* had been searched, on the pretext that they had met a delegation of the 2,500 drivers of 'match-boxes' (horse-drawn taxis) who were on strike. They were released after their identities had been verified. The new 'communist' mandates were invalidated at the end of 1936.

The League of Internationalist Communists for the Construction of the Fourth International

In Cochinchina, the police operations of 1930-1931 and 1932 against the two wings of the communist movement were followed by a further police round-up of members of the Indochinese Communist Party (PCI) which was in the process of reconstructing its apparatus and rethinking its policies.

Lu sanh Hanh was among the 163 newly arrested. From his position on the Saigon City Committee, influenced by the Left Opposition, he had led a dozen Communist Party comrades into opposition and launched a new paper. Then, on 9 October 1932, he was arrested, and sentenced in September 1933 to 15 months in prison. As soon as he was freed he renewed contact with Ho huu Tuong. They, together with Ngo van Xuyet and Trinh van Lau (an ex-pupil of Ta thu Thau), founded the League of Internationalist Communists for the Construction of the Fourth International (Doan the cong san quoc te chu nghia, phai tan thanh De tu quoc te). This was the name adopted since 1933 by the International Left Opposition when they found it impossible to continue activity 'under the same roof' as Stalin. In October this organisation launched a theoretical review, *Cach mang thuong truc* (*Permanent Revolution*) and an agitational sheet, *Tien dao* (*Vanguard*), whose first practical action was to support the drivers' strike of December 1935.

The French colonisation of Indochina:
Prisoners sentenced for protesting against French taxes, 1908 (top);
The Bank of Indochina's headquarters in Saigon (above);
a state-owned opium factory in Saigon (opposite, top) and silk milling
(below).

Nguyen van Linh   *Lu sanh Hanh*

Some of the Vietnamese Trotskyist leaders: Nguyen van Linh and Lu sanh Hanh (above) were members of the October group; Ta thu Thau (right) and those opposite, of the La Lutte group.

The young Ta thu Thau

Phan van Chanh

Tran van Thach

Tran van Si

Phan van Hum

To the revolutionaries' dismay, Stalin had on 2 May 1935 signed a non-aggression pact with the Conservative Republican foreign minister of France, Pierre Laval. This pact disarmed them, since it officially approved France's build-up of a military strength sufficient to maintain its security. They saw the French Communist Party obediently endeavour to extinguish all anti-militarist sentiment and accept the integrity of the tricolour Empire; they saw the PCI align itself with the French Communist Party for the defence of 'France threatened in Indochina'.

The 'legal' Trotskyists of *La Lutte* maintained an enforced silence in line with the agreements made when the organisation was formed. This made it urgently necessary to make a radical criticism of the Comintern's new line, and of the PCI — which was evolving towards collaboration and allowing itself to be dragged, by professional revolutionaries trained in Moscow, in a direction contrary to its spirit. The League of Internationalist Communists again took up the Oppositionists' critical arguments; they added that the Communist Parties should not allow themselves to be reduced to the role of auxiliaries of Russian diplomacy, that if imperialist war broke out, the duty of communists was to transform it into civil war and that the USSR could be defended only by the revolutionary activity of the proletariat.

In May 1936, the French Popular Front's electoral victory once again heightened the crisis of the PCI. In the midst of stormy working-class struggles in France there arrived at the head of the state, the imperial power which ruled Indochina, a government of 'socialists' and 'radicals', headed by Leon Blum and Marius Moutet — and supported by the Communist Party's votes in parliament. This government proposed not to give up imperialist domination, but only to 'renovate the colonial system'.

Stimulated by strikes and factory occupations in France following on the electoral victory of the Popular Front, and influenced by Trotsky's perspectives for the French working-class movement, the League of International Communists launched an urgent agitation. (See 'The French Revolution Has Begun', declaration of 9 June 1936, in Trotsky, 1974, p. 131.) It was necessary, said the League, to create a mass revolutionary party prepared eventually to launch the local workers' movement into action in conjunction with the metropolitan workers' movement. It declared:

Fellow workers, peasants and soldiers of Indochina!
The proletarian revolution is reaching boiling point in France.

Hundreds and thousands of workers are on strike and occupying the factories and they are preparing a general strike.

Let us stand up again: elect your delegates in each workshop, each factory, each village, each province; fellow workers and peasants, set up your action committees everywhere. Unite! Launch the general strike in unison with the French proletariat!

Long live the total independence of Indochina!

For the confiscation of the rice plantations and lands of the landowners and their handing-over to the peasants!

Long live the French and Indochinese proletarian revolution!

Union of Workers' Committees, League of Communists.

This leaflet was distributed on 11 June 1936. The same day, the core leadership of the League of Internationalist Communists was locked up.

Again there were tortures at the Sûreté, reported in the *Dépêche d'Indochine* newspaper. Fruitless complaints were submitted by the lawyers. On 31 August, Lu sanh Hanh and Ngo van Xuyet were sentenced to 18 months and one year's imprisonment respectively, the teacher Trinh van Lau and the worker Ngo chinh Phen to eight months, the printer Van van Ky, the college student Pham van Muoi and the coolie Vo van Don to six months suspended; the worker Van van Ba was acquitted.

The Popular Front and the Indochinese Congress

The year 1935 had thrown a harsh light on the Comintern's rightward turn, first with the Laval-Stalin pact of 2 May, and then with the Seventh Congress in July-August which dictated to the Communist Parties their immediate tasks: the 'main enemy' was fascism, Popular Fronts must be created and the call for the overthrow of capitalism abandoned. The PCI marched in step with the French Communist Party: it dropped the struggle for national liberation and agrarian reform from its programme, and eliminated from its speeches (with a few exceptions, vestiges of the old line, up to March 1937) the expressions 'class struggle' and 'French imperialism'. After the electoral victory of the Popular Front in May 1936, it went as far as advising the trade unions, peasant unions and communist youth to dissolve themselves.

With a parliamentary Commission of Inquiry proposed by the Popular Front government in Paris, to ascertain the wishes of the Indochinese people, the Constitutionalists could only think in terms of a small Reception Committee to present the views of the nation. But

Ninh was inspired by a more ambitious idea, and so was *La Lutte*: to express the popular will in action committees in accordance with the June appeal of the League, which was still refused a voice:

> Organise in the factories, the agricultural estates, in the towns and villages, to form action committees. Their tasks? To get the masses to formulate their demands, to elect delegates to the Indochinese Congress. (*La Lutte* leaflet.)

The action committee of the *La Lutte* group, inspired by Ninh, Tuong, Thach, Hum and the Stalinist Nguyen van Nguyen, was the heart and soul of the propaganda campaign for action committees. It distributed, among others, a pamphlet by Tao, *Cho duoc thuc hien Dong duong dai hoi* (*To create the Indochinese Congress*), and another by the Trotskyist Dao hung Long, *Cach lam viec cua mot uy ban hanh dong* (*How an Action Committee Functions*).

The action committees spread like wildfire. On 30 September the Sûreté estimated their number at 600 in Cochinchina, of which 285 were legal, the others underground. About 200 committees were under the direct influence of *La Lutte* in the Saigon-Cholon region. The Trotskyists Nguyen van So and Dao hung Long were organising those of the suburbs of Cau Ong Lanh, Cho dui, Cau kho, Cau mui and Choquan; Ho huu Tuong and Edgar Ganofsky that of Dakao and Nguyen van Cu and Nguyen van Chuyen that of the school children of Saigon. Our comrades also organised some in the provinces; Tran hai Thoai at Ca mau, Nguyen van Dinh at Giarai, and so on.

The *Militant*

The Constitutionalists, responding to Ninh's appeal, had participated on the Committee which called the Indochinese Congress — but on condition that they had a majority on it and that the number of worker and peasant delegates be limited to less than a quarter of the total! Unacceptable demands, but accepted nevertheless!

Ho huu Tuong, who was opposed to collaborating with them in the Congress, published independently, from 1 to 21 September, the first Trotskyist weekly in the French language, *Le Militant*. He called on the workers and peasants to beware of the bourgeoisie, at the same time publishing texts from Trotsky on the united front and the counter-revolutionary character of the Popular Front. He reminded the paper's readers of the seriousness of the present situation: permanent repression in the country (the sentencing in August of the Internationalist

Communists for the Fourth International, and of the communist peasants of Duc hoa); the outbreak of the civil war in Spain on 19 July; the burden of Russian foreign policy; the first Moscow trials on 19 August — all finding no mention in *La Lutte*. He reminded the 'legal' Trotskyists that to co-operate with the Constitutionalists came near to class collaboration.

Strikes broke out on 26 November at the Arsenal and the naval base. Workers came out in sympathy on 7 December at the tramway workshops, and on 15 December on the railways. *La Lutte* supported the strikers by collections in the markets and factories and among the peasants.

While continuing activity with the *La Lutte* group, Ho huu Tuong brought together the clandestine militants in the Bolshevik-Leninist Group for the Construction of the Fourth International, explaining his position in the *Tap chi noi bo (Internal Bulletin)* of 15 November 1936. This group also became known as the 'October group', after the journal *Thang moi (October)*, which had been launched by Ho huu Tuong in 1931. On 1 December the group issued the illegal paper *Tho thuyen tranh dau (Workers Struggle)*, Its second number addressed young conscripts in these terms:

Comrade soldiers! In a few days you will be in uniform. As French subjects they will teach you the use of arms. This is what Lenin said on the subject: 'Accept the rifles and learn to use them! The proletariat must learn to bear arms, not in order to kill their foreign comrades, as the enemies of society command, but to turn them against the country's capitalists.'

We are fighting for your right to read workers' papers and to form Soldiers' Committees. Rally under the red flag of the Fourth International, for the dictatorship of the proletariat.

The trade union work of the two Trotskyist groups was reflected from November onwards in the paper *Lien hiep (Union)* and resulted in the formation of the Lien uy tho thuyen (General Workers' Federation) in the spring of 1937.

On 14 September 1937 the Constitutionalists left the Indochinese Congress of their own accord, accusing *La Lutte* of raising the labouring classes against the owners and disturbing public order. On 19 September Moutet, now Minister for the Colonies, ordered that all legitimate and legal means, even prosecutions, be used to maintain order. Repression against the action committees, until then held back, was intensified, with arrests and imprisonments. Employers sacked workers who belonged to committees; everywhere *notables* and militiamen harassed any villager who seemed rebellious. The Sûreté arrested Thau and Ninh on 28 September and Tao on 3 October. Jailed as common law prisoners, the three wrote a joint letter to the French Socialist prime minister Léon Blum, on 26 October:

> We are now in prison for having been and for being on the side of the Popular Front. The acts of which we are formally accused: articles appearing in *La Lutte* of 24 September in the case of Ninh and Thau, a pamphlet in the Annamite language entitled *Dong duong dai hoi* (*Indochinese Congress*) in Tao's case.

They were freed in November, after 11 days' hunger strike. When the Popular Front government's envoy to Indochina, the Radical minister Justin Godart, arrived in Saigon on 1 January 1937, thousands of workers and employees demonstrated, chanting: 'Democratic liberties! Trade union freedoms!' On the arrival of the Governor General Jules Brévié on 15 January, police cordons blocked all roads into the town to the thousands of peasants who were converging from the outskirts to present their grievances. Godart and Brévié met similar processions on the road to Hanoi.

Following an appeal in *La Lutte* on 7 January, the Preparatory Committee of the Indochinese Congress resumed its activity under the name of 'Central Committee for Demands'. The action committees experienced a brief revival.

On 26 February a telegram from Brévié warned *La Lutte* supporters to cease 'all political agitation', under threat of 'sanctions'. Already on 22 February a poster of the Central Committee had been confiscated by the police. The banned action committees retreated into the shadows and evolved into underground Stalinist and Trotskyist cells which were to be at the centre of the unprecedented wave of generalised strikes in 1937.

The French parliamentary Commission of Inquiry was finally buried in the Senate session of 17 July 1938: it had never been to Indochina!

The workers' and peasants' movement of 1937

In 1937 the strike movement for workers' demands reached its highest point. Workers and coolies, toiling people, unorganised and subject to unbridled exploitation, rose up in their misery, prompted by the militants. Godart noted:

The underlying cause of the social ferment is the poverty of the masses, aggravated by the rise in the cost of living, all too often wilfully ignored by employers whose decisions are taken far from the colonies and dictated by a cold concern for the reduction of 'general costs of production' . . . Rice and basic food prices have risen considerably — by 85 per cent between October and December 1936. (Godart, Report to the Minister for the Colonies, 10 March 1937.)

In January and February the strike was almost 100 per cent among the workers of the rice-processing plants and distilleries of Cholon; it shook the cotton industry and coal mines of Tonkin, and spread to the nerve centres of Cochinchina and Annam; the Arsenal struck from 6 April to 12 May, the railways from 3 July to 10 August. The most impressive strikes among the craft workers were those of the poorest, such as pottery workers and pit sawyers. Also effective were the strikes of dockers, sugar refinery labourers, rickshaw coolies and 'match-box' drivers, of coolies and day labourers in the plantations and rice-fields . . . all risking the sack, and the Chinese workers risking deportation as well. In the course of this movement, at first spontaneous and then organised, workers and coolies set up action committees and strike committees under Trotskyist rather than Stalinist influence. They demanded wage rises, an eight-hour day, the legalisation of trade unions, democratic liberties and an end to brutality and fines; they were not deterred by the fact that striking remained illegal and that any clandestine workers' association was classed as a secret society and membership was punishable.

Any native worker or employee who goes on strike without giving at least two weeks' notice is liable to six days' to two years' imprisonment . . . (Articles 41 and 43 of a Decree of 1930, *La Dépêche d'Indochine*, 22 October 1930.)

According to *La Lutte*, 242 strikes by workers, 56 by agricultural workers or peasants, 23 by shopkeepers and seven by other employees broke out in Indochina between 1 August 1936 and 1 February 1937. To stem the movement, the Blum-Moutet decree of 30 December 1936 reduced the working day to nine hours for the year 1937 and eight hours for 1938, granted five days' paid holiday per year, increased to ten days from 1938, restricted the working week to six days (but the obligatory weekly rest day could not be paid to day workers) and banned night work for women and children.

These measures were to apply to agricultural workers only after agreement by the Chamber of Agriculture (composed of native or French landowners)! 'Obligatory labour' was forbidden, but persisted, disguised as 'allowances' which could be bought back. Unions remained illegal and workers' representatives were not recognised, the factory inspectorate being entitled to represent the workers in all proceedings against employers or bosses. The workers therefore remained at the mercy of those who held economic power.

The concessions granted by the Popular Front government were meagre, and yet the bosses — French, Annamite or Chinese — tried to get around them. In order to inform the exploited of their new rights, *La Lutte* published the pamphlet *Che do lao dong Dong duong (The Labour Regulations in Indochina)*, calling on them to organise to prevent this legislation remaining a dead letter.

The workers sacked for striking got no support from the factory inspectorate. The Sûreté continued to arrest the more combative strikers and the courts continued to sentence them for 'interfering with the right to work'.

In the protectorates (that is, Tonkin and Annam), the impact of the Decrees was minimised, using the pretext of 'the rights of the protected monarchies'; in Cambodia a punishment of one year's prison for all strikes was added.

The peasant movement did not match the extent of the workers' movement. But *La Lutte* supported it and publicised its demands: the action committees encouraged them. The demands were no longer limited to the abolition of corvées (unpaid labour) and personal tax and the reduction of land-rent; they now included wage increases for sowers, reapers and threshers, an end to the appropriation by the powerful of reclaimed land with no title deeds. Petty regulations harassed the tobacco growers and gave the *notables* and militiamen the opportunity for new abuses; this provoked a movement of hundreds of small cultivators in the provinces around Saigon and ended with dozens of convictions. Nevertheless, between March and May 1937, it was with cries of 'Long live the Popular Front' that the Stalinists participated in peasant demonstrations throughout the countryside.

Like the Stalinists, the Trotskyists concerned themselves with the agrarian problem. Trotsky had already raised this with his followers from the birth of their group in 1930. But having come late on to the peasant scene, already worked on by the Thanh nien since 1926, slandered by the Stalinists ('the Trotskyists despise the peasants') and numerically weaker, they found it difficult to become established.

Nevertheless it was to Ta thu Thau that the deprived peasants of Rachgia turned, in May 1937, to defend them against the Governor; and the Trotskyists were not without influence in the action committees in the southern countryside.

The end of the Popular Front and the split of June 1937

After the arrests of Thau, Ninh and Tao in September-October 1936, the (Trotskyist) majority of the *La Lutte* group launched a full-scale attack on the Popular Front: it was sabotaging the Indochinese Congress, forgetting its promises of reforms, it was increasing the misery of the masses by devaluing the piastre, it had not lifted its repressive measures and had continued the employment of reactionary top officials. The Stalinists, frightened by this hardened tone, which they called 'Trotskyisation', withdrew solidarity from the organisation, in an Open Letter of 17 December 1936, and boycotted the paper.

In an international context the Trotskyist-Stalinist collaboration in *La Lutte* was truly paradoxical. In Moscow the Russian Trotskyists were being called 'slimy vipers' and were being imprisoned, deported and massacred; how could the Trotskyists of Indochina escape Stalin's condemnation? A new Moscow trial had just ended at dawn on 1 February 1937, with the execution of 13 internationally renowned revolutionaries whose names had been dragged through the mud.[3]

Nevertheless Thau persisted in a precarious unity within the *La Lutte* group; that is why Tuong resumed publication of *Le Militant* on 23 March 1937 as an 'organ of proletarian defence and Marxist struggle', with the slogan on the masthead 'Workers of the World Unite'. It reiterated the Trotskyist principle of the united front — to march separately and strike together; it reproduced Trotsky's article 'The Decisive Stage'; published Lenin's *Testament* and a theoretical article on the permanent revolution; denounced the deceptions of the Moscow trials and, in June, drew up a balance sheet — 'Twelve Months of the Blum Government, Twelve Months of Anti-Working-Class Politics'.[4]

The new municipal elections in Saigon, on 18 and 25 April 1937, united Tao, Thau and Mai — whose councillorships had been invalidated — in a common campaign for the last time. They were re-elected. The influence of the *La Lutte* group on the middle-class layers of Saigon-Cholon had remained intact.

On 19 May 1937 the French Communist Party intervened abruptly in the form of a letter from one of its foremost leaders, Marcel Gitton:

On the basis of the instructions for you that we have received, concerning the attitude to be adopted towards the Trotskyists in Indochina, we consider impossible the continuation of the collaboration between the party and the Trotskyists.

Ten days later the Stalinists in Saigon launched the paper *L'Avant-Garde* (*The Vanguard*) in which, faithfully echoing Moscow, they labelled the Trotskyists 'twin brothers of fascism'. The Trotskyist Thau and the Stalinist Tao were in prison at the time, following the strike at the Arsenal. Released on bail on 7 June, Tao proposed to Thau that they should cease attacking the Popular Front, the necessary condition for collaboration.

Thau replied to him on 9 June with a counter-proposal: the Trotskyists should suspend all criticism of the Popular Front for three months and would only renew it if the Blum-Moutet government continued to refuse an amnesty, political and trade union rights and the purging of reactionary local officials. This proposal had hardly been rejected before the Stalinists slammed the door on any further collaboration. *La Lutte* from then on became a Trotskyist organ. *Le Militant*, which would have duplicated this function, therefore ceased publication.

On 11 July 1937 the International Secretariat for the Fourth International wrote to the comrades of *La Lutte* and *Le Militant* that the period for a united front paper was over, the Stalinists having broken the alliance despite major concessions. *La Lutte* must now appear as the organ for rallying the masses (as a united front of all the exploited), must popularise the most winnable concrete demands — amnesty, economic demands, and so on — without ever giving up basic principles. *Le Militant* must reappear for the education of cadres and for building of the revolutionary leadership.

On 2 July Ta thu Thau and some of his comrades were brought before the courts under the press laws (see below page 52), and jailed for two years. The International Secretariat learned of these arrests on 28 August, and declared itself against the entry of the Indochinese Trotskyists into the French Socialist Party, the party of the imperialist 'government clique'; such entry would be of no help either to their safety or to the revolutionary movement. It advised the expansion of the illegal organisation and an increase in its publications.

The split engendered a great deal of lasting popular support for *La Lutte*. The Stalinists accused the Trotskyists of stirring this up. Tran van Thach put the record straight in a long letter published by *Le*

Flambeau d'Annam (*The Torch of Annam*) and then by *La Lutte* of 22 August 1937. On 29 August *La Lutte* published Gitton's letter, the French seaman who brought it having confused the names Thau and Tao, and handed it by mistake to our comrade. The Stalinists accused the *La Lutte* people of having stolen it and of betraying the secrets of their conspiratorial correspondence like 'the common cops (flics) that they are'. But to no avail.

Trotskyism grows in the Indochinese working class

The Sûreté noted in February 1937: 'The influence of the revolutionary agitators favourable to the Fourth International has grown in Cochinchina, particularly in the working class milieux of Saigon-Cholon.' In July it added: 'The worker element has been won more by the Trotskyist party than by the PCI.'

The Trotskyists had won over young militant workers and attracted sympathisers in about 40 enterprises: among the dockers and postal workers, in the Arsenal, on the railways and trams, in the FACI Company (Forges Ateliers et Chantiers d'Indochine), in the East-Asiatic Company, in the Water and Electricity Company, in the Manufactured Rubber Company, in the Portail, Ardin and L'Union print works and in the three large bus depots of the town; in Cholon among the workers of the Distilleries de l'Indochine, the porters in the rice mills of Hiep xuong, Duc hiep, Hang thai and Extrême-Orient; in the provinces, on the dredging sites of Mytho, and in the potteries, brick works and sugar refineries of Giadinh, Thudaumot and Cholon. Their trade union activities took in the Mytho and Travinh areas.

On Saturday evening, 29 May 1937, in Binh hoa xa, a suburb of North Saigon, the Fédération Générale Ouvrière (General Workers' Federation) held a conference of workers' delegates from 44 enterprises to agree its constitution. The Sûreté immediately raided the conference and rounded up about 60 people for identity checks, among them our comrades Dao hung Long, Ta khac Triem, Vo buu Binh and Vo thi Van. This did not prevent them from being at the centre of 50-odd strikes.

On 22 June 1937, 45 of the delegates met on the initiative of Tran van Thach to elect a Trade Unions Steering Committee. The Stalinists of *L'Avant-Garde*, with Nguyen van Tao, had their meeting at 34 rue d'Alsace-Lorraine. Shortly afterwards the offices of both Committees were raided and closed down by the Sûreté. Their organisers were tried in September. Here is how the official history related the event, with its usual dishonesty, in 1975:

> The colonialists used Tran van Thach, Nguyen van So and others to persuade a number of people to set up a Committee at 133 rue Lagrandière in Saigon in opposition [to ours]. The majority of the workers, seeing through the reactionary character of Tran van Thach and Nguyen van So, did not follow them. (Vietnam State Publishing House, 1979, p. 292.)

Naturally, the author conjures away the penalties inflicted on our comrades when he mentions those inflicted on Tao and his colleagues.

Ta thu Thau and his comrades were arraigned before the courts on 2 July for offences against the press laws, having been shamelessly informed on by the French Communist Party leaders, Jacques Duclos and Henri Lozeray, from April 1937, and again in July in the columns of *L'Humanité*, where Deloche wrote: 'The Communists will not hesitate to publicly denounce the Trotskyist provocateurs in Indochina'. Our comrades were sentenced to two years' imprisonment, to which the Court of Appeal added five years of residence ban (which stopped them from living in their own locality) on 11 August. This was the beginning of an uninterrupted suppression of our press as it sought to develop the unity in action of the workers. The same comrades were sentenced in September to one year in jail and ten years' residence ban. On appeal, on 10 November, the prison sentence was doubled. Contrary to what the informers of *L'Humanité* had hoped, Tao was implicated in the last two trials and given the same sentences as Thau.

On 24 July, on the eve of the strike at the Manufactured Rubber Company, the Sûreté arrested three of its organisers in whose homes the police had found copies of illegal papers, *Lien hiep (Union)* and *Tien quan (The Vanguard)* — which was the new title of *Tho thuyen tranh dau (Workers Struggle)* since February — as well as copies of *Quan chung (Masses)* from Paris. Seven more of our comrades living illegally were also put under lock and key.

At dawn on 2 September 1937 there was a further round-up of Trotskyists and their sympathisers in Saigon. Among them were Ta khac Triem who, together with Vo thi Van and Kieu cong Que, had organised small Fourth Internationalist groups in Annam, in the districts of Mo duc and Duc pho in the Quang ngai, and also in Tonkin, during the strikes on the Transindochina railway. Also rounded up were Ngo van Xuyet — who, after his release from prison in June published the pamphlet *Vu an Moscou (The Moscow Trials)*, also banned — and Nguyen van Soi, at whose home the police seized gelatine printing equipment and stencilled copies of leaflets. Among these was the *To hieu trieu* (*Appeal*) of the Workers' Federation of Saigon-Cholon of 26 March 1937, which opposed the PCI and its 'Guidelines on the new (working-class) organisation of the party'. 'We prefer strong mutual societies [mutuelles] . . . to red workers' associations pursuing a strictly revolutionary goal but attracting only a small number of members', said the Appeal.

On 7 September 1937, Nguyen van Cu, formerly managing editor of *Le Militant*, was given a six months' suspended sentence. On 9 September, 27 organisers of trade union committees were prosecuted for illegal association; only Nguyen van So was acquitted. Tao and six of his comrades, as well as Tran van Thach, Le van Thu, Vo thi Van, Dao hung Long and Nguyen van Cu were immediately sent to prison for terms varying from two months to 15 days; the others received suspended sentences.

On 18 November there was a new trial of Trotskyists: Le van Oanh, Duong van Tu, Nguyen van Tien, Nguyen van Man, Doan van Truong and Ta khac Triem were sentenced to one and two years in prison, and from 10 to 15 years' residence ban. Nguyen van Nho, Nguyen van Trong, Duong van Tuong and Nguyen van Soi were given six month sentences. On appeal, on 18 January 1938, the sentences were significantly reduced and Truong and Tuong were acquitted.

Marius Moutet wrote at the end of 1937: 'I recognise the complete legitimacy of most of the Indochinese strikes but the Communist Trotskyists prolonged and embittered them.' (AOM, Slotfom III, 59.)

The quoc ngu press was again put down. In November 1937, the Cochinchina Association of Annamite Journalists published *The control of the press in Indochina*, and sent it to Nguyen the Truyen, president of the Rassemblement colonial (Assembly of the Colonised). They pointed out that the journals *Than chung*, *Trung lap*, *Dan quyen*, *Viet nam* and *Phu nu tan van* had disappeared; *Phong hoa* had been banned; and *Ngo bao*, *Dan nguyen*, *Hon tre*, *Khoe*, *Tieng tre*, *Nhanh lua*, *Tuong lai*, *Nu luu tuan bao*, *The gioi tan van*, *Duoc nha nam* had been suspended.

Though actively engaged in practical work among the workers, and in spite of the repression against them, the Bolshevik-Leninists and *La Lutte* did not neglect to publish pamphlets popularising their ideas in quoc ngu — pamphlets which were often confiscated, for example *Bien chung phap pho thong* (*Dialectics Made Simple*) by Phan van Hum, *Ngay I thang tam va nan de quoc chien tranh* (*1 August and the Danger of Imperialist War*), *Vi sao ung ho Mat tran binh dan Phap* (*Why Support the French Popular Front?*), and so on.

The Vietnamese Trotskyists were supported in Paris by a group of sympathisers who had launched the *Quan chung (Masses)* on 15 September 1936 as a reaction against the first Moscow Trial on 19 August[5] and against the reformist degeneration of the Third International. These sympathisers, who kept in contact with *La Lutte*, published news of the strikes in Indochina and of the arrests and sentences being handed out under the Popular Front administration. They were joined on 1 October 1937 by the Indochinese group which, in *Quoc te IV (Fourth International)*, explained how the Comintern, through its theory of 'socialism in one country', had come to betray internationalism and the class struggle, by forcing the Communist Parties to support the policy of rapprochement with certain imperialist powers:

> The Third International people . . . are urging the Annamite masses to support the 'democratic' imperialisms against the Germany-Italy-Japan bloc. They forget that in the eyes of the Annamites, the word 'democracy', the French tricolour and the 'Marseillaise' are identified with the brigandage, assassinations and exploitation of French imperialism in Indochina. (*Quoc te IV*, November 1937.)

7

HOW THE STALINISTS 'DEFENDED INDOCHINA' UNDER THE FRENCH TRICOLOUR 1938-1939

In May 1938, the French government launched a loan of 33 million piastres for the 'defence of Indochina',[1] and decreed the conscription of 20,000 natives into the French imperialist forces. The Stalinists Nguyen van Tao and Duong bach Mai joined with the Constitutionalists in exhorting the population to subscribe to the loan, and to volunteer *en masse* to support 'French democracy' against the menace of 'Japanese fascism'. On 1 July 1938 the PCI Central Committee lectured its initiates in a circular:

> The envious looks cast by Japan on the Island of Hainan directly threaten Indochina's security. The PCI approves of the measures taken in the face of the fascists' territorial ambitions.

For the Stalinists, the colonial state became a possible ally. Their patriotic fibre, dormant between 1930-1935, started to stir again, down to its roots . . . 'the race'! On 1 April 1939 an article in *Dan chung* (*The People*) headed 'The Trotskyists are selling themselves to Japan and Fascism', claimed:

> The party of the Third International supports national defence as a matter of life-and-death for the Annamite race (Phai De tam het suc lo ngai cho su con mat cua noi giong dan Nam Viet ma ung ho quoc phong).

The Stalinists linked survival to support for the oppressors! Some people in the PCI showed such excessive zeal for the loan that they proposed dividing the 100 piastre bonds into coupons of ten piastres and five piastres accessible to the purses of the poor. Others rebelled against collaboration with the colonial regime and were suspended (such was the case of three members of the Cantho local committee in August 1938).

Our comrades' declarations took the opposite standpoint to that of the Stalinists: against the imperialist war, against war taxes, against the resulting worsening of living standards:

> M. Nguyen van Tao asks the proletarians to make sacrifices to support 'national defence'. If the capitalist countries are quarrelling over the loot, if they are tearing each other to pieces, the proletarians are not so stupid as to support one such country against the other or to kill their class brothers who live in the same conditions as them. Their duty is to take advantage of the war between the capitalist nations to emancipate the proletariat. Proletarians, close ranks in the workers' and peasants' front!
>
> United anti-imperialist front of the French and Japanese proletariat, of the populations of Korea, Formosa, North Africa and other colonies . . .
>
> While the people endure poverty and misery they have nothing to defend. They show us the rice-fields, the lands, the houses . . . but when we look closely we see that these spendours, these beautiful things and riches all belong to the big bourgeois. Among the ten new categories of taxes are those which fall on sugar and matches, two daily requirements . . . 'National defence'? Why load it on to the backs of the poor?
>
> (Popular black humour talked of the 'Third International box of matches' (hop quet de tam) when its price went up from 1 cent to $1^1/_2$ cents). (*Tranh dau*, 19 May 1939.)

The Governor General, Jules Brévié, congratulated himself on Tao's position:

> While the Stalinist Communists believe, with Nguyen van Tao, that the interests of the Annamite masses drive them closer to France . . . the Trotskyists, under the auspices of Ta thu Thau, are not afraid of pushing the natives to revolt so as to turn a possible war to their advantage in order to obtain total liberation. (AOM, NF330.)

It was the latter position which corresponded to popular sentiment. Hostility to military service was traditional, and the campaign to recruit an extra 20,000 riflemen brought this hostility to life — as shown by the disorders at the centres where lots were drawn for conscription, the self-mutilations and the prosecutions for incitement to refuse enlistment.

It was because they, in common with the Constitutionalists, had supported 'the defence of Indochina' and the war effort that the Stalinists of Cochinchina were repudiated at the colonial elections of April 1939.

The Stalinists and Trotskyists clash in the elections[2]

The beginning of 1939 saw an exceptional respite for the press and in Cochinchina as a whole. A decree by Edouard Daladier, the Radical French Prime Minister, on 30 August 1938 had abolished the requirement to obtain preliminary authorisation for publications in the vernacular, censorship was abolished and confiscations became less frequent. The Perrier decree of 4 October 1927 which outlawed 'manoeuvres and acts compromising public security or which led to serious political unrest' seemed to have been forgotten.

Our comrades redoubled their efforts, knowing nothing except that the truce would be short-lived. From 9 October, without waiting for Ta thu Thau's release from prison, *La Lutte* became bilingual. The *Tranh dau-La Lutte* defended the workers and famine-stricken peasants who had seized the granaries in Baclieu province and had started hunger marches at Rachgia, Ca mau and Soctrang. At the same time it clarified its political position towards Moscow, as the following sub-title indicates: 'It's time to take the offensive internationally against Stalinism — L. Trotsky'.

The organisation also began its modest Van hoa tho xa (Cultural Publications), which barely had time to distribute Ta thu Thau's pamphlet, *Tu De nhut den De tu Quoc te* (*From the First to the Fourth International*).

In Tonkin the Tia Sang (Spark) group, which was of the same mind as the October group, had two periodicals: the *Thoi dam* (*The Chronicle*) and then the *Chinh tri tuan bao* (*Political Weekly*) which replaced it on 14 January 1939. It also issued some pamphlets in the short-lived *Su that* (*Truth*) series.

Since 27 October 1938 the October group had, with Ho huu Tuong, been producing the trade union weekly *Thay tho* (*Employees and Workers*), which was supported by militants in the Posts and Telegraphs, teaching, public works and railways. In September 1938, in agreement with the illegal Bolshevik-Leninists, it restarted publication of the monthly *Thang muoi* which had folded after the arrests of 1932. In January 1939 it published the Statutes of the Fourth International,[3] and in February it published the theses of the permanent revolution as applied to Indochina, as well as an appeal to all the De tu (Fourth internationalists) scattered throughout Cochinchina, Annam and Tonkin to unite to create the Fourth Internationalist Party. The same appeal was issued by the *La Lutte* group in February 1939 (special Tet edition of *Tranh dau*).

The October group published new pamphlets in quoc ngu: *The Stalinist Faction and the Soviet Union, Reply to the Stalinists on behalf of comrade Bac giang, Marxism or Pacifism* and *Who Organised the defeat of the Chinese Revolution?* On 13 January it launched a weekly agitational, the *Tia sang*, with the intention of supporting the coming electoral campaign of *La Lutte*.

Two months before the elections to the Colonial Council — held on 16 and 30 April, on the eve of Annamite New Year (Tet) — Ta thu Thau, Nguyen van Tao and Nguyen an Ninh were freed, just short of completing their two-year sentences. Six Trotskyists stood in the elections against the Stalinists, headed by Tao, and against the Constitutionalists. The *Tranh dau* of 31 March published the Trotskyist election programme: a radical revolutionary statement and manifesto, recalling the heavy Stalinist responsibility for the defeats of the German proletariat in 1923 and 1933, of the Estonian proletariat in 1924, of the Chinese in 1925-1927 and the Spanish in 1936-1939. It reminded its readers that when the PCI diverted the class struggle towards national unity within the framework of French imperialism, it was acting, like all the world's Communist Parties, as an instrument of Russian diplomacy.

The election programme called for an Indochinese Constituent Assembly to be elected by universal suffrage, the granting of democratic liberties and an amnesty for all political prisoners; on the economic and social front it demanded the 40-hour week with social security and unemployment benefits, the building of schools, hospitals and cheap housing; the cancellation of debts and land rent for the small owners and poor peasants for the duration of the crisis; exemption from taxes for peasants holding no more than five hectares, the handing over of communal lands to the poorest and the abolition of taxes on oxen and buffaloes.

The revolutionary perspective, a transitional programme leading towards international socialism, consisted of the following steps: against commercial secrecy, the setting-up of factory committees and peasant committees to control the activities of banks and industrial, commercial and agricultural enterprises; next, the nationalisation of banks, large industry, big agricultural enterprises, transport and postal communications under workers' control; redistribution of the estates of the banks, the church and landowners among the poor peasants; the task of doing away with feudal exploitation to be given to the committees of poor peasants; against war, the formation of an Asian Soviet Federation; establishment of the dictatorship of the proletariat by a workers' and peasants' government. Such a programme could drive away many voters — but it did not matter whether people were elected or not, if great hopes could take root in the popular consciousness. Posters and leaflets promoted the campaign; they denounced the loan and the new war taxes.

Thau, Hum and Thach were elected despite their meetings having been banned.[4] The Democratic Front candidates of the Stalinists were defeated everywhere; the discontented electors labelled them as 'pro-government'.

The repression was unleashed on 8 June 1939, and it was in prison that Thau, Hum and Thach learned that their election had been invalidated by the authorities on 24 October.

Nguyen ai Quoc urges the PCI to 'politically exterminate' the Trotskyists

Nguyen ai Quoc (the future Ho chi Minh), living in China after returning from the USSR in 1938, reacted to his party's defeat, and the Trotskyists' successes, in a letter of 10 May 1939 to his 'beloved comrades' of Tonkin about 'the repugnant face of Trotskyism and the Trotskyists'.

It was the first of three 'lessons', each more delirious than the last, which were soon to be published by the Hanoi Stalinist paper *Notre Voix* (*Our Voice*).

In a report to the Comintern in July, he reiterated his loyalty to Moscow's views:

No reconciliation or concession is possible in relation to the Trotskyists. They must by all means be unmasked as agents of fascism; they must be politically exterminated (tieu diet).

His appeal to murder was noted. The Trotskyists were to be

physically exterminated by his acolytes when they had power, in 1945.

Repression and war

The PCI's appeal for class unity (doan ket giai cap) in the Democratic Front did not seem to have been heard. Workers, coolies and peasants continued to struggle for their demands, not only against the colonial exploiters and Chinese bosses, but equally against the Annamite bourgeois and landowners. The Trotskyist papers *Tia sang* and *Tranh dau* continued to support them.

The repressive Perrier decree of 4 October 1927 was re-applied. This decree, described by the journalist and anti-imperialist Daniel Guérin as 'villainous', had always been used against the press, even the legal press — except on the memorable occasion when the Saigon Appeal Court refused to do so on 19 May 1936. Now the decree was again invoked on a large scale: first, in Tonkin, from 28 April. Three journalists on the *Thoi dam* (*News Chronicle*) — Thai van Tam, Nguyen uyen Diem and Bui duy Tu — were sentenced (Tam died in prison in Annam during the war). At Bacninh, the publications of the Fourth International were seized.

In Saigon, on 8 June, the day the strike at the Arsenal started, the Sûreté raided and searched the premises of the Trotskyist papers *Tia sang* and *Tranh dau* as well as those of Stalinist papers and arrested journalists and managers. Other *Tranh dau* militants were rounded up at the print shop as they prepared a special issue calling for a demonstration on 14 July — among them Tran van Si who died two years later in the Poulo Condore penal colony. With *La Lutte* closed, Ta thu Thau, still at liberty, tried to continue his propaganda in other sympathetic papers including *Dan moi* (*The New People*), *Sanh hoat* (*Life*) and *Su that* (*Truth*). The Communists for the Fourth International circulated a new underground sheet, *Cach mang* (*Revolution*).

An increasing number of 'legals' were now in prison — but the illegals remained active. In August, the militants of Thudaumot, the Internationalist Workers of Giadinh and the Communists for the Fourth International united as the Bolshevik-Leninists of the Fourth International and once more took over the publication of *Cach mang*.

On the night of 23-24 August 1939 the Hitler-Stalin pact was signed.[5] This was the prelude to the Nazi troops' entry into Poland on 1 September and to France and Britain's war on Germany, declared on 3 September. Trotsky declared in Mexico on 19 September:

Even complete idiots should now understand that the Moscow trials, in which the Bolshevik old guard was destroyed, accused of collaborating with the Nazis, was only a camouflage for the preparation of Stalin's alliance with Hitler.

In Cochinchina in September 1939, a week after the great massacre started in Europe, the comrades of the Bolshevik-Leninists of the Fourth International distributed appeals to soldiers at Thudaumot entitled 'Do not fire on your worker comrades in the ranks of the enemy army'. They set up cells of three members each responsible for propaganda against recruitment. In his report of 30 November 1938 to the Governor General, the Governor of Cochinchina wrote that there were 'abstentions at the special drawing of lots'. (AOM, NF 1820.)

The poem 'Den sap' ('The Candle'), composed by the nationalist leader Phan chau Trinh at a labour camp in 1908, was still topical:

> Five times moulded, ten times remodelled, is that nothing?
> Honour the candle that always resists and does not break.
> One draws on its few inches of wick,
> One rolls and rolls again its envelope of wax.
> But the candle, it burns to light up the dark night,
> Its only concern is to illuminate.

On 26 September 1939 the Communist Party was banned in France; this ban was extended to Indochina. On 29 September, the Sûreté carried out a huge round-up all over the country: 323 searches, seizure of 2,223 books and pamphlets, and 26,316 copies of papers; 121 arrests of Stalinists and 55 of Trotskyists or sympathisers, among them Nguyen van So, Tran van Thach, Phan van Hoa, Ho huu Tuong and Doan van Truong. Dissolution orders hit the friendly societies and the committees of workers' delegates. In December 1939 and February 1940 there were searches and arrests at the secret premises of the newly-born Trotskyist papers *Tieng tho* (*Workers Voice*), *Cong nong* (*Worker and Peasant*) and *Cong san* (*Communism*) and at the homes of two members of the Bolshevik-Leninist group. Documents, in particular an anti-war declaration signed by an Anti-Imperialist Worker and Peasant Committee, were confiscated. Despite this, underground activity continued. *La Dépêche d'Indochine* of 3 April 1940 reports: 'Subversive leaflets are raining down in rue Frère Louis and rue d'Arras; it is the work of Trotskyist elements'. There were nine further arrests, on 13 June, of Trotskyists and sympathisers in the east of the country.

Trials followed. On 5 September, the *Tia sang* reported new victims:

Dao hung Long, Nguyen van Cuong, Le chanh Dinh, Nguyen van Nam and the elderly Edgar Ganofsky were given sentences from five months' to two years' imprisonment plus ten years' residence ban. In November, Ngo van Xuyet and Nguyen van Canh were condemned to eight months and six months jail.

At the trial, from 22 February to 9 April 1940, of 79 'communists' (members of the Third and Fourth Internationals, sympathisers, workers' delegates, and the like), Ta thu Thau, Tran van Thach, Ho huu Tuong and Phan van Chanh were sentenced to prison terms of three to five years, plus ten years' residence ban and loss of civil rights. From 24 April instructions were given to hold all trials of 'communists' in camera. Military tribunals sometimes took over from the civil courts. Even the charges remained unknown to the press and the population.

Defence industry employers had the right to hold on to employees they might need, and there was an instance of 82 coolies on a rubber plantation who were sentenced to months of imprisonment for refusing to sign a new contract when their old one expired.

Political prisoners whose terms of imprisonment were ending, and 'suspects' classed by the Sûreté as 'a threat to public order', were confined to their homes without means of subsistence or sent to 'special labour groups' (the concentration camps of Bara and Talai in the mountains and forests of Bienhoa). In 1940-1945 there were 1,726 Stalinist and Trotskyist communists, and 490 nationalists, living under these conditions. Ngo chinh Phen and Dao hung Long were exiled to Nossi Lava in Madagascar.

While the Trotskyists were leaving for the Poulo Condore penal colony on the same boats as the Stalinists, Trotsky was assassinated by one of Stalin's henchmen, on 20 August 1940 in Mexico. The crime had been preceded on 25 May by an unsuccessful attempt, by the Mexican painter Alfaro Siqueiros, another henchman.

'I am sure ... of the victory ... of the Fourth International. Go forward!'

It was with the above words that Trotsky — still lucid for some hours after the assassin struck him with an axe — expressed his unwavering confidence in the working class. (See the account of Joseph Hansen, his close collaborator.) On 12 September 1939, a week after war was declared, having forecast his own fate and conscious of the potential disarray of working-class revolutionaries, Trotsky wrote during a discussion with American comrades in Max Shachtman's group[6]:

The second imperialist war poses the unsolved task on a higher historical stage. It tests anew not only the stability of the existing regimes but also the ability of the proletariat to replace them. The results of this test will undoubtedly have a decisive significance for our appraisal of the modern epoch of proletarian revolution. If, contrary to all probabilities, the October revolution fails during the course of the present war, or immediately after, to find its continuation in any of the advanced countries; and if, on the contrary, the proletariat is thrown back everywhere and on all fronts — then we should doubtless have to pose the question of revising our conception of the present epoch and its driving forces. ('The USSR in War', 25 September 1939; in Trotsky, 1971, pp. 3-26.)

On 27 February 1940, Trotsky drew up his Testament, in which he declared:

For 43 years of my conscious life I have remained a revolutionist; for 42 of them I have fought under the banner of Marxism. If I had to begin all over again I would of course try to avoid this or that mistake, but the main course of my life would remain unchanged. I shall die a proletarian revolutionist, a Marxist . . . My faith in the communist future of mankind is not less aredent, indeed it is firmer, today, than it was in the days of my youth. . . . Life is beautiful. Let the future generations cleanse it of all evil, oppression and violence, and enjoy it to the full. (Trotsky 1958, pp. 165-167.)

But oppression and violence had many long years in front of them.

In Indochina, the colonial power believed that its repression of the revolutionary movement had 'established order' for a long time to come. But it was only the calm before the storm.

8

FROM 1940 TO 1944

The fifth decade of the century witnessed the near-disappearance of the Trotskyist movement in Vietnam, under the combined blows of the Stalinists and of the colonial power.

The Hitler-Stalin pact of August 1939 marked the USSR's defection from the camp of 'democratic' imperialisms which Stalin judged too weak. The PCI aligned itself with this new Russian foreign policy and ended its collaboration with the French colonial power 'in defence of Indochina' against Japan. It again spoke the anti-imperialist language it had used in 1930-1935. In November 1939 it spoke of 'the preparation of insurrection for national liberation', replacing its slogan of Democratic Front with that of a National United Anti-Imperialist Front of the Indochinese Peoples. This front would fight — supported by the USSR, 'fortress of world revolution' — against imperialist war, for the overthrow of the colonial regime and the native feudalists, for the independence of Indochina and to establish an Indochinese Republican Democratic Union. As in the period of the Democratic Front, the agrarian revolution remained absent from this programme.

In the PCI's eyes the colonial regime suddenly became once more a 'militarist and police' regime, as though French colonialism had not always been such. The party, although seriously disorganised at the start of the war, retained a considerable rural potential in the old network of popular action committees set up during the Indochinese Congress movement of 1936-1937, which had continued some sort of secret existence. Its change of line allowed it to resume contact with a population disappointed with its previous policy of support for the French war effort and violently opposed to conscription of youth and the sending abroad of Annamite soldiers. The PCI no longer exhorted people to join the army and now went along with the popular discontent, the opposition to taxes and requisitioning.

Both before and after the Hitler-Stalin pact, the Trotskyists saw the coming conflict between French Indochina and Japan as an imperialist war. The Fourth International's partisans fought against this war, within a perspective of its transformation into a revolutionary civil war. Putschist action should also be avoided, as Ta thu Thau had written in *La Lutte* in August 1937:

> While we were still a small minority in 1930-1931 we did not hesitate to react against the infantile insurrectionism of the Stalinists, exposing the wrong road on which they travelled. Internationally, our tendency combated the bureaucratic insurrectionism of the Stalinists and denounced the tactical errors of the 'Third Period' and of 'social fascism'. (*La Lutte*, 29 August 1937.)

In June 1940 the French state capitulated to Hitler, and the Japanese demanded of the local colonial regime that it close Tonkin's frontier with China to equipment destined for Chiang Kai-shek. On 22 September the Japanese army attacked Langson and three days later the French-Indochinese garrison laid down its arms. On 27 September, Japanese troops occupied Tonkin. Siam laid a claim to two Laotian regions and a Cambodian province, and started a war of skirmishes on the banks of the Mekong, causing the colonial government to send troops to its frontiers.

Peasant insurrection in Cochinchina[1]

The PCI saw it as necessary to act before soldiers won to the party were sent into battle. The insurrection was decided on. The country committee for Indochina had since July been planning an armed uprising directed by a 'military high command' with 'self-defence groups' and preceded by an insurrectional general strike; it fixed the time of the insurrection as the night of 22 November. A manifesto signed by the 'Provisional Government' emphasised that what was involved was not the setting up of soviets (class government) but of a Popular Government of the Democratic Indochinese Republic.

The Sûreté, alerted by its informers, apprehended the organisers, Ta Uyen and Phan dang Luu, on 22 November 1940, and also rounded up 'suspects' in Saigon-Cholon, particularly some soldiers of the Camp des Mares (O Ma). The army, navy and gendarmerie were put on a war footing. Despite all this, the insurrection was launched at 22.00 hours, simultaneously on Saigon-Cholon's outskirts, in Giadinh,

PREMIÈRE ANNÉE — N° 1   LE NUMÉRO 0 $ 03   Mardi 1er Septembre 1936

le militant

Organe théorique paraissant le Mardi

Administration — Rédaction : 15, rue Martin des Pallières -:- SAIGON

A TOUS.

NOUS aurions voulu, pour ce premier numéro de notre journal, ne pas faire de déclaration solennelle et ennuyeuse.

Pour se justifier, pour justifier son activité antérieure dans le seul but de soutenir une popularité ébranlée, l'homme politique petit-bourgeois attache beaucoup d'importance à de telles déclarations, déclarations qui sont en quelque sorte des plaidoiries pour lui.

Le militant marxiste n'a pas à se préoccuper des choses aussi futiles.

Le militant marxiste se dévoue à la lutte de classe du prolétariat. Dans cette lutte, il se contente d'une parcelle de la popularité dont jouit le prolétariat dans son ensemble. Dans cette lutte, en des moments où le prolétariat est bafoué, calomnié, le militant marxiste accepte courageusement toute l'« impopularité » que subit sa classe. Il n'a pas à conquérir ou à défendre sa popularité personnelle. Aussi n'a-t-il pas besoin de perdre son temps pour des futilités chères au philistin petit-bourgeois.

On peut raconter des choses les plus invraisemblables, les plus absurdes sur son compte. On peut tisser autour de son activité politique tout un réseau de mensonges et de calomnies. On peut l'accuser de tous les maux terrestres et infer-

naux.

Lorsqu'il avait à conquérir pour ses idées une place sous le soleil, lorsqu'il voulait que son mouvement « perce », le mi   marxiste se défendait quelqu.... C'était plutôt pour avoir une base pour un bon départ.

Mais les temps ont changé. Les armes forgées dans l'arsenal de la calomnie et du mensonge ne l'atteignent plus.

Nous ne sommes plus en cette période où l'on comptait dans le mystère, pour croire naïvement que les masses acceptent encore d'emblée tout ce que les comploteurs mystérieux leur chuchotent à l'oreille. Nous ne sommes plus en cette période où l'on s'enfermait entre les quatre murs d'un bureau de rédaction, absorbé par une activité journalistique sans ra-

Camarade ! As-tu fait voter dans ton Comité d'action un ordre du jour protestant contre la répression et réclamant pour nos frères terrorisés du Tonkin et de l'Annam la libre expression de leurs pensées et de leurs desiderata ? C'est là ton devoir. Sois vigilant !

cines profondes dans les masses, pour croire naïvement que celles-ci ne puissent pas contrôler les « canards » lancés et qu'elles ne puissent pas leur couper les ailes.

Les masses s'éveillent de leur torpeur. Et quand les masses s'éveillent, elles n'acceptent plus tout rond en métal pour monnaie courante. Les masses n'ont pas le temps de faire de la théorie, moins encore celui de croire aux absurdités. Elles apprennent tout dans l'action. Et maintenant que tout le monde est descendu dans l'arène, elles peuvent voir de près chacun de nous, suivre pas à pas notre activité. Nous ne craignons pas les masses. Au contraire ! Nous gagnons à ce que les masses nous connaissent.

Il faut dire aussi qu'actuellement, c'est la mêlée. Et dans la mêlée ceux qui emploient les armes à deux tranchants de la calomnie se blessent les premiers. Nous n'employons pas de telles armes. Que d'autres en usent, nous n'avons rien à y perdre !

Aussi le militant marxiste a-t-il infiniment avantage à suivre tout droit son chemin et à laisser dire les gens. Son activité dans les masses sera un feu de haute température qui réduira en cendres tous les châteaux de cartes.

Propaganda: the first number of Le Militant (above) published by the October group in September 1936; La Lutte (opposite), published jointly by the Stalinists and Trotskyists, challenging the disqualification of its candidates in the March 1936 Colonial Council elections

Troisième année : N° 34   LE NUMÉRO 6 CENTS   Samedi 22 Février 1936

la lutte

administration — rédaction
99, rue Lagrandière — Saigon

Le seul droit du gouvernement — et il est déjà exagéré — est de ne pas afficher à la porte des bureaux de vote les noms des candidats n'ayant pas fait régulièrement leur déclaration de candidature. Tao, Thach, Nguyen, Tuong ont fait des déclarations régulières. Ils sont donc candidats et d'autant plus candidats qu'en définitive ce sont les électeurs qui décident

Malgré le coup de force du Gouvernement, Tao et Thach
sont candidats quand même, et légalement

Opinion unanime
de cinq avocats de Saigon

Votez en bloc

Dans la 2e circonscription

Pour :

Duong-bach-Mai,
Nguyên-van-Tao,
Trân-van-Thach.

Dans la 1re circonscription

Pour

Phan-van-Hum,
Hô-huu-Tuong,
Nguyên-van-Nguyên.

candidats de l'opposition ouvrière

NOS CONSULTATIONS JURIDIQUES

Tao & Thach
maintiennent leur candidature

Le chef de Cabinet du Gouverneur a refusé d'enregistrer les déclarations de candidature de Tao et Thach. Il a même refusé ce qu'un honnête homme fait généralement quand il reçoit quelque chose. Il a refusé de délivrer un récépissé attestant qu'il a reçu les pièces que lui et bien il rangeait dans ses dossiers.

Nous avons été consulter trois avocats français et deux avocats annamites. Leur modestie ne nous a pas autorisés à donner leurs noms à nos lecteurs.

Voici les deux questions posées :

1° Un fonctionnaire préposé au service de réception et d'enregistrement des déclarations de candidature est-il

qualifié pour préjuger de la validité d'une candidature qui se présente et pour refuser la délivrance du récépissé ?

2° Les candidats ainsi évincés par le Gouvernement munis du constat d'huissier, peuvent-ils faire leur campagne électorale comme tout le monde, avec les avantages que la loi met à la disposition des citoyens en période électorale ?

Nous avons obtenu partout invariablement une réponse négative à la 1re question et une réponse affirmative à la seconde

Nous remercions sincèrement les avocats consultés de nous avoir assurés qu'ils nous appuieront sans réserve sur ce point.

(VOIR LA SUITE EN 3e PAGE)

APPEL

ÉLECTEURS,

La longue durée de la crise actuelle qui est surtout une crise du régime capitaliste rend chaque jour les conditions d'existence toujours misérables de la classe ouvrière tandis qu'elle aggrave singulièrement celles des classes moyennes : petits propriétaires, petits commerçants, fonctionnaires, employés, artisans.

En temps de prospérité bourgeoise comme en temps de crise, le sort du prolétariat indochinois est d'être exploité avec la férocité caractéristique du colonialisme sans qu'il lui soit reconnu le droit de se défendre.

Ni organisation syndicale, ni droit de grève, ni lois sur les accidents du travail, ni indemnités de renvoi, ni interdiction du surmenage, ni allocations au chômage, ni assurances sociales. Aucune conquête du mouvement ouvrier d'Occident ne trouve accès dans ce pays.

La classe ouvrière est tenue dans un esclavage implacable par la bourgeoisie qui, diminuant les salaires, congédie, maltraite physiquement sans tolérer la moindre résistance des exploités. Dans tous les conflits de classe, la loi bourgeoise force invariablement le travailleur à s'incliner devant les intérêts sacrés de la bourgeoisie.

Avec vigilance le gouvernement capitaliste veille à détruire tout effort que tente le prolétariat pour l'amélioration de son existence et son émancipation progressive. La répression s'acharne, interdit de se réunir, met l'évolution des masses vers la pleine conscience de leurs droits. D'innombrables militants ouvriers se meurent dans les bagnes ou le régime est atroce.

L'oppression qui étouffe la classe ouvrière facilite sa surexploitation. Depuis la crise. Les salaires déjà très bas des ouvriers des villes et des champs baissent sans arrêt. Réduits de 50 à 80 %, ils ne leur permettent plus de se procurer le minimum indispensable à leur existence. Le manque d'embauche fait des victimes en nombre considérable et sans cesse grandissant. Une paupérisation démente et suraiguë se meut par de l'impuissance organique un régime social qui condamne au chômage et à la faim.

La sécheresse contre les salaires la bourgeoisie franco-annamite s'efforce dans la mesure du possible à se décharger sur les travailleurs du poids de la catastrophe économique. Car la moyenne bourgeoise des industriels et des gros propriétaires se débat et détruit elle-même entre les griffes du grand capital, payant ainsi ses erreurs et ses ambitions démesurées.

Moyenne bourgeoise contre capital financier : une des contradictions de l'organisme capitaliste. Mais pour le prolétariat bourgeoisie et haute finance sont des ennemis de classe qu'il doit combattre avec la même énergie. C'est par une lutte sans répit dirigée et contre l'une, et contre l'autre qu'il défend ses droits contre ses exploiteurs pour un temps divisés.

La classe ouvrière n'est pas la seule que écrase la crise du régime. Les classes moyennes en souffrent de plus en plus.

Le petit commerçant désespère devant la diminution de la clientèle dont le pouvoir d'achat est fortement réduit. Ses affaires empirent par suite de la raréfaction du crédit, banques et haut négoce l'abandonnant à son sort. Victime de la politique de la déflation, il voit par contre ses charges diminuer dans une mesure insignifiante. Ceux qui se disent ses défenseurs dans les

Nhà xuất-bản «CHỐNG TRÀO-LƯU»

Những sách sắp xuất-bản :

1. — LIÊN-BANG SÔ VIẾT 1937.
2. — CUỘC TRANH-BIỆN GIỮA TA-THU-THÂU
   VÀ NGUYỄN-AN-NINH VỀ MẶT-TRẬN
   BÌNH-DÂN.
3. — SỰ THAY ĐỔI CỦA ĐỆ-TAM QUỐC-TẾ.
4. TROTSKY.
5. — TỪ LÊNINE ĐẾN STALINE.
6. — LỊCH-SỬ ĐỆ-TỨ QUỐC-TẾ.

Hãy đọc :

TIẾN TỚI CÔNG-HỘI . . . . 0 $ 08
CÁCH LÀM VIỆC CỦA MỘT ỦY-BAN
HÀNH-ĐỘNG. . . . . 0 $ 10

Thơ và Mandat đề cho :

Ngô-văn-Xuyết
108, Rue Lacotte
SAIGON

NHÀ XUẤT BẢN
CHỐNG TRÀO-LƯU
═══ 1937 ═══

ĐỆ-TỨ
HỠI VÔ-SẢN HOÀN-CẦU, PHẢI CÙNG NHAU LIÊN-HIỆP

QUỐC-TẾ
CỘNG-SẢN, CÁCH-MỆNH
LỜI NÓI ĐẦU.

Propaganda: the cover of Vu An Moscou (The Moscow Trials), a pamphlet published in Saigon in 1937 (above); De Tu Quoc Te (The Fourth International) a journal published by Vietnamese refugees in France after the second world war (right); Tranh dau, the newspaper of the Trotskyists of La Lutte in 1938-1939 (far right)

        Tập báo này viết ra cho những chiến-sĩ cách-mệnh muốn
tranh-đấu cho cuộc cách-mệnh xã-hội ở Đông-dương và ở trong
thế giới được toàn thắng.

        Tập báo này đề giải bày tư-tưởng của nhóm người Việt-
Nam theo con đường cách-mạng Bolchevick-Léniliste của Lénine đã
tạo ra. Nhóm Bolchevick-Léniliste Việt-nam là một nhóm đã
họp thành trong trường chiến-đấu tại Pháp chống lại Đế-quốc tư-
bản. Các phần-tử của nhóm đã gia-nhập theo đệ-tứ quốc-tế ở. Đệ-
tứ quốc-tế là một đảng độc nhất phấn đấu cho cuộc giải-phóng
các thuộc-địa và phấn-đấu cho cuộc cách-mệnh xã-hội hoàn-cầu.

        Từ trước tới nay nhóm chúng có thể cho ra một cơ-quan
ngôn-luận nào là vì còn phải bận nhiều việc phấn-đấu hàng ngày
và còn phải huấn luyện tổ chức chính-trị trong nhóm.

        Song đến ngày nay, mặc dầu nhóm còn nhiều việc phải
hoàn-thành, nhóm nhận thấy cần phải cho phát hành tờ báo này
vì thế rằng trong đám Việt-kiều ở Pháp cũng như trong quần-
chúng ở Đông-dương, cần phải vạch ra một con đường chính-trị rõ
rệt, cần phải nêu lên những chuẩn-đích xác đáng để đạt tới và
những phương-pháp để đạt được những chuẩn đích ấy.

        Hiện giờ khẩu hiệu "chống với Đế-quốc" đã thành ra
không đầy đủ, còn cần phải biết phân biệt rõ ràng, ai tuyên-chiến
với Đế-quốc, ai tranh đấu đến cùng để đánh đổ Đế-quốc, còn ai
tuyên-chiến với Đế-quốc nhưng rồi rốt cuộc lại đi theo Đế-quốc
để đàn áp đến thợ và dân cày.

        Cuộc tranh-đấu của nhóm Bolchevick-Léniliste chúng tôi
chống lại Đế-quốc không phải là một cuộc tranh-đấu bác-huyền.
Chúng tôi tranh đấu không phải dưới bảng trường giai Việt-nam
hưởng lợi và tự-do bóc lột quần chúng lao-công trong xứ. Chúng

tranh đấu

SỐ ĐẶC BIỆT MÙA XUÂN

ĐỌC TRONG SỐ NÀY:
Kiến thiết chánh đảng Đệ-tứ
1938, năm toàn thắng của
fát-xít
Chúng tôi đấu với cuộc
tuyển cử quần hạt.
Phan-tì Hữu từ báo Tự-Do
Từ án Moscou 1936-1938,
bị hành án ... đình trong
... điện của Léon Trotsky
Ba tháng ở bót Catinat
của Tạ Thu-Tứu

THỢ THUYỀN ! NÔNG - DÂN !

HÃY TỔ-HIỆP THÀNH ĐẢNG ĐỆ - TỨ ĐÔNG - DƯƠNG

MÙA
XUÂN
Ở
PARIS

Tỉnh sổ cũi năm

1938,
năm toàn thắng
của fat - xít !

1939,
năm tranh đấu
của vô - sản !

1938...
Cái nấm nhông
đặc biệt của các
đế-quốc fát-
xít.

năm «xu» sự
sự toàn bình
thế-giới, của vô sản giai cấp
hoàn cầu.

Từ đầu năm cuối năm đen
nuông nó sung sự hông nổ của
dân chúng, các nước yêu trên
quả địa cầu này, dân Âu phải
mất được, xứ Tiệp bị của
manh. Quảng châu toàn thủ,
cách mạng Tây-ban-nha sắp
nửa vào

Tháng ba: Hitler chiếm
Áo-quốc

Vừa đầu năm tới ao hùng sắp
từa trên đầu dân chúng Áo
Tháng 4 « 19 » Hitler vào
ấu ranh đưa vào Áu trong
một bài diễn văn dục lại nhà
ở Opéra kroll (berlin).

Tôi tuyên bố phát xít tuyên bố
sẽ đang vô lực sẽ sắp xếp
nước Áo về Đức

Tôi thành tưởng độc tài Schuss-
chung cầm quyền nước Áo
trong sức ấy là tên sát nhân
để bắt giết thợ thuyền thành
Vienne một cách dã man, tàn
nhẫn.

Vậy mà, trước thái độ khẩn
khích của Hitler, anh chàng
lại bọ một, nhường bộ luôn, anh
(Còn tiếp qua trương 11)

RENAULT

Ở in 1938 — Thợ thuyền trong hãng Renault
đình công chiến xưởng.

Những đảng Cộng-sản lại đưa ra khẩu hiệu
đầu hàng : « Phải biết giữ một cuộc đình công».

Hời các phần tử xu hướng Đệ-tứ ở Đông-dương!

KIẾN THIẾT CHÁNH ĐẢNG

HIỆN tại liệt cường đế quốc đã bị nạm
vào chổ sản tư quán đầu. Tranh
giành nhau thị trường, tranh giành
nhau thuộc-địa, tranh giành nhau
nguyên liệu, tranh giành nhau nhơn
công, tóm lại tranh giành nhau sự
sống ở dưới bóng mặt trời, lê-quốc
phải liều mạng đâm đầu vào chổ chết, họa chiến
tranh xông đến không biết giờ phút nào ở trước
mắt ta.

Nước phát-xít độc-tài, phải gây chiến tranh
mới tồn tại được. Điều ấy đã hiển nhiên. Năm rồi
Hitler đã làm cho liệt-cương cuồng loạn hồi tháng
Septembre. Năm nay Mussolini hầm hầm gây sự
với nước Pháp. Hai tướng độc-tài bắc, Ý, đầu chỉ
bề trong có quyền lợi mâu-thuẫn nhau, bề ngoài
cũng phải nương dựa ý y nhau để chống với những
nước gọi rằng « dân chủ ». Cái « chánh trực »
(Còn tiếp qua trương 12)

Cholon, Mytho and Tan an provinces on the borders of the Plaine des Joncs; it involved the Mekong delta and the provinces of Vinhlong, Travinh and Cantho, and spread to Soctrang. The insurgents stormed the administrative centres of Hocmon, Vungliem and Tambinh, and attacked the belt of small forts around Saigon-Cholon and the posts held by Annamite militiamen, capturing some rifles. Municipal buildings, offices of the councils of *notables*, were set on fire; some *notables* and officials known for their cruelty were struck down or abducted, their arms confiscated and their houses burnt.

The guerrillas tried to block roads and canals, destroy bridges and cut telegraph wires and communications; to get arms they attacked patrols. The rising shook the whole of western Cochinchina — the very same regions where large scale peasant risings, and no less severe repression, had taken place in 1930-1931. It reached the provinces of Rachgia, Longxuyen and Baclieu towards the end of November and finally flared up on the night of 13-14 December with the attack on the lighthouse on Poulo Obi island by 40 insurgents.

Martial law was proclaimed. French troops of the 9th and 11th regiments of colonial infantry, the Foreign Legion, the air force, the militia and police agents were sent against the insurgents. The Plaine des Joncs was surrounded and then bombed from the air. Entire villages were machine-gunned and then raked over by the police. Cambodian rifle regiments operated in the western provinces of the delta; raping and pillaging went unpunished.

The insurrection was put down by the same methods as had been used ten years before in February 1930 at Co am, Tonkin, at the time of the soldiers' mutiny at Yen Bay, and in September 1930 against the soviets of Nghe Tinh in North Annam. In the county town of Travinh, where the author was in forced residence, one saw at night the militiamen bring back dead and wounded peasants heaped on lorries; the province's chief was wounded. R. Bauchar, a French eye-witness not without some regard for the Annamites, describes the cruelty of the repression north of Mytho:

> A battalion of the Foreign Legion, a company of Tonkinese troops, and a mechanised unit, some marines . . . carried out a mass search, arresting suspects and firing on those who attempted to fight or flee. The air force violently bombed the centres of resistance . . . In four days they were crushed . . . and the ringleaders shot. (Bauchar, 1946, p. 71.)

Official figures gave the numbers killed in action as more than 100 insurgents and about 30 from the repressive forces, including three French. The thousands of non-combatant villagers who were massacred are not included. Official figures said 5,846 people were apprehended; the prisons were full and excess prisoners were piled into barges where, under sheet metal decks, overheated by a burning sun, they died like flies. Franchini related:

> An infectious epidemic called hospital gangrene spread among them. The stench spread for two or three kilometres around. (Franchini, 1977, p. 112).

It was in one of these prison-barges that our comrade Trinh van Lau died, having been captured by the Sûreté on 17 December.

In September 1941, some Frenchmen, on leaving Indochina, told of what they had witnessed:

> Rows of prisoners, men and women, sitting with their feet shackled to a long rod; obliged to sit continually thus while awaiting their trial, subject to blows and insults from their guardians . . . the methods used to force the suspects to talk were: electric wires attached to their sexual organs, ants introduced into those of the women . . . the disgust of the airmen, ordered to bomb and machine-gun the villages near the Plaine des Joncs . . . the summary convictions repeating the events of Yen Bay ten years earlier. (Hertrich, 1946, p. 22.)

Paul Isoart draws up the following balance sheet of the judicial repression: 221 death sentences, of which 181 were carried out; 216 hard-labour sentences; prison sentences counted in thousands (Isoart, 1982, p. 13). Ta Uyen died under torture in December 1940, and Phan dang Luu was executed in May 1941. Some activists who had been in prison since long before the insurrection, such as Ha huy Tap and Nguyen thi Minh Khai, the only woman political prisoner, were shot on the orders of the French Admiral, Decoux, who ruled Indochina by agreement between the Vichy government[2] and the Japanese.

The tragedy had repercussions within the PCI. The Sûreté noted the decision of a new Cochinchina country committee, in January 1941, to condemn to death the secretaries of the previous country committee and of the inter-provincial committee of Cantho, guilty of having launched a hopeless insurrection (see note 1 for this chapter). As far as we know, any mention of this internal trial in the PCI is missing from the party's official history.

The Japanese occupation

Although France had been defeated, its colonial apparatus remained intact. The Vichy government made it more totalitarian than ever. The arrival in Vietnam of Japanese troops in September 1940 through northern Tonkin and Haiphong was followed in July 1941 by a 'mutual defence' agreement, signed in Vichy. This legitimised the peaceful occupation of all Indochina by the Japanese. Admiral Decoux's government became 'the guarantor of security behind Japanese lines and of internal order in Indochina'.

Economic agreements signed from May onwards covered deliveries of rice, maize, rubber and coal to Japan. Decoux conscripted labour for the Japanese forces' strategic building works (railways, camps, airfields). He ordered industrial farming, set up a monopoly over the collection of crops, and gave the Japanese troops massive allocations of piastres. Inflation, destitution, rationing, black-market speculation and profiteering cruelly hit the poor. This culminated — after raging typhoons, the crumbling of the dikes in Tonkin and American bombardment of the Trans-Indochina railway to prevent the delivery of rice from Cochinchina — in a famine which killed between one and two million of Tonkin's people in 1944-1945.

What can be said about the 'protective tutelage' of the country by Admiral Decoux — who, on the day his administration was kicked out by the Japanese, 9 March 1945, held a stock of 500,000 barrels of paddy for export?

Double occupation, doubled exploitation! And, also, a two-fold attempt at seduction.

From Decoux, there was a conciliatory policy towards the local rulers under French protection (the kings of Cambodia and Laos and the emperor of Annam); the setting up of a consultative Federal Council of 25 natives 'chosen for their loyalty to France'; for 'native élites' came the 'opening-up' of 'functions of administration and management, that is, positions of authority' after the purging of hundreds of French 'malcontents, freemasons and Jews', and equality with the French officials. A relative freedom of the press, abolished in 1939, was restored, allowing a 'controlled' intellectual life in literary circles; the educated youth were wooed, and organised in branches of the 'Youth of the French Empire' with the building of schools and camps, spectacular torch races, and parades in uniform — all under the motto 'obey and serve', and pervaded with the cult of the 'venerated Marshal' [Pétain].

From the Japanese side, there was a promise of aid to the colonial peoples of Asia to free them of the European yoke and admit them to the 'economic co-prosperity sphere of Great Eastern Asia', limited support for politico-religious sects and illegal nationalist groups such as the Phuc Quoc of Prince Cuong De and the opposition of the Kempeitai (Japanese police) to certain arrests by the French Sûreté.

The outlawing of the 'communist' movement from 1939, the crushing of the peasant rising of 1940, and the execution or detention of Stalinist and Trotskyist militants, had sown confusion and distrust among the population. Coolies, workers and peasants would not put themselves in danger . . . except in their struggle to survive, to get their daily bowl of rice, to demand the sale of the cloth, rice, matches and soap which were not on the markets.

According to official figures there were 18 strikes in the north in 1943-1944; in the printshops, Bank of Indochina, enterprises in Hanoi, the shipping line Namdinh-Hanoi, textile mills of Namdinh — and at the air base of Gialam after the Japanese murdered a woman day-labourer. There was also occasional desperate opposition in the villages to the able-bodied men being requisitioned for work, as in the Thanhhoa area in November 1943. In Cochinchina 24 strikes were noted between May 1942 and June 1943, particularly in the rubber plantations of Bienhoa. In October 1943, 500 coolies on the Long thanh plantation went on strike after one of their workmates was murdered by a French overseer. There were similar actions in the Japanese clothing and boot factories for the army and military camp sites. In the port of Saigon the workers were bold enough to protest against the Japanese soldiers' brutalities as well as about the food.

Nationalist resurgence

From the moment of their arrival the Japanese were busy propagating the myth of 'Great East Asia' over the radio, in the cinema, through quoc ngu journals such as Tan A (New Asia), with exhibitions showing the early victories in the Pacific and by Japanese language courses. On a visit to Saigon in July 1943, the retired Japanese general, Matsui, declared that 'Japan would liberate the countries of Asia, against the will of the Americans, French and English'.

For the time being, the French administrative apparatus was kept on and given the task of maintaining order — but the Japanese also gave protection to the Cao dai and Hoa hao religious sects and the tiny nationalist groups which had appeared since 1940. In the south, there was the United Revolutionary Party of the Annamite People, an offshoot of the Viet nam phuc quoc; in the North, the Dai Viet (Great Viet) founded by the novelist Nguyen tuong Tam, the Dai Viet quoc xa (National Socialist Great Viet) and the Viet Nam ai quoc (Patriotic Viet). These tiny groups of conspirators reflected currents among radical intellectuals who hoped to end French colonisation by leaning on Japanese power.

After the bombing of Pearl Harbour on 8 December 1941,[3] the Kempeitai, to protect these groups more effectively, established itself in Indochina as a police force parallel to the Sûreté.

After the Japanese reverses in the Pacific and the German setback at Stalingrad, there appeared, in the quoc ngu press that Decoux tolerated, alongside a new appreciation of the ancient culture, a new anticipation of independence linked to a victory of the Allies. (Since Hitler's invasion of the USSR it, too, had been in that camp.) On 7 August 1943, Huynh tan Phat's Saigon weekly, *Thanh nien*, announced its intention to encourage a 'national consciousness'. It sought to activate popular forces whose intervention 'will enable the country to enter a new stage in its history', the union of the three Kys (Tonkin, Annam and Cochinchina) into one free country.

A 'patriotism' that transformed itself into open nationalism had no place in Decoux's scenario; the *Thanh nien* was suspended towards the middle of 1944.

The Cao dai sect, which first appeared in Cochinchina in 1925-1926, was built by a fraction of the Cochinchinese bourgeoisie ill-at-ease with its subordinate position in the colonial apparatus. It tried to create for itself a transcendental domain in which it would recover its pre-eminence and restore the lost morale of three religions — Buddhism, Taoism and Confucianism — by remoulding them into one religion called Cao dai-ism (from the name of Cao Dai, Supreme Being). The sect's initiators were mainly high officials and landowners. (See Werner, 1976; Savani, 1966.)

The sect's organisation was modelled on those of the Catholic hierarchy (with a Holy See) and of the colonial administration. It recruited rapidly among the rural milieux of landed gentry and notables. Both Constitutionalists and nationalists hoped to use it to build points of support for themselves among the peasantry mobilised since 1930 by the Nguyen an Ninh movement, the Thanh nien and the Indochinese Communist Party. Despite internal conflicts, the Cao dai already had 350,000 followers in 1932. The European war and the French defeat were interpreted and explained in lyrical poems, spirit messages and prophecies announcing the imminent end of French oppression as confirmed in the stars.

In August 1940, Admiral Decoux ordered that the Holy See of Tay ninh and most of the provincial pulpits be shut down. In July 1941 the sect's Pope was deported to Madagascar and in September the Holy See was occupied by troops. In September 1943, the high official Tran quang Vinh, 'civil attaché' to the Japanese police, joined the Phuc quoc. The Dai Viet and the Dai Viet quoc xa, two of the nationalist sects which had emerged recently, united with this movement under the name of Viet nam phuc quoc dong minh hoi. The sect paid for Japanese protection by recruiting coolies for the shipyard of Vinh hoi (Saigon); its followers were given military training by Japanese instructors.

Another sect, the Hoa hao, appeared only in 1939. Taking its name from the home village of its founder, it grew so rapidly that from August 1940 it was persecuted by the regime. (See 'Notes sur le Phat giao Hoa hao', in Savani 1966.) Huynh phu So, son of a rural *notable*, started, at the age of 20, to preach a version of Buddhism based on simplicity, fraternity and forgiveness, ascetic ideals conforming to peasant poverty and linked to ancestor worship. Disguised as a beggar, a pedlar, a minstrel, a holy man or a cripple, he told his prophecies to anxious crowds along the banks of the Mekong river and right up to Tonkin.

From 1940 his prophecies began questioning the colonial set-up. He was banned from living in the province of his birth, Chaudoc, to which flocked villagers from far and wide to be converted or miraculously cured of ailments. He was arrested in August 1940 and confined as a mental patient in the Cho quan hospital; there he converted his doctor, Tran van Tam.

When the Sûreté tried once more to arrest this mad monk, the Japanese police took him under their wing. His sect grew again, but away from the non-violence it had preached. Its faithful received military training in the corps of native auxiliaries raised by the Japanese. They made themselves knives, spears and swords and talked of seizing power. The master himself, only two years before his death, was dragged into the violent events of 1945. He was to be assassinated by the Vietminh in 1947.

Colonel Savani of the Deuxième Bureau noted that under cover of the Hoa hao some 'anti-French and defeatist pamphlets' attributed to the Trotskyist 'Phan van Num' were distributed. But the evidence indicates that this was Phan van Hum, whose writings were anti-imperialist but not anti-French. (Savani, 1966, p. 11.)

The Vietminh

In 1946, Ho chi Minh was to say to Daniel Guérin: 'All those who do not follow my line will be broken.'

The line he established was one of hedging, of secret diplomacy in search of state support (Chinese, Russian, American, French even); the proletariat had no place in it. It was what the Bolsheviks had always fought against. Ho chi Minh offered aid for aid; he cordially welcomed the French army. But his power was only tolerated long enough for him to put an end to his internal opposition — that is, until late 1946 when the French war against his regime began. He succeeded only in postponing the armed confrontation with 'Free France' and its new conquistadores.

From 1940 onwards, while the Japanese were wooing the Annamite nationalists, the Guomindang was gathering Annamite refugees who were scattered over the two Chinese provinces bordering Tonkin, with the intention of enrolling them as political and military auxiliaries in the event of future anti-Japanese operations by the Chinese in Vietnam.

Some 500 émigré members of the Phuc quoc of Prince Cuong De — who, after a vain attempt in September 1940 to install themselves in Tonkin behind Japanese lines, had sought refuge in Guangxi province — were integrated into the Guomindang army. In Yunnan, nationalists who had escaped after the VNQDD's 1930 Yen Bay putsch, had for some time been competing with PCI emigrés for influence over 2,000 or so of their compatriots who lived alongside the Hanoi-Kunming railway line. (The line was under French jurisdiction as a result of the Franco-Chinese treaty of 1885.) The nationalists were regrouped around Vu hong Khanh, under Guomindang protection. The communists, who accused them of being tolerated by French imperialism, were secretly brought under the command of Nguyen ai Quoc, then an instructor-officer in the Eighth Route Army.[4] The purpose of this activity was to facilitate a second Guomindang-Chinese Communist Party alliance against the Japanese invasion. To avoid antagonising the Guomindang, Quoc operated under the name of Ho Quang.

Only a small Trotskyist group, at Kunming, remained outside the Guomindang's sphere of influence. It was, as always, the target of Stalinist calumny:

> Profoundly influenced by Ta thu Thau with his pseudo-revolutionary theories which were capable of fooling the masses, it [the Trotskyist

group] carried out propaganda and agitation among our émigré compatriots, inciting them to take to the streets to demonstrate against France and to demand a reduction of taxes from the Chinese authorities. We have fought it energetically everywhere [i.e. slandered it shamelessly]; so its plot (am muu) [*sic*] got nowhere and it was completely isolated. (Hoang van Hoan, 1986, p. 127.)

In the Guomindang's mobilisation of the émigré nationalists, Nguyen ai Quoc saw an opportunity for the PCI to rebuild its forces, which had been hit by the French repressions of 1939-1940. It did so by dropping the communist label and adopting that of an old nationalist group, the Vietminh, which had been recognised by the Guomindang at its inception.

The Vietminh had been set up in Nanking in 1936 — with the participation of émigré PCI members — by two former companions of Phan boi Chau, one of whom, Nguyen hai Than, was a trusted confidante of the Guomindang. Its name had been shortened from Vietnam doc lap dong minh hoi (Alliance for the Independence of Vietnam) — and it had had, until then, only a shadowy existence.

In October 1940, Pham van Dong, Vo nguyen Giap, Hoang van Hoan and three other of comrades of Quoc's travelled to Guilin in the Guangxi, to request from General Li Jishen recognition of this ghost organisation. They described themselves as nationalists fighting 'Japanese aggression' from within their country, and therefore potential allies for the Guomindang.

The butcher of the insurrectionary workers of Canton in 1927 welcomed these petitioners with open arms. Evoking his obedience to the dying wishes of Sun Yat-sen — support for 'weak and oppressed peoples' — he granted them the right to remain in the 'Fourth war zone' whose command he shared with Zhang Fakui, the other perpetrator of the Canton Commune slaughter. On the initiative of Quoc, who remained well in the shadows, a 500-dollar banquet was offered to Li Jishen's secretary — at the Comintern's expense — 'so that he might respect us and help us all the more', according to Hoang van Hoan.

Provided with passes franked with the stamp of 'the Sino-Annamite Operational group' ('Hoa Nam cong tac doan'), the delegation made its way to Jingxi to take part in a conference organised by the Chinese generals. This united the leaders of the émigrés under the chairmanship of Nguyen hai Than in the Viet nam dan toc giai phong dong minh (Alliance for National Liberation). Its 'political cell' — entrusted to another Guomindang loyalist, Truong boi Cong — welcomed these young compatriots. A month later (10-19 May), the PCI Central Committee met with Quoc in the woods of the Pac po (Cao bang) frontier region. The resolution finally adopted proclaimed the birth of the new Vietminh, whose objective was 'to drive out the French and Japanese fascists and re-establish the complete independence of Vietnam', in 'alliance with the democracies that are in struggle against fascism and aggression'. This nationalist front adopted a red flag adorned with a yellow star; its final aim, unlike the other nationalist groups formed in exile in China, was the 'formation of a democratic republic of Vietnam' which would grant universal suffrage, bourgeois democratic freedoms, political and social equality between men and women, the rights of ethnic minorities to separation.

The class struggle and the agrarian revolution were excluded from this programme. For its authors it was necessary not to frighten the bourgeoisie and landowners, whom they wanted to rally to their cause. To the peasants, the 'arms' of the future revolution, they promised only the 'confiscation of the property of the imperialists and traitors, reduction of land rents and interest rates, the abolition of the personal (poll) tax and division of the common lands' - crumbs from the rich man's table. To the workers, the programme offered the eight-hour day, social security and pensions . . .

On 22 June 1941 Hitler broke his pact with Stalin and propelled him into the camp of the democratic imperialisms. The Vietminh rediscovered its anti-fascist language, and defined its aims in a manifesto of 25 October as follows: 'unity of all the social classes', 'collaboration with anti-fascist French elements, destruction of colonialism and fascist imperialisms'. This theme was elaborated again in a pamphlet: 'ally ourselves to the democracies which are fighting fascism and aggression; build a democratic republic'. In a leaflet of 10 October 1942 it extended a 'fraternal hand' to the French Gaullists of Indochina. (Devillers, 1952, p. 110.)

The Vietminh's structure was hierarchic and authoritarian like that of the PCI and its predecessor, the Thanh nien. A new term was coined, cuu quoc (national salvation) and all organisations controlled by the Vietminh included it in their titles. The trade unions became 'Workers for National Salvation', the women's associations 'Women for National Salvation'. The to (basic cells) became 'to cuu quoc' ('national salvation cells'). At the top the Tong bo ruled, and its circular of 15 November 1942 declared: 'The cadres decide everything.' While the secretariat of the Vietminh was held by Quoc and that of the PCI by Truong Chinh, it was no less true that the PCI was the only brain.

For party militants, Quoc translated into Chinese *The History of the Communist Party (Bolshevik) of the Soviet Union*; for members of the Vietminh, he adopted the patriotic language of *Thanh nien*. In his poem 'Lich su nuoc ta' ('Our Nation's History') circulated in 1942, he declaimed:

> The history of Vietnam shows it,
> Its people were gloriously heroic.
> It fought the North, it pacified the East.
> Invincible are the sons of the Dragons and the grandchildren of the Immortals.

Inspired by Mao Zedong ('political power comes out of the barrel of a gun'[5]), Quoc had for a long time been envisaging the conquest of power through a peasant war, which he called a 'revolutionary war'. He counted in the first place on aid from the Guomindang for building groups of guerrilla fighters in the Viet Bac (region of Higher Tonkin). When the time was ripe, he would extend guerrilla operations southwards, launch armed risings of the 'national salvation' associations and establish the Vietminh's power in each liberated region, as the Chinese Communist Party had done. He would thus finally establish a sole power in the whole country.

In order to get military training for his Vietminh cadres in China, he agreed to co-operate with a Guomindang project ('Hoa quan nhap Viet') 'to infiltrate Chinese troops into Viet', which Zhang Fakui, military Governor of the Guangxi, had been preparing since the summer of 1942. Quoc directed about 300 Annamites from his zone to the Daiken military training camp, and a hundred or so into the military school at Nanning, in Guangxi province.

He justified his policy of compromise thus, in a circular of 21 December 1941:

> It is possible that Chinese troops will soon enter the country [Vietnam] to fight the Japanese . . . our tactic consists of making an alliance with the Chinese troops against the Japanese and the French, on the basis of assistance by equals (binh dang tuong tro) [*sic*].

It was also necessary to defend the Vietminh's abandonment of the slogan of class struggle. Thus the PCI general secretary, Truong Chinh, wrote in January 1942: 'The fighting movement of the working class does not yet measure up to its role of vanguard of the revolution.'

(Truong Chinh, 1942.) More than 70 future cadres of the Vietminh were trained in guerrilla warfare, sabotage and espionage in the Guomindang camps and military schools at Jingxi, Tiandong, Nanning and Daiken.

Nguyen ai Quoc manoeuvres with the Guomindang

Nguyen ai Quoc was arrested for Vietminh fractional activity damaging to the Nguyen hai Than group:

> The official history relates that on 13 August 1942, comrade Nguyen ai Quoc, under his new name, Ho chi Minh, went to China . . . to try to obtain international aid. After travelling on foot for half a month he was arrested at Tuc vinh (Guangxi) and imprisoned by the local authorities of the Chiang Kai-shek clique on 29 August. (Vietnam State Publishing House, 1976, Vol 1, p. 555.)

Forty-four years later, Hoang van Hoan lifted the veil over the purpose of 'the President's voyage':

> Up until now very few people have known. . . . Some say that President Ho's journey to Chungking was to meet the Chinese communists and not Chiang Kai-shek. . . . Those who were more or less informed avoided talking about it, because they thought this journey was a right deviation, an unprincipled compromise. (Hoang van Hoan, 1986, pp. 232-233.)

Be that as it may, having tried to go over Zhang Fakui's head to directly seek aid from Chiang Kai-shek under the neutral and unknown name of Ho chi Minh, Quoc found himself in Zhang's jail in Liuzhou. He was still there when, in October 1942, the latter again called together the leaders of the rival Annamite organisations — the Dong minh hoi, VNQDD, Phuc quoc, Vietminh and seven other small groups — and insisted that, if they wanted help, they would have to unite under Nguyen hai Than in an alliance of Vietnamese revolutionary parties, the Viet cach (shortened from Viet nam cach menh dong minh hoi). No representative of the Vietminh was elected to the Executive Committee.

Nguyen hai Than received 100,000 Chinese dollars per month to organise espionage and sabotage against the Japanese in Tonkin. The groups based in China that made up the Viet cach had hardly any roots in Viet nam. Only the Vietminh had any presence there through its 'national salvation' cells, and guerrilla groups established among the discontented ethnic minorities of Tho, Man, Meo, Tay, Nung, in the heavily-wooded, chalky massifs of Langson and Caobang provinces.

It should be noted that, when the French lost Langson in September 1940 under the blows of the Japanese army, local rebels had, in their hundreds, attacked the stations of the native Guard, seized arms from those that fled and extended their revolt. French troops only completed reconquest of the region in December. In the process, the Phuc quoc nationalists lost their commander, Tran trung Lap, and dispersed towards China.

Meanwhile a young Tho, 32-year-old Chu van Tan, who had sparked off the Bacson (Caobang) revolt, had survived, and joined the Vietminh with his partisans. They made up the bulk of the guerrilla units and self-defence groups, and were led by Vietminh militants who came from the Guomindang military schools of Guangxi.

It was therefore only the Vietminh who could furnish reliable information to Zhang Fakui. It was thanks to this that the detained Ho could communicate with his active comrades, particularly with the Vietminh section in Yunnan, and participate, in March 1944, in a new congress of the Viet cach called by Zhang Fakui in Liuzhou. There, with Pham van Dong, he represented the Vietminh; like Nguyen truong Tam of the Dai Viet, he was accepted as a delegate even though under lock and key.

Though the Vietminh's 'fractional activity' was vigorously criticised, the union 'for the liberation of Vietnam' survived and a Provisional Republican Government of Vietnam, presided over by the elderly Truong boi Cong, was set up under the auspices of Zhang Fakui, with Nguyen hai Than, Vu hong Khanh, Ho chi Minh, Bo xuan Luat (leader of the Phuc quoc party, who was exiled in China) and others.

Illusion and compromise: Franco-Indochinese entente

Having taken note of the Algiers Declaration of 8 December 1943, dealing with the future status of Indochina, Ho chi Minh established contact with representatives of the 'Free French'.[6] Two Vietminh delegates travelled to Kunming on 29 April 1944 to meet the French consul, Royère, and propose a 'Franco-Indochinese entente' for the democratisation and independence of Indochina 'in the shortest possible time'; as a quid pro quo they promised collaboration by the Vietminh, including military collaboration, in the coming struggle of

'Free France' against Japan. The VNQDD and the Dong minh hoi denounced this attempt at a secret compromise with French imperialism. In any case the proposal was not endorsed by De Gaulle: on 16 June, all he promised, in return for Vietminh collaboration, was autonomy within the framework of a 'French Federation uniting all the French nations'.

On 6 August, the Vietminh announced that it would come to power thanks to the political vacuum which would result from the conclusion of the war in the Pacific and the defeat of Japan:

> Germany is on its knees and its defeat will bring about that of Japan, which will not be able to resist the general offensive. . . . When the Chinese and Americans penetrate into Indochina . . . we will then not need to seize power, as there will no longer be any. We shall form a government which will reign wherever our enemies, the French and Japanese, are not in control. (Circular of the Vietminh, 6 August 1944, quoted in Devillers 1952, p.111.)

Ho chi Minh, freed on 9 August 1944, aimed to set up two guerrilla bases along the frontier. He begged Zhang Fakui for a thousand rifles, 25,000 Indochinese piastres for the first two months' supplies, a permanent pass confirming his status as a delegate of the Viet cach on a mission in Viet nam, and a revolver for his own protection. He was given the pass and 76,000 Chinese dollars; on 20 September he left Liuzhou for the Tonkin frontier, accompanied by 18 Vietminh cadres.

In his 'Letter to my fellow countrymen' (October 1944) Ho expressed his confidence in 'China, which will help our movement for national liberation concretely and with all its strength' ('Trung quoc se tich cuc giup do cuoc dan toc giai phong cua chung ta') (Vietnam State Publishing House, 1976, Vol. 1, p. 586).

In November Ho's guerrillas attacked the posts of the native Guard in the frontier zone, in order to get arms. The Decoux government ordered reprisals, which hit local people accused of aiding and abetting the guerrillas. Under French officers, the native Guards and Tonkinese riflemen combed the area, burning villages, destroying granaries and firing on suspects. No doubt it was this moment of extreme barbarity which prompted the writer J.M. Pedrazzani to report: 'In the space of two weeks [Decoux's] special tribunals condemned several hundred suspects to death.' (Pedrazzani, 1972, p. 111.)

Elsewhere, Jean Sainteny recalled the 'excessively brutal reprisals carried out by the Vichyist troops in North Tonkin', when he wrote on 19 May 1945, that the Vietminh were prepared to 'collaborate with General de Gaulle's men'. (Devillers, 1988, p. 59.)

The reprisals did not succeed in putting an end to the uprising; it spread to the whole of High Tonkin. The Resident-in-Chief and the military command prepared a new punitive operation for 12 March 1945. It did not take place: the French military and administrative apparatus was overturned by the Japanese three days before. While the French armies of Generals Sabatier and Alessandri were retreating towards China under Japanese pressure, the Vietminh was able to tighten its grip on the three military zones of Langson, Caobang and Ha giang and to organise a 'security zone' ('khu an toan') in the Tuyen quang.

The Provisional Government of the French Republic, set up on 10 September 1944, confirmed the declaration of war against Japan of 1941, and decided to form immediately an expeditionary corps for the Far East (that is for the reconquest of Indochina). While the Japanese, on the day of their coup in Vietnam, 9 March 1945, declared themselves ready to satisfy 'the ardent desire for independence so dear to the peoples of Indochina', the French Communist Party newspaper, *L'Humanité*, wrote on 13 March:

> France must step up its efforts to send its forces to the Far East, to collaborate with the Allies and the peoples of Indochina in the liberation of this area [sic] . . . for the betterment of Franco-Indochinese relations.

In reply to the Japanese taunt, the Provisional Government of the French Republic promised a new status for Indochina in its declaration of 24 March. It would no longer be a territory of the French Empire — the term annoyed the American president, Franklin D. Roosevelt — but a member of a French Union. Within this Union, an Indochinese Federation would be presided over by a French Governor General, who would chose his ministers 'from among the Indochinese as well as from among French people resident in Indochina'. The word 'independence' was never uttered.

Ho chi Minh seeks aid from the US secret service and entente with France

It was at the end of 1944, according to Hoang van Hoan, but on 29 March 1945 according to Devillers, that Ho, who was still living in China, went in his turn to Kunming. He offered the military co-operation of the Vietminh to General Chennault of the Office of Strategic Services, the wartime secret service of the US, predecessor of the Central Intelligence Agency. Chennault was commander of the American Air Force in South China; Ho offered to supply him with useful information and promised to organise a helicopter landing ground within the Vietminh maquis, as a 'rescue relay'; his guerrillas had just saved an American airman who had crashed in the jungle.

Chennault made Ho a gift of 'six pistols, 20,000 rounds, a supply of medication and some money. Uncle Ho refused the money but . . . he counted on rapid and more substantial aid from the United States'. (Hoang van Hoan 1986, p. 246.)

After this 'diplomatic' encounter, Ho did not miss any opportunity to flaunt a photo of himself standing next to the OSS general and autographed by the latter, to give the impression that the Vietminh had obtained the backing of the Americans (see Brocheux et al., 1982, p. 207). Convinced that strength attracts waverers, Ho had already used a similar ploy to make people believe the Chinese had prioritised giving support to the Vietminh: all over the Caobang region pennants were exhibited, imprinted with greetings from Zhang Fakui and Li Jishen to the Liberation Alliance formed at Jingxi in April 1941.

Ho chi Minh at last entered Tonkin in May 1945 and established himself in a 'security zone', under the protection of Chu van Tan's guerrillas. The Americans immediately made contact with a Vietminh which — no longer having to fear Decoux's repressive forces — had grown considerably. They supplied it with modern arms, Colt 45s, Thompson sub-machine guns, grenades, ammunition, advisers, instructors and radio sets. Soon, Ho agreed to the parachute drop at his headquarters of an American team led by Major Thomas. It arrived at Tan trao on 16 July. Through Thomas, Jean Sainteny, who was at Kunming, received Ho chi Minh's reply to the Algiers Declaration of 24 March: Ho accepted that the French would grant independence to Vietnam only after a delay of five to ten years — and that in the meantime they would appoint a French Governor General for the Indochinese Federation.

By these compromises and manoeuvres the Stalinist party was merely sowing illusions about a possible understanding with French imperialism and its allies for the gradual attainment of 'national liberation'. And what liberation? Would the coolie-slaves of the rubber plantations, the workers in the mines and factories, the serfs of the rice-fields be liberated, when the Stalinists declared forthrightly on 11 November 1945:

The communists, as vanguard militants of the race are . . . willing to place the interests of the Motherland above those of class. (*La Republique*, no. 7, Hanoi, 18 November 1945; quoted in Devillers, 1952, p. 195.)

The Trotskyists remained convinced that a communist party should be the vanguard of the proletariat, and that the liberation of the country could be achieved only by a victorious armed insurrection of the workers supported by the poor peasants. They were also convinced that this would mean confrontation with the imperialists and the native bourgeoisie and landowners, auxiliaries of the colonial power. They were convinced, too, that this struggle would need to be supported by the revolutionary workers of France and would end only with the worldwide overthrow of the capitalist system and through a really communist consciousness. National liberation, without the taking over of the factories by the workers and without mastery of the peasants over the land, would be only a change of masters for the exploited, the overwhelming majority of the population; the power to appropriate the labour of others would remain.

History has proved them right. The Stalinist Tran van Giau has himself recently written:

Why have we, revolutionaries and resisters, created an unequalled bureaucratic state? The province of Thanh hoa alone has more officials than had the whole colonial apparatus of the old Indochina. How can the country maintain such a state? I am over 70. I have never in my whole life seen the peasants as miserable as now; they have nothing left to eat after the harvest. This is because they have to maintain a state as over-developed as it is ineffective. (Tran van Giau, 1988; quoted in *Le Monde Diplomatique*, April 1989.)

The peasants, too, have spoken for themselves. In April 1989, *Le Monde Diplomatique* reported that:

. . . between July and December 1988, one demonstration after another has taken place in Ho chi Minh City. The peasants and fishermen from the Mekong Delta and the coast were demanding the return, in accordance with recent legislation on small holdings, of lands and boats wrongfully confiscated by local cadres at the time of forced collectivisations.

9

AFTER THE COUP OF 9 MARCH 1945

On 9 March 1945 French colonial rule, which had been established in Indochina for over 80 years and had successfully resisted the desperate efforts of generations of conspirators and peasant risings, collapsed overnight. The Japanese replaced the French at the head of an apparatus of domination, while presenting themselves as liberators. On 11 March, under Japan's auspices, the emperor Bao Dai proclaimed the independence of Vietnam and his 'determination to collaborate with Japan'; he was followed on 13 March by the king of Cambodia and on 8 April by the king of Laos.

Cochinchina, however, remained a colony and was given a Japanese Governor, Minoda. In Saigon on 18 March, the Cao dai sect (whose paramilitary groups had taken part in the coup de force), the Phuc quoc, and the Viet nam quoc gia doc lap dang (National Party for the Independence of Vietnam, a new party of bourgeois and officials) greeted the liberation in progress within the framework of Great Far-Eastern Asia. They called for unity behind 'victorious Great Japan'. The Cao dai sect, which disposed of some 20,000 men in military formations (Noi ung nghia binh), prepared the return to the Vietnamese throne of Prince Cuong De.

The master of the Hoa hao sect declared: 'The foe who massacred our fathers [that is, France] finds himself in irons'. He urged his fellow country people to bend their efforts towards the independence of the country in national unity, so as to 'avoid the risks of a civil war'; he urged the native agents of the Sûreté and soldiers who had deserted to hand in their arms to the Japanese military; he urged thieves and pirates to repent, and promised to all the pardon of the new authorities. While awaiting the coming of the king-buddha (Phat Vuong), the sect organised its own 'security groups' (bao an), assumed some *de facto* power in Chaudoc province, and helped the poorest at the expense of the rich. Minoda made sure they remained within limits which did not affect the harvest.

On 17 April, an imperial government was formed at Hue by Tran trong Kim, a scholar approaching 60, a former inspector of primary schools, whom the Japanese had protected from French repression. It was composed of men with no political past: doctors, lawyers, teachers and engineers.

Tran trong Kim's Minister for the Economy, Dr Ho ta Khanh, related that it was the Stalinist, Tran van Giau, who urged him to accept this appointment, but the official history, drawn up with the help of this same Giau, alleges that:

> The band of Trotskyists . . . in order to obtain power . . . told Ho ta Khanh to co-operate with the puppet pro-Japanese administration . . . and sent Ta thu Thau to Hue as adviser to Tran trong Kim in the hope that he would succeed him. (Vietnam State Publishing House, 1960, vol. II, p. 221).

This government faced a tragic social situation: Tonkin and north Annam were in the grip of a terrible famine. Bereft of material resources or armed forces, it adopted only timid measures (freedom of union organisation and of assembly). It was in jeopardy from its inception. The Vietminh forces put an end to it as early as August.

Immediately after 9 March, the Japanese tried to revive Decoux's Youth and Sports (Jeunesse et Sports) movement, by transforming it into the Vanguard Youth (Jeunesse d'Avant-Garde). On 15 April, the youth who just the day before had been shouting 'Maréchal nous voilà!' ('Marshal [Pétain] we are with you!') acclaimed the Japanese victory in the vast assembly at Cholon to celebrate 'Great Far-Eastern Asia'.

On 25 May in Saigon the cultural attaché Iida, recently appointed by Governor Minoda as Commissioner for Youth and Sport, called together the leaders of this movement (lawyers, teachers, engineers and doctors), among them Dr Pham ngoc Thach. He urged them to transform this creation of 'the French colonialists' formed 'in order to distract the youth from their patriotic duty' into a new enterprise, where each member would become 'a militant prepared to build the complete independence of the Viet nation within the framework of Great Far-Eastern Asia'.

The leaders of the thus-constituted Thanh niem tien phong (Vanguard Youth), placed on the road to power, paraphrased Iida's speeches, calling on the youth to join it irrespective of class (but making no mention of Great Far-Eastern Asia). Failure to join was 'equivalent to lack of affection for one's motherland' (Nguyen ky Nam, 1964, p. 64).

Enrolment took the form of an oath of obedience to one's superiors. A uniform, flag and anthem were adopted and the movement structured: 'each factory, office, workshop, school and public service soon had its section'. It involved a general mobilisation of all those eligible (13 years and above), from the urban centres to the deepest countryside. Its tasks were maintaining order (armed mainly with sharpened bamboo stakes), civil defence (clearing up after bombings, collection of corpses and assistance to the wounded), aid to victims of famine in the north, literacy campaigns and hygiene. On 1 July the first 'mass oath taking', a great spectacle enacted by some 3,000 people, took place in Saigon in the presence of Minoda and Iida, under the flag of the Hue Court. On 3 July a delegation of 38 students, who had the task of training new recruits, was received by Bao Dai, who conferred on Dr Thach the title of Xu truong thanh nien (Dean of the Youth) and Representative of his Youth Minister in Saigon. On 27 July Madame Dr Ho vinh Ky set up the Phu nu tien phong (Vanguard Women's Section) for the education of peasant women.

The Vanguard Youth, envisaged by the Japanese as a supplementary force, gradually became the *de facto* power. In August Dr Thach brought them over to the Vietminh, thus allowing the Stalinists to easily supplant the less numerous and less organised nationalist groups and to take power.

The surviving Trotskyists regroup underground

In Cochinchina the *Tranh dau* (*La Lutte*) group had had an important following. Its leaders had been in the Poulo Condore penal colony throughout the war and Tran van Si was laid to rest there. The other Trotskyists, like all the political prisoners who survived, were sent into enforced residence in all four corners of the country, under police surveillance. Tran van Thach and Ho huu Tuong went to Cantho, Phan van Hum to Tan uyen and Ta thu Thau to Longxuyen. Ho huu Tuong defected, declaring that after four years of meditation in prison he was no longer a Trotskyist or a Marxist.

From the day after the coup of 9 March 1945, the country was under Japanese martial law. Evading surveillance by the Kempeitai, the Japanese secret police, Ta thu Thau left Longxuyen for Saigon.

He was soon joined by former comrades of *La Lutte*, Tran van

Thach, Phan van Hum, Nguyen van So, Le van Thu and Phan van Chanh. In a world in flames and full of upheavals it seemed to them that, despite their small numbers, the moment had come to reorganise themselves as a workers' revolutionary party (Dang tho thuyen cach mang), ready to act together with their comrades in Annam and Tonkin.

To carry out this decision, Ta thu Thau departed secretly for the north in May and contacts were immediately renewed locally with workers.

The influence of the *La Lutte* group had far from disappeared in Cochinchina. It was necessary to regroup and revive the spirits of its action committees which had been stifled by the repression. Among those who dedicated themselves to this task in Saigon-Cholon were Le van Vung and Nguyen thi Loi, former organiser of the illegal teachers' union. Under cover of his position as a lawyer, Hinh thai Thong renewed contacts in the west (in Mytho, Bentre, Cantho and Travinh) with former readers of *Tranh dau* who were close to the peasantry.

When their paper restarted in August and September its print run went as high as 15,000 or 20,000, so well did its contents reflect its readers' aspirations and the possibilities of action. For his part, Lu sanh Hanh was secretly regrouping former comrades of the Thang muoi and Tia sang groups. He reconstituted these as the League of Internationalist Communists which, as early as 24 March, distributed a manifesto which stated:

> The coming defeat of Japanese imperialism will set the Indochinese people on the road to national liberation. The bourgeoisie and feudalists, who today spinelessly serve the Nippon High Command, will tomorrow serve the Allied imperialist states in the same way. The petty-bourgeois nationalists, with their adventurist line, will also be unable to lead the people towards victorious revolution. Only the working class, fighting independently under the banner of the Fourth International, will be able to carry out the tasks of the revolutionary vanguard.
>
> The Stalinists of the Third International have already abandoned the working class in order to ally themselves miserably with the 'democratic' imperialisms. They have betrayed the peasants and no longer mention the agrarian question. If, today, they march together with the foreign capitalists, they will again help the national exploiting classes crush the revolutionary people when the time comes.
>
> Workers and peasants! Unite under the banner of the Fourth International!

Some comrades from Tonkin came to work with the League in Saigon, and reported that after the 9 March coup, their appeal to the workers and peasants of Tu ky to fight the imperialists had been heeded.

Like the *Tranh dau* Trotskyists, those of the League aimed their efforts towards the workers, particularly in the tramway workshops of Go vap, where some 400 workers formed a works committee and were able to force the Japanese military administration not only to increase pay but to recognise their 11 elected delegates.

In Tonkin in 1943, the underground paper *Ngoi sao Do* (*Red Star*) had denounced the dissolution of the Comintern on 15 May 1943 as a favour to the Allies by Stalin.[1] In 1945 in Haiduong province, Nguyen te My and other internationalist militants, Tiep, Luong, Vinh and Sam, organised the Vo san thuong truc cach mang dang (Party of Permanent Proletarian Revolution) together with their comrades Chanh Dao from Binh giang, Doan from Haiduong, Diem from Thanh hoa and Sinh from Camgiang. It published the paper *Viet dan tuyen* (*Viet People's Front*); one of its leaflets called on the workers and peasants to prepare the struggle against Japanese imperialism and, at the same time, condemned the overtures of the Vietminh to Moscow's imperialist allies.

In the Dan phuong region other comrades organised themselves in the Dang tho thuyen xa hoi (Socialist Workers Party) and secretly circulated *Chien dau* (*Combat*) with the help of the printer Luong duc Thiep. It carried the symbol of the Fourth International, a globe crossed by the lightning of world revolution in the shape of a figure four. In the mines of Hongay-Campha and as far afield as Tien yen, Mongkay, the student comrades Nguyen ton Hoang, Phan thanh Hoa and Tuan countered the Vietminh's patriotic propaganda by calling on the miners to take their fate into their own hands.

The Vietminh did not wait to take power before assassinating those they called 'Trotskyist reactionaries' — as witnessed by the following official account, in which cynicism is combined with triumphalism:

One evening, at the end of June 1945, the rice-fields were flooded and so the individual Nguyen huu Dung, known as Ba De, took the ferry to get from Ninh giang to his home village of Uc tai (Tu ky) for his father's birthday. One of the youth comrades spontaneously took a sampan and followed him. They both arrived at the same time at the landing stage at Uc tai. Ba De went ashore first; our comrade followed him, and at an isolated spot suddenly put an end to the life of this reactionary with a pistol shot. (Vietnam State Publishing House, 1960, vol 2, p. 243.)

Ba De was a young Trotskyist who had been working tirelessly in Ninh giang, Tu Ky, Thanh ha and Haiduong. In Annam, the surviving Trotskyists in the Moduc and Ducpho districts of Quang ngai also tried to reorganise themselves after March 1945; the majority of them were massacred in September that year, at the same time as Ta thu Thau.

10

THE SO-CALLED REVOLUTION OF AUGUST 1945

After 230,000 Japanese people had been killed by the nuclear bombs dropped on Hiroshima and Nagasaki, on 6 and 9 August 1945 respectively, Emperor Hirohito ordered his subjects to cease fighting on 15 August.

Ta thu Thau left Hanoi for Saigon, where his comrades of *La Lutte* were awaiting him and where his life as a militant had won him great popularity. The Vietminh arrested him at Quang ngai and killed him.

The US president Harry S. Truman, the British prime minister Winston Churchill and Stalin had agreed at Potsdam in July that northern Indochina should be occupied by the Chinese, and the south by the British, who were to accept the surrender of the defeated Japanese.[1] The Chinese troops did not arrive until 10 September. In the interval, the power vacuum and a certain indifference by the Japanese allowed Ho chi Minh's guerrillas to enter Hanoi on 18 August. On 27 August, Vo nguyen Giap started negotiations with Jean Sainteny, who had arrived on 22 August as representative of the Free French Provisional Government together with an OSS mission.

Faced with the imminent threat of a return of the French, the Trotskyists called on the people to demonstrate and called for the arming of the population. Meanwhile, Ho chi Minh was making secret overtures to the new imperialist France. It was in this context that the murder under torture of the Trotskyist teacher, Tran tien Chinh, took place in the Vietminh prison of Backan.

The revolutionary upsurge

At the same time, outside the control of the Vietminh, the 30,000 miners of Hongay-Campha elected councils to manage production. The largest and most exploited concentration of the Tonkinese proletariat was in these collieries. They took control of the public services of the district, railways, and telegraph communications, and applied the principle of equal wages for all at all levels of manual and intellectual work. Throughout the existence of this working-class commune, from the end of August to November 1945, a new order reigned, without police. The Japanese troops, whose commanders had surrendered, seemed indifferent to the situation. With the former management pushed aside, the miners maintained the economic life of the region, carried on a struggle against illiteracy and tried to develop some sort of social security system.

The movement remained isolated and Ho chi Minh's guerrilla forces encircled the area. Nguyen Binh, their commander, made the most of the need for unity and promised to maintain the status quo. This meant nothing; as soon as he could, he arrested the workers' delegates S, Lan, Hien and Le, and replaced the councils by a new hierarchy. Soon, after three months of effort, the military-police government of the 'Democratic Republic' ruled over the district. (See N. Van, 1950.)

The movement was no less powerful in the rural areas.

In numerous provincial centres and villages, notably in North Annam (Nghe an, Thanhhoa) and in Tonkin (Bacninh, Thaibinh), the People's Committees . . . ordered . . . the distribution of the land, the confiscation of the goods of the rich. (Devillers, 1988, p. 181.)

Ho chi Minh reacted by holding back the peasants who — impelled by a still-unchecked famine, and remembering the PCI's slogan of 1930, 'the land to those who work it' — rejected national unity with the landowners and pressurised their people's committees to launch an agrarian revolution which would encourage them to increase production and guarantee that the harvest would not be diverted to speculators.

A circular issued in November to the provincial committees reminded them that 'the rice-fields and cultivated lands will not be redistributed'. Order No.63 on the 'organisation of people's authority' spelt out the re-establishment of a pyramidal hierarchy similar to those of the old Thanh nien, of the PCI and of the Vietminh: the executive committee of each country would be responsible for executing the orders of the government, and each body of the pyramid would control the bodies immediately below it.

In Annam the Tran trong Kim government had been unable to resolve the problems of famine and poverty, and was in practice supplanted by the Vietminh guerrillas. On 23 August it formally handed over power. On 25 August Bao Dai abdicated and Ho chi Minh appointed him 'Supreme Adviser to the Provisional Government of the Democratic Republic'.

The Vietminh and its guerrillas had not yet appeared in Cochinchina. From 16 August onwards the Japanese began to relinquish the direct administration of the country. Minoda named Tran van An of the Phuc quoc 'President of the Council of Cochinchina' and Kha van Can of the Vanguard Youth 'Prefect of Saigon-Cholon'. On 19 August he handed power over to Ho van Nga, who had been appointed as the provisional Imperial Delegate of the Tran trong Kim government, the Nam ky (Annam) having finally been restored to the Empire of Vietnam by the Japanese as a last resort.

This Imperial Delegate, congratulating himself on the unification of the Empire, freed all political prisoners and abolished the poll tax. On 23 August, the same day that the Tran trong Kim government in Annam abdicated, he followed its example — and made way for the Stalinist party.

Mass demonstrations in Saigon

On 14 August seven parties and nationalist groups — the National Party for the Independence of Vietnam, the Vanguard Youth, the Civil Servants' Federation (Fédération des fonctionnaires), the Group of Intellectuals, the Group of Buddhist Anchorites (Tịnh do cu si) and the Hoa hao and Cao dai sects — met to form a National United Front, 'for Vietnamese independence, against French imperialism and all foreign aggression' (mat tran quoc gia thong nhut). This Front published a Manifesto in the *Hung Viet* of 17 August.

The *La Lutte* group, which, despite what the Stalinists said, did not belong to the Front, participated — as did the League of Internationalist Communists — in its demonstration of 21 August against the return of the French.

For the first time, from the morning onwards, a real human mass choked the Boulevard Norodom from the Botanical Gardens to the Governor's Palace, and then marched in good order along the central arteries of the city as far away as the populous quarter of Cau Ong Lanh. The National Party for the Independence of Vietnam, the Cao dai and Vanguard Youth marched under the flag of the Royal Court of Hue and the Hoa hao under its own deep purple banner.

The Trotskyists marched under the flag of the Fourth International.

The *La Lutte* group and the League did not intermingle; each carried its own slogans inscribed on posters and banners. *La Lutte*'s were 'Action committees in the towns and villages! Arm the people! National Assembly elected by universal suffrage! Organise unions in the factories, public services and agricultural estates! For a workers' and peasants' government!'

The League's were 'Down with imperialism! Long live world revolution! Long live the Worker and Peasant Front! People's committees everywhere! Forward to a People's Assembly! Arm the people! Land to the peasants! Nationalisation of the factories under workers' control! Forward to a workers' and peasants' government!'

Already two days before, the workers of the Ban co quarter (in Saigon) had spontaneously formed the first people's committee in the south; the next day those of the Phu nhuan quarter had elected theirs and declared themselves 'the sole legal power of the quarter'. At the same time the Vanguard Youth committees were affirming their readiness to die for freedom in front of their yellow flag with a red star.

Thus almost everywhere embryos of power, with tendencies as yet undifferentiated, were springing up; the popular dynamism seemed irresistible. The people's committees were multiplying. A provisional central committee of about 15 members of the League established itself at 9 rue Duclos in Tan dinh; it was guarded by armed workers, and had its own printshop and military nuclei. The Japanese collapse opened up possibilities for the 'arming of the people', with gifts from deserters, munitions and arms from the black market, and so on.

For its part the *La Lutte* group organised some 18,000 militants and sympathisers. *Tranh dau* reappeared as a daily, with a print run of over 15,000 copies. Multiplying its contacts with the workers in the Saigon-Cholon region and the provincial centres, *La Lutte* organised its armed groups. The Cao dai sect offered to put itself at its disposal, with 900 rifles and four 45mm guns, received from the Japanese, and the Hoa hao, reorganised as the Democratic Socialist party (Dang dan xa) also sought an alliance with it for a joint armed struggle against the reinstatement of the old masters. The *La Lutte* group accepted neither of these offers.

It was at this moment that the representatives of the Vietminh in Cochinchina (the PCI's Country Committee) came on the scene. On the very evening of 21 August, cars with loudspeakers toured the streets of Saigon with the slogan 'Everyone behind the Vietminh!' ('Ung ho Vietminh!') The Vietminh, almost unknown, came out of the shadows and introduced itself in a leaflet:

The Vietminh has been closely linked with the Allies in fighting the French and the Japanese. We are the friends of Russia; China is with us heart and soul; America dreams of trade and not of conquest; in England, [Labour leader Clement] Attlee is Prime Minister and leans to the left. It will be easy for us to negotiate. (Nguyen ky Nam, 1964, p. 51.)

Soon the Vietminh called for a demonstration on 28 August.

On 22 August, the National United Front held a plenary conference of all its seven component organisations, but Dr Pham ngoc Thach, leader of the Vanguard Youth, defected; some hours later banners, posters and leaflets announced that as from the evening of 22 August, the Vanguard Youth was part of the Vietminh.

On 23 August, the National United Front, shorn of the component which had been most disciplined and well rooted in the population, agreed to talks with the Vietminh at 14 Boulevard Charner. The *Hung Viet* of 24 August published the following capitulatory communique:

After talks between the National United Front and representatives of the Vietminh Front, agreement on co-operation for the following three objectives has been reached:
- ☐ Total independence of Vietnam;
- ☐ Setting-up of a Democratic Republic;
- ☐ Immediate actual power to the Vietminh.

The National United Front joins the Vietminh en bloc and will participate in the demonstration on Saturday 25 August. [The Vietminh, thus reinforced, advanced its demonstration by three days.]

The Vietminh was able to take power without striking a blow, thanks to the decisive support of the Vanguard Youth. According to Dr Thach it had, in August, 200,000 members in the Saigon-Cholon region, of whom 120,000 were in the factories, workshops and offices. They were powerfully led and obedient, as this communiqué of 14 August from the Civil Servants' Federation shows:

The Federation has organised self-defence groups jointly with the Vanguard Youth in each office . . . . All officials pledge themselves to obey the decisions of the Administrative Council.

A resolution of postal workers organised in the Vanguard Youth stated:

The personnel voted for its own mobilisation against the return of the French colonisers; the orders of our leaders — even for a general strike — must be carried out without hesitation. Those who infringe them will be severely punished by the self-defence groups. The dictatorial powers of the leaders will end when the Viet have finally conquered. (*Hung Viet*, 18 August 1945.)

A week later the Vanguard Youth, under the aegis of Dr Thach, went over to the Vietminh lock stock and barrel. On the evening of 24 August, its self-defence groups, armed mainly with knives and bamboo pikes, seized control of their own public service installations and mounted guard in front of the Central Post Office, the Treasury, the palace of the Governor of Cochinchina, the police stations, the Sûreté, the fire station, the power station of Choquan and the waterworks.

They were careful to avoid 'storming' the palace of the Governor General, the Bank of Indochina, the powder magazine, the port and the aerodrome, which were all held by the Japanese. The Vietminh had already sounded out the situation on the night of 22 August by persuading Minoda's Annamite appointee to hand over power locally to them. The Japanese troops had not reacted.

The *de facto* power of the Stalinists

When the peasants from the surrounding countryside began to crowd into the city for the next day's demonstration, the stage had already been set by the architect Huynh tan Phat, nephew of Huynh van Phuong. A seemingly huge column had been erected in front of the Saigon town hall at the corner of Boulevard Charner and Boulevard Bonard; the names of the members of the Provisional Executive Committee of Nam Bo (Uy ban hanh chanh lam thoi Nam Bo) had been inscribed on it in large characters.

Out of nine members, there were seven Stalinists.

President and Military Affairs	Tran van Giau
Foreign Affairs	Pham ngoc Thach
Interior	Nguyen van Tao
Labour	Hoang don Van
Political Inspection of the West	Nguyen van Tay
State Security (quoc gia tu ve cuoc)	Duong bach Mai
Economy	Ngo tan Nhon
Propaganda and Youth	Huynh van Tieng
Finance	Nguyen phi Oanh

The whole of Saigon was astonished: none of the nationalists of the National United Front, which had just surrendered to the Vietminh, were on the list.

Thus, in the space of a week (18-25 August), Ho chi Minh and his supporters had made themselves masters of the three Kys (countries); the Japanese surrender had helped their rise to power by sowing confusion among the nationalists who had banked on a Japanese victory. The bourgeoisie and landowners were reassured; private property remained. And the workers and peasants who might want to break their chains were warned that they would be crushed by the new rulers.

Tran van Giau

Who was this Tran van Giau, head of the new government? He was a Cochinchinese, born in 1911 in Tan an, and a former pupil of Ta thu Thau. He studied at the Toulouse Lycée in 1928-1929 and then at the University. Expelled from France in 1930, after Yen Bay, he went to the Stalin School in Moscow from which he graduated in 1932 with a thesis (in French) on 'The Agrarian and Peasant Question in Indochina'. He did a course in the Red Army (so he confided to the author when they were both confined in 1936 in the Maison Centrale prison in Saigon) and returned to Vietnam with the task of reconstructing the Communist Party of Indochina (PCI). On 19 April 1935, after the party's Macao Congress,[2] he was arrested in Saigon. According to the monthly police file for the second quarter of 1935, his statements to the examining magistrate resulted in the arrests of 167 party members and sympathisers, 113 of whom were not detained. Sentenced to five years on 24 June 1935, he was transferred to Poulo Condore on 29 July.

In his review *Hoa Dong* (*Peace and Equality*), Ho huu Tuong related that when Giau's fellow convicts reproached him with having talked too freely he justified himself in these terms:

> If the Sûreté had tortured me to death the party would have lost a leader. My statements saved me from being tortured; a few years in prison spread between several comrades was the price for my life. (Quoted in Ba phuong Lang, 1974, pp. 251-2.)

Under the French Popular Front government, Giau was brought back to Saigon in June 1936 and there completed his sentence. He was then interned in the Talai camp in 1940. He was said to have escaped in 1941 — and resurfaced in 1944 when he was contacted by the French Sûreté superintendent J. Duchêne, head of the clandestine Gaullist resistance network which was working against Decoux, and which sought contact with Vietnamese intellectuals on de Gaulle's behalf. Professor Paul Isoart of the university of Nice writes:

> According to the evidence of the police officer, he [Tran van Giau] agreed to distribute papers and pamphlets in which he would explain why the Indochinese should from now on trust democratic France; he would also form groups of partisans who would be used for supportive resistance missions (intelligence, supplies, sabotage, assistance to parachutists and neutralisation of pro-Japanese groups). (Isoart, 1982, p. 39.)

Giau has never publicly admitted to his secret relations with Duchêne and the role to which he was assigned, nor to the help he received (some revolvers and a duplicator). At the beginning of 1945 he reconstituted the country committee, infiltrated the Vanguard Youth and won over Dr Thach, who was to become his tool in the seizure of power. At the beginning of September he was removed from the presidency of the *de facto* government and reprimanded by Hanoi for not having 'followed the line', for having 'committed the error of using the Japanese' and for failing to give his government an appearance of national unity. The emissaries from the north told him to dissolve the Vanguard Youth in favour of the National Salvation Youth (Jeunesse de Salut National).

Giau and his acolyte, Duong bach Mai, took on the pirates of Binh xuyen as Sûreté agents and personal bodyguards. They had offered them a stock of arms stolen from the Japanese.

Was this permissible? Let us consider what Frederick Engels wrote:

> If the French workers, in every revolution, inscribed on the houses: 'Death to thieves!' and even shot some, they did it not out of reverence for property, but because they rightly considered it necessary above all to get rid of that gang. Every leader of the workers who uses these scoundrels as guards or relies on them for support proves himself, by this action alone, a traitor to the movement. (Engels, 1956, p. 14.)

The demonstration of 25 August 1945

In calling the demonstration of 25 August, the Stalinist party had in mind a general show of support for Vietminh rule, and therefore for its legitimacy. It was not unaware that spectacular gatherings of crowds galvanise and inspire. Giau was to centre his speech around the general aspiration of the day, which was both profound and simple: national independence.

From the early morning the whole native population of Saigon, from the palm-leaf huts of the outskirts to the Europeanised town centre, began to assemble on Boulevard Norodom where a platform has been erected behind the Cathedral. It was on this stage that Giau, revolver in belt, was to address the crowd. The humble people of the inner suburbs, Giadinh, Govap, Thi nghe and Khanh hoi, converged on the town centre. It was already full of peasants who had arrived during the night from the rebellious centres of Ba Diem, Hoc mon, Duc hoa and Chodem, mobilised by Stalinist militants who were just back from the prisons and camps.

It was a human ant-heap under a sea of Vietminh flags with yellow stars on a red background. No police intervened. The fuse had blown. They may all have been filled with differing expectations. But they all wanted to see the end of the colonial regime and were ready to throw themselves into a struggle with an uncertain outcome.

From the platform Giau unleashed on to the crowd a speech which was almost an echo of that of Ho van Nga on 19 August: an appeal for unity of all, in and for the nation, for a better life, for independence and democracy — but within a republic (whereas Ho van Nga envisaged it within the bosom of the Empire).

Giau added: 'Today the people have endorsed us; it must therefore help us against the agitators and provocateurs.' To whom was he alluding if not to the Trotskyists?

At noon, from the balcony of the town hall, Dr Thach read out the list of members of the *de facto* government to a prolonged storm of applause.

The League of Internationalist Communists aroused the enthusiasm of the ordinary people with its slogans, 'Land to the peasants! The factories to the workers!' To the Stalinists' cries of 'all power to the Vietminh', the League members replied: 'all power to the people's committees!', and marched past to the song of the International which clashed with the March of the Vanguard Youth (Len dang) lauding 'the millennial heroism of the Viet people'.

The *La Lutte* group was more restrained. We have not been able to trace any copies of *Tranh dau* for August-September 1945, and we continue to seek them. But we can already say that this group did not want to exclude itself from a united front of anti-imperialist struggle.

It tried to be accepted by the PCI, which was deeply rooted in the peasantry, in a joint military action, while maintaining its political independence and defending in its press the perspective of 'permanent revolution'.

The absence during the long years of war of any proletarian revolution anywhere in the world encouraged it to restrict its immediate demands to national independence and agrarian reform. It kept its distance from the League by declaring that it had no relations with it.[3]

Phuoc, a young 17-year-old member of the *La Lutte* group points out that the central committee of *La Lutte* had obtained the agreement of the Stalinists to set up a workers' self-defence militia — whose command would be under the control of the government which, in return, would supply it arms and ammunition:

> Our comrades forgot all their mistrust of the Stalinists. That is why they relaxed their efforts to create soviets in the towns, to transform the factories into fortresses and to prepare for civil war. (See page 163.)

People's committees had been organised almost spontaneously in the Saigon-Cholon region. In response to an appeal by the League of Internationalist Communists, they elected delegates to draft a joint declaration; it was distributed on 26 August. They asserted that they wanted to maintain independence in relation to political parties; the need for a united front against imperialism, they stated, should not cut across the masses' freedom of action; and they condemned all attempts to interfere with the autonomy of decisions by the workers and peasants, the mainspring of social change.

The peasants of the west and the power of the Vietminh

Japan's defeat disorientated the nationalists who had banked on its success. In the provinces as in Saigon those to whom the Japanese had partially handed over power acted out the same scenario: they bowed down to the Vietminh, which proclaimed itself to be on the right side for achieving independence, the Russo-Sino-Anglo-American side. They handed over the archives and registers, the seals and the funds to the Vietminh committees, who were supported by the Vanguard Youth and by massive peasant demonstrations. They ordered their militiamen and Sûreté agents to hand in their arms.

Between 25 and 28 August the Vietminh committees reorganised the apparatus of repression under a new label, State Security (Quoc gia tu ve cuoc).

To the peasants' satisfaction the Vietminh had a number of cruel *notables*, sadistic policemen and hoarders shot. They ordered the landowners to lower rents. But the rights of private property were respected.

In several provinces — notably Mytho, Travinh, Sadec, Long xuyen and Chaudoc — the landless peasants, remembering the PCI's slogans of 1930-1931, believed this was the end of their serfdom. Before the Vietminh took over they attacked the particularly harsh proprietors and their possessions. The official history says:

> In Travinh, the peasants began to share out the land, the livestock, the agricultural implements. In order to conciliate the landed owners, the Vietminh stopped these actions and forced the peasants to hand back what they had taken. This made the Vietminh unpopular among the poor peasants. (Vietnam State Publishing House, 1960, Vol II, p. 355.)

In Mytho province, the peasants sought the services of the surveyor Thu, a supporter of *La Lutte*, to help them fairly divide up the seized land. Thu was arrested by the Vietminh; the author met him in October in the church-prison of Song xoai, Tan an. It was obvious that the Commissar of the Interior, Nguyen van Tao, was aiming at the Trotskyist spokesmen for the landless peasants, day labourers, servants and coolies when he wrote:

> Those who have pushed the peasants into taking over the landed estates will be punished without pity. The communist revolution which will resolve the agrarian problem has not yet happened. Our government is a democratic and bourgeois government even though the communists are in power. (*Tin Dien*, No. 5, Saigon, 12 February 1946.)

Had Tao forgotten that the distribution of the land and rice-fields to the landless peasants was, according to the theory of the PCI in 1930, a task for the bourgeois-democratic revolution before going over to the socialist revolution? He had regressed to the period of the Thanh nien — when the theory stated that 'national revolution' (landowners included) came first.[4]

On 23 October 1945 *Co giai phong* (*Banner of Liberation*), the newspaper of the PCI central committee of Hanoi, called directly for murder in its article 'The Trotskyist bands must be put down immediately'. It stated:

> In Nam Bo, they [the Trotskyists] demand the arming of the people — which frightens [sic] the British Mission. They demand the full carrying-out of the tasks of the bourgeois-democratic revolution (essentially the agrarian revolution, distribution of the rice-fields and land to the peasants) with the aim of splitting the National Front and provoking the opposition of the landowners to the revolution.

At the end of October the leaders of the *La Lutte* group were executed by firing squad at Ben suc. The executioners were Duong bach Mai's men.

The illusions of the Stalinists

Let us return to Saigon where Jean Cédile, representative of the 'New France', had been since 24 August, when the British RAF had dropped him by parachute. In a discreet interview he granted Giau, Tao and Dr Thach on 27 August, he proposed the Algiers Declaration of 24 March as a basis for discussion. This first step towards the Stalinists' compromising with the French aroused the anger of the nationalists of the former National United Front.

Now installed in the Governor of Cochinchina's palace, Giau and his government obsequiously prepared for the reception of an (imagined) Allied Mission. A communiqué of 29 August ordered the population to 'work together with the government to solemnly receive the Allied Mission; let each building, public or private, be decked with the colours of the four allied nations, with the national flag of Vietnam in the middle.' (Nguyen ky Nam, 1964, p. 217.)

In the streets of Saigon, banners saying 'Welcome to our Allies' intermingled with those expressing the general sentiment 'Independence or death' when Brigadier-General Douglas Gracey, commanding an Anglo-Indian force, arrived on 6 September to take control of Vietnam on the Allies' behalf.

Later Gracey was casually to remark:

> I was welcomed on arrival by Vietminh. I promptly kicked them out.
> (*Journal of the Royal Asian Society*, July-October 1953.)

On 30 August, at a conference in the Saigon town hall, Tran van

Giau's government summarised the balance sheet of its five days in power. The press and representatives of various political currents were present. The journalist Nguyen ky Nam reported a stormy confrontation between Giau and the Trotskyist Tran van Thach.

> 'Who elected the Provisional Executive of the Nam Bo?' asked Thach.
>
> Giau's inappropriate and menacing reply was: 'We are provisionally taking over the government at this stage; later, we will hand it to you.
>
> 'As for my political reply, I'll meet you elsewhere' he said, as his hand went to his revolver. (Nguyen ky Nam, 1964, p. 2, and *Tin Dien* (*Dispatches*), no. 19, 22 February 1946.)

The events of 2 September

On Hanoi's orders a demonstration was organised by the provisional executive committee of Nam Bo on 2 September, to celebrate the independence declared that day by Ho chi Minh. It was also intended as a show of strength by Giau who, unable to control all the armed groups, had, on 28 August, called for them to be reorganised into a 'popular army' (dan quan).

The crowds began to assemble before 9 a.m. in Boulevard Norodom (renamed Boulevard of the Republic) to hear Ho chi Minh proclaim the independence of Vietnam at 2 p.m. The platform, which had been up since 25 August, was occupied by government dignitaries who were to watch the subsequent march-past of the disciplined ranks of demonstrators and of the four divisions of the 'popular army'.

Only the First Division, under direct government control, was well-armed and well-trained, being made up of the former native Mobile Guard. The other three were under their own command: the para-military formations of the Cao dai made up the Second; the Third, commanded by Nguyen hoa Hiep of the VNQDD, a graduate of the Whampoa military academy, was composed of the auxiliaries (nghia dong quan: Giyutai) recruited by the Japanese army in July and since demobilised; the Fourth comprised the self-defence groups of the Hoa hao.

As the radio had broken down it was Giau himself who harangued the crowd at 2 p.m.; he not only called for rejoicing about independence but also threatened:

> A number of traitors to our country are building up their numbers, in order to help the enemy . . . we must punish the bands which, by creating

disorders within the Democratic Republic of Viet nam, give the enemy a pretext for invading us [sic]. (Quoted in Nguyen ky Nam, 1964, pp. 219-220.)

These threats were aimed at the Trotskyists but also at all those — Hoa hao, Cao dai, VNQDD, and so on — who had not completely fallen in line. The hour for the march-past arrived. Above the moving multitude, the national flags intermingled with those of the Allies. Banners in English, Russian, Chinese, French and Annamite, proclaimed: 'Down with French colonialism! Rather Death than Slavery! Welcome to the Allied Mission! Total Independence for Vietnam!' An unusual inscription 'Assault Committee of Assassination' (Ban am sat xung phong) was displayed by bare-chested tattooed men; Duong bach Mai's cut-throats were present. The bulk of their band, the Binh xuyen pirates, controlled the Y-shaped bridge between Saigon and Cholon.

Towards 4 p.m. rifle shots rang out as the human river, singing and shouting slogans, flowed past the cathedral. They seemed to come from the Mission House. Apparently a group of French colonialists, resolved to preserve imperial domination, were responsible. The crowd panicked and fled in all directions, but some armed groups pounced. Father Tricoire, the kindly prison chaplain, was stabbed and finished off with a revolver shot on the square in front of the cathedral.

The *La Lutte* group was there, a moral and political presence with the flag of the Fourth International and several thousand militants and sympathisers. A veteran member of *La Lutte*, Le van Long, came down the steps of the Mission House, grasping a Frenchman by the collar and handed him over to Duong bach Mai's Sûreté.

By now scattered rifle fire was coming from Boulevard Bonnard, from the central market and from all directions. The 'popular army' returned it in a no less random way. Calm returned only at dusk in the rain. The toll was five French killed and dozens of wounded.

Had not Giau's armed ostentation with his 'Four Divisions' been as provocative to the French colonialists, emboldened by the imminent arrival of British troops, as the desperate calls by the Trotskyists for the arming of the people?

The Stalinists' final manoeuvre

On 3 September Duong bach Mai released all the French suspects; and Giau forbade all carrying of arms, whether knives, pikes or rifles, except by army personnel or the men of the Sûreté.

The League of Internationalist Communists demonstrated in the central market; its leaflets called for the strengthening of the people's committees and the arming of the people to fight the imperialists, whether they be labelled fascist or democratic. The land to the peasants and the factories to the workers! For the complete independence of Indochina!

The Stalinist paper *Dan chung* accused the Trotskyists of being traitors to Vietnam (Viet gian). Nguyen van Linh went to its offices to protest about this incitement to murder.

On 4 September, the British made the Japanese Marshal Terauchi responsible for the maintainance of order. On the 6th, the British Mission arrived. On 7 September, news of Ta thu Thau's arrest in Quang ngai was posted up in front of the offices of *Tranh dau* at the junction of rue Garros and rue Lagrandière. The *La Lutte* group challenged Giau on this.

Giau informed the press that the Japanese headquarters insisted on the dissolution of the popular army, banned all 'subversive' political activity, all demonstrations not previously authorised by the Japanese army and all carrying of arms, including knives and pikes. He accused the League of Internationalist Communists of having given the 'foreigners' cause to strike a blow at Viet sovereignty by their call to the population to demonstrate at the Saigon market for 'arming the people'.

On 8 September, 17 parties or groups, assembled in the Cochinchina Governor's palace, were invited to broaden the Provisional Executive Committee of Nam Bo by Hoang quoc Viet, one of two emissaries from Hanoi and the man who had organised the surveillance of Ta thu Thau during his journey to the north. He proposed to transform the provisional executive into the Popular Committee of Nam Bo (Uy ban nhan dam), and proposed the non-party lawyer Pham van Bach as its president.

A list of about 20 people, including Huynh phu So, the Mad Monk (Hoa hao), Phan van Hum and Tran van Thach (of the *La Lutte* group), Ho van Nga, and even a Constitutionalist, Duong van Giao, was presented for selection. Nearly all the existing members remained on the Committee; there were only three new members including the Mad Monk. On the next day, Phan van Hum learned that he had been nominated as a reserve member but refused to participate in this government.

On 9 September, Giau replied to the *La Lutte* group's challenge in a press communiqué:

Ta thu Thau's arrest in Quang ngai does not concern the provisional executive committee. The Popular Committee [of Quang Ngai] can, and has the right to, judge Ta thu Thau.

The headquarters of the Hoa hao in rue Miche in Saigon were raided. The Mad Monk managed to escape arrest, ordered by Giau who had opposed his inclusion in the CPN.

The Hoa hao rose in revolt at Cantho and were crushed. The poet Nguyen xuan Thiep (Viet Chau), whom the Vietminh took for a Trotskyist, was executed; so were the Mad Monk's brother, Huynh phu Mau, and the son of the Hoa hao chief in Cantho. As early as 27 August the Vietminh had arrested some 300 Hoa hao faithful at Chaudoc (one was executed), and, on 30 August, had arrested leaders of its provincial sections.

On 10 September, the Popular Committee of Nam Bo, which had been ejected from the Governor's palace by the British, installed itself in the town hall and appointed a committee to organise relations with the Allies. Among those nominated to serve on it, four would soon be assassinated by the Vietminh: they were Tran van Thach, Phan van Chanh, Huynh van Phuong and Madame Ho vinh Ky.

On 12 September, Gracey ordered the Gurkhas to occupy the more important police stations. Then the Bank of Indochina, the Treasury, the aerodrome, the power stations and waterworks were occupied while the expeditionary corps arrived in small instalments.

The League of Internationalist Communists and its people's committees distributed a manifesto opposing the Stalinist government's capitulation to the British threats. On 14 September Duong bach Mai had their headquarters surrounded, and arrested all the assembled delegates of the people's committees and seized arms and typewriters. Thus he prepared himself to carry out the 'physical extermination of the vanguard of the revolutionary proletariat' (Lu sanh Hanh, 1947).

Gracey allowed a measure of rearmament by the French, and the French Colonel Rivière, who had landed with the British a week earlier, created a battalion from formerly interned soldiers from the barracks of the Fifth Regiment of Colonial Infantry.

On 16 September, the Popular Committee of Nam Bo held a press conference. It protested that measures adopted in favour of the workers had been ignored, at the difficulties the Compagnie Franco-Asiatique des Pétroles was creating for it, and at the ill-will of the French merchants.

On 17 September, the Popular Committee called for a general strike

The Trotskyists in 1945: Ta thu Thau, who was killed by the Stalinists in Quang ngai (right); the street named after him in Saigon (above); this picture was taken in 1984, one year before its name was changed to Luu van Lang street. A contingent of Fourth Internationalists on the mass demonstration in Saigon on 21 August 1945 (opposite). The zig-zag symbol is that of the Fourth International; behind is a contingent of nationalists, with a banner saying 'national liberation'.

Defeat of the Saigon workers, 1945:
A contingent of the Stalinist party on the demonstration of 25 August, with
their slogans 'Long live the Allied Commission! Long live total independence
for Vietnam!' (top); Prisoners of the Saigon Sûreté on 23 September 1945
(above, and opposite).

and banned sales of all goods and services to the French; anyone working would be looked on as a traitor. Saigon was paralysed. To the intense annoyance of the settlers there were no more 'boys', nor cooks; no waiters in the hotels, nor rickshaw coolies in the streets. The docks were deserted and transport at a standstill.

About a hundred French soldiers entered the Arsenal and left with lorries full of arms and ammunition.

On 18 September, Gracey ordered the Japanese to maintain order between the Annamites and the French.

On 19 September, Cédile called a press conference:

> The Vietminh does not represent the popular will. It is incapable of maintaining order and preventing looting. First, order must be restored. Then we will set up a government consistent with the Algiers Declaration of 24 March.[5]

On 20 September, Gracey forbade the carrying of arms and closed the Annamite press, had the Vietminh's posters ripped off the walls, and reminded the Stalinist police that they were merely auxiliaries of the British forces.

On 21 September, Gracey declared martial law against sabotage and looting. The *La Lutte* group urged non-combatants to evacuate the town. On 22 September, the British took control of the Saigon prison and freed the Vietminh's French prisoners; they handed over the militants of the League of Internationalist Communists to the French Sûreté. Gracey allowed Cédile to rearm 1,400 soldiers of the Colonial Infantry.

The Popular Committee of Nam Bo stuck up posters urging the population to disperse to the countryside and to 'remain calm as the government hopes to begin negotiations'.

The Saigon uprising of 23 September 1945

On the night of 22-23 September, the French, supported by the Gurkhas, reoccupied the police stations, the Sûreté, the Treasury and, towards 4 a.m., the town hall, which had already been evacuated by the Nam Bo Popular Committee.[6] The firing stopped at about 6.30 a.m. British correspondents, in particular that of the *Daily Telegraph*, circulated reports of the cruelty meted out that night by the rampaging French; of a 'chasse aux Annamites' ('Annamite hunt'); of the way in which Annamite captives — youths and women — were piled into the town hall and the post office, kneeling on the floor with their arms brutally shackled above their heads. Gracey ordered the troops of the 11th Regiment of Colonial Infantry back to their barracks and Cédile, much to the annoyance of many colonists, condemned the barbarous conduct that night of the unbridled French.

Saigon rose on the night of 23-24 September. In the poorer quarters trees were cut down, vehicles overturned and furniture stacked in the streets to improvise barricades. The movement spread to the suburbs of Khanh hoi, Caukho, Ban co, Phu nhuan, Tandinh and Thi nghe and encircled the city. The insurgents attacked the port commissariat. On 24 September the soldiers carried out searches in all the houses in the town centre and the sailors in those by the docks. In the afternoon the insurgents counter-attacked; one group penetrated into the town through rue de Verdun and occupied the central market, and from Boulevard Bonnard kept the town centre under fire. Another group advanced from the Chinese quarter up the Boulevard de la Somme, towards the market, which was burning on the night of 25 September.

There was no water or electricity. On the night of 24-25 September about a hundred French from Cité Heraud were frightfully massacred. This was the reaction to the whites' contempt for the 'natives' and to the boasts by certain colonists that they would 'skin the Annamites to make sandals' once order had been restored under the French tricolour.

In their operations to break the encirclement of the town — which was soon to be short of food — the French, supported by the Gurkhas, did not spare poor people's palm-leaf huts. The Saigon suburbs were soon in flames.

Fierce battles rage at the bridge-heads which are joined by revolutionary Japanese deserters. Workers and Trotskyist militants fight under the banner of the Fourth International in the first battles at Dakao, Ban co, Caukho, Ngasau, Cho quan, Vinh hoi, Chanh hung, Thu thiem, Thinghe, Phu nhuan, Gia dinh, Cayqueo, Govap and Nhabe. In the Thinghe sector, out of 214 fighters, all Trotskyists, 210 are cut down. On the third day of the fighting, Tran van Giau orders, via leaflets, the disarming of all the resistance fighters of *La Lutte* who are fighting without orders from his government. (*La Lutte* group, 1948.)

The workers' militia of the Govap tramways, organised by the League of Internationalist Communists and comprising about 60 fighters, took part in the uprising independently of any governmental authority. Although the 400 or so workers at the tramway depot belonged to the Confédération Générale du Travail du Sud (a creation of Giau's for controlling the Saigon-Cholon workers),[7] they rejected both the Vietminh flag and the label 'Workers of National Salvation' (Cong nhan cuu quoc). Their militia, whose leaders Tran dinh Minh and S. had been elected, fought under the red flag and to the tune of the 'Internationale' and the 'Marche des Ouvriers, Paysans et Soldats' ('March of the Workers, Peasants and Soldiers'). The militia's first casualty was a tailor, Ho van Duc, native of Mytho. Tran van Nghi, who belonged to the 'Volunteers of Death No. 1 Group', was wounded at An phu Dong.

Threatened with annihilation by the armed Vietminh groups, the militia withdrew to the Plaine des Joncs. There it was protected from decimation by the Third Division, led by Nguyen hoa Hiep of the VNQDD who was opposed to the totalitarian repression by the Stalinists. During this withdrawal it lost a score of comrades in battles with the French troops, including Chi Quy, a woman nurse, Dong, Thien, Tran van Thanh, Nguyen van Huong, Tran quoc Kieu and six comrades from the plantations of Tayninh.

Nguyen van Linh, Le Ngoc, Nguyen van Nam and Ngo van Xuyet had withdrawn towards Thuduc and met together at the last hamlet in Tanlo, to draft a text explaining the political and military perspective of the League, and in particular of the workers' militia. They were determined to mount an armed defence if they faced arrest by the Stalinist cops, who had been in Thuduc since 26 September. They rejoined the militia in its retreat towards the Plaine des Joncs, a particularly poor peasant area where many had, ostensibly, rallied to the Cao dai cult or that of Phat Thay of the Hoa hao to escape the French repression of 1940.

In October, pursued and machine-gunned by French planes, the fighters of the Third Division and the militia, retracing the steps of the rebels at the time of the French conquest, plunged into this immense area of desolate swamps. Ngo van Xuyet was arrested by Vietminh guards on the banks of the river Vaico while on a mission to the Western region; this arrest was ordered by one Trong, a former teacher and pedlar of Chinese medicines, who had been promoted Chief of Tan an province a month previously.

Ngo van Xuyet was imprisoned with about 30 other 'suspects' — including a 'mad woman' accused of irreverence towards Tinh truong Trong — in the Temple of the Tutelary Spirit of Myphuoc. Summary executions were regular occurrences: three Catholic suspects who had fled Tan an, which was retaken by the French troops, were shot. So were two former agents of the French Sûreté who had been taken on to act as Vietminh river police and had engaged in provocations. Meanwhile there could be heard, through the wooden partition which separated the prisoners from the adjoining room, the cries of a poor peasant family who, on returning home with their harvest of sweet potatoes, had been accused of spying and were being kicked and punched.

After being transferred to the palm-leaf covered church at Songxoai, which had been turned into a prison, the author met up with friends belonging to *La Lutte* from Mytho, among whom was the surveyor Thu who had helped the peasants parcel out the land they had seized. All the political internees, who were there in the charge of a Vietminh cadre who had returned from Poulo Condore, were liberated by the Third Division when it passed through. Tran dinh Minh was killed on the My loi front on 13 January 1946. The workers Le Ngoc, Le Ky and Le van Huong were assassinated as 'traitors to Vietnam' by the Vietminh in the Hocmon region.

'The Trotskyist band must be immediately struck down'

Saigon was choking to death. Awaiting the arrival of the expeditionary force, Cédile proposed a truce to the provisional executive committee of Nam Bo, which was still hoping for negotiations; the truce was to be from 2 to 10 October.

On 3 October, the *La Lutte* group, which was circulating the paper *Khang chien (Resistance)* in Cholon province, called on the population not to entertain illusions in diplomacy and to continue the armed struggle against imperialism.

The Stalinists had not waited to begin the repression of the Trotskyists. In Cochinchina it had already started during the insurrection. Duong bach Mai's men had killed Le van Vung, secretary of the Saigon-Cholon regional committee, as he was returning home.

The violent crimes of the Stalinists rose to a peak throughout Cochinchina during the month of October. The perpetrators were Duong bach Mai's men in the east and those of Nguyen van Tay, another of the Stalinist leaders, in the west.

All our comrades at Thudaumot, Bienhoa, Mytho, Tan an and Cantho were exterminated. Among them were Hinh thai Thong, who was chairing an interprovincial meeting, and our delegates from the villages and cantons. Hinh thai Thong was disembowelled; his body was discovered at Quon long (Chogao-Mytho) in 1951 together with that of Ho van Nga, in a mass grave of hundreds tortured by the Vietminh.

A part of the *La Lutte* group retreated, still in combat, towards the west. It was disarmed at Chodem and disappeared. This was the execution centre where the government of Tran van Giau, itself in retreat, was established. The Trotskyist Huynh van Phuong and the Constitutionalists Bui quang Chieu and Duong van Giao were put to death there.

Tran van Thach, Phan van Hum, Phan van Chanh, Ung Hoa, Le van Thu and Nguyen van So regrouped the survivors of Thi nghe and about 30 fighters at Xuan truong (Thuduc).

Eight years previously, Duong bach Mai had written in *La Lutte*:

> In the situation peculiar to Indochina . . . any break in our united front of struggle . . . will kill the combative ardour of our people. We don't overestimate the Trotskyists. However, along with their errors of sterile revolutionism, we also loyally recognise, until fresh orders, that there still remain anti-imperialist elements among them that deserve our support. (*La Lutte*, 6 June 1937.)

In 1945, these 'fresh orders' had arrived. First, the Trotskyists arrested at Xuan truong were disarmed. Then Thach, Hum, Chanh and So were arrested and taken to Thudaumot where they were shot, possibly at Kien an. This was just when Hanoi was ordering that 'the Trotskyist band must be immediately struck down' (*Co giai phong*, 25 October 1945).

Hanoi's official history mentions these arrests, with three inexactitudes (Vietnam State Publishing House, 1960, Vol. 2, p. 319). The *Tranh dau* leaders were not 'in hiding' but had withdrawn in the course of the fighting; they were publishing not the *Doc lap* (*Independence*), but the *Khang chien* (*Resistance*); and the arrests took place at Xuan truong and not at Di an. The killing of these comrades is passed over in silence. As for the teacher, Nguyen thi Loi, he was killed in cold blood at Can giuoc at around the same date.

A dispatch from Captain Gordon, government commissioner attached to the Saigon Permanent Military Tribunal reported:

> Towards mid-October 1945, Duong bach Mai ordered the arrest at Cap Saint-Jacques [now Vung Tau] of Le thanh Long, leader of the Vanguard

Youth of Cap Saint-Jacques and former editor of the paper *La Lutte*; then his detention at Baria for some days; and then his execution by firing squad at Bienhoa. (Quoted in Chaffard, 1969, p. 111.)

In 1947, Mai was in Paris, having been left there as head of the Delegation by Ho chi Minh after the Fontainebleau Conference.[8]

Trotskyist activity after the return of French colonial rule

By the end of October 1945, the workers' movement was dissipated. Most of the Trotskyist leaders had been killed. The nationalists, too, suffered repression at the hands of the Vietminh.

This opened the way for the return of French imperialism — and in November 1945 General Leclerc landed in Saigon with a substantial military force. Vietnam was divided at the 16th parallel: the south was controlled by the French Admiral d'Argenlieu, the north by the Vietminh, who accepted the presence of allied garrisons — first Chinese and then French — while they tried to negotiate with France.

On 6 March 1946 Ho chi Minh signed an agreement with France which 'amicably' welcomed the French army into the north and provided for the reunion of the three Ky (Tonkin, Annam and Cochinchina) by means of a referendum. He stated his readiness to accept 'full co-operation within the French Union, leading to eventual independence'. But French colonialism sought to reassert its direct rule across the whole country, and as a step in this direction, an 'autonomous republic of Cochinchina' was proclaimed on 1 June 1946 by the colonists and bourgeois Annamites. Its first president, Nguyen van Thinh, committed suicide on 10 November and was succeeded by the Cao dai-ist, Le van Hoach.

War broke out between France and Ho's 'Democratic Republic of Vietnam' in December 1946 and continued until the French were defeated in 1954.

Phan hieu Kinh and Ung Hoa, Trotskyists who had survived the 1945 massacre, restarted *Tranh dau*, the organ of the Vietnamese proletariat, on 1 December 1946; in it they reproduced the *Communist Manifesto*. They wrote of 'the disappearance of comrades', among whom were Ngon from the Arsenal and Nguyen van Tien, former manager of *Tranh dau*, freed from Poulo Condore — but without denouncing the assassins. They reported Ngo chinh Phen's and Dao hung Long's return from exile in Madagascar. After several issues the weekly was banned by Le van Hoach's government.

Nguyen van Linh of the League of Internationalist Communists managed to renew contact with the Parti Communiste Internationaliste, the French section of the Fourth International, on 9 July 1947. 'If our group has survived the savage Stalinist persecution, it is in order to continue the struggle', he wrote; he understood neither 'the purely intellectualist attitude of [Pierre] Naville and [David] Rousset', nor 'Rimbert's opportunism' and demanded that the group be 'informed about the men as well as about the events'.[9] He introduced Lu sanh Hanh, who arrived in Paris in 1947, as 'delegate from the Saigon section, who might participate in the work of the international leadership and of the PCI'. This is from a letter, addressed to Raymond Molinier and Yves Craipeau. It never reached Molinier, who had gone to Latin America, and was not replied to. (In the Archive of the International Secretariat of the Fourth International, Fo. 455.)

The League of Internationalist Communists was soon to suffer a mortal blow. In January 1950, three leaders of the Communist League of China — Peng Shuzhi, his companion Chen Bilan and Liu Jialiang — came to join it in Saigon. This Chinese Trotskyist organisation, which in 1948 had 380 worker and student members, sought closer collaboration with its Vietnamese comrades. Several months later, these Chinese comrades, together with Nguyen van Linh and Liu khanh Thinh, were invited to take part in a secret conference in the Vietminh military zone of Bienhoa — a conference supposedly organised by Trotskyist sympathisers to discuss the participation of the Trotskyists in the resistance. Linh, Thinh and Liu Jialiang fell into the trap on 13 May. They were never seen again and the Vietminh radio accused them of being 'agents of French imperialism'. (See N. Van 1950.)[10]

11

AND TODAY?

The movement of the Fourth International in Indochina fought for action by the coolies, workers and poor peasants within the perspective of the world proletarian revolution, the only one capable of achieving a 'true and complete' solution to the national problem and the agrarian question, and of going beyond them towards socialism. This movement practically disappeared — in the battle against colonial reconquest, but mainly as a result of the methodical assassinations of its spokespeople by the Stalinists, who could not tolerate their intransigence in the class struggle, their rejection of unity with the bourgeoisie and landowners and their internationalism opposed to Stalinist nationalism.[1]

The proletariat, small in number and barely awakened to a revolutionary consciousness, was unable to lead the national liberation struggle. Millions of peasants carried the Stalinist party to power, paying a frightful price in deaths and suffering — only to find themselves, in the end, conscripted and enslaved by the national bureaucracy ('quan lieu', literally mandarinate) as a labour force necessary for the primitive accumulation of capital.

'National independence' has turned out to be dependence; Vietnam, having become a satellite of the so-called Soviet Empire, became embroiled in the conflict between the two great 'communist' party-states for hegemony over south-east Asia: its inflated 'communist' army, supplied by the Russians, chased the 'communist' Pol Pot, protégé of the Chinese, from Cambodia and occupied it for a decade (1979-1989).

With the help of the Chinese and Russians the new dominant caste or class of the so-called 'Socialist Republic of Vietnam' arose from the 'cultured middle class' to replace the bourgeois and landowners at the head of a hierarchic party-state in which the working class is today still numerically very weak. It has since then exercised its dictatorship over the producers who still enjoy neither collective ownership of the means of production, time for reflection, power to make decisions, expression of their own interests nor the right to strike. While poverty and social inequality persists, the bureaucratic order rules with its military-police repressive apparatus, with its 'prebendary nomenklatura motivated mainly by careerism'. (Boudarel, 1983, p. 32.)

After March 1956, and Khrushchev's report on Stalin's crimes, some poets and writers in Vietnam ventured to break the seeming consensus. On 15 December that year, Ho chi Minh issued a decree banning all publication of oppositional views, punishable by up to life imprisonment. Some peasant revolts shook the regime, such as those in Nghe an in November 1956, and were cruelly repressed.

After the unification of the country in 1975, and the agrarian reform carried out by the bureaucracy, demonstrations like those of the peasants and fishermen of Camau, in the Mekong delta and on the Plaine des Joncs openly defied oppression. Social unrest became such that internal criticism within the party finally broke into the open in the person of Le quang Dao, member of the executive commission of the party's central committee and president of the National Assembly:

A dictatorship exercised by the Party has replaced the class dictatorship of the whole working people . . . this has resulted in a totalitarian regime based on privileges . . . a regime of social injustices which drives the people to revolt. (*Dai doan ket*, 8 December 1989.)

In November 1990, Bui Tin, 'war hero' and the editor of *Nhan dan* (*The People*), organ of the central committee of the Communist Party of Vietnam, broke with his government and testified to the political and economic crisis gripping the country:

The present state of the nation worries every Vietnamese . . . Bureaucracy, irresponsibility, egoism, corruption and fraud thrive under the insolent rule of privileges and prerogatives. ('Petition d'un citoyen', (A citizen's plea), *Chroniques Vietnamiennes*, No. 10-11, Paris, 1991.)

Russian aid (oil, steel, fertilisers, cotton) is drying up; Chinese aid will only be given in return for submission; appeals for foreign capital and a market economy are being discussed on the Planning Commission. In December 1990, the vice-premier Vo van Kiet admitted in front of the Hanoi National Assembly that the economic crisis risked becoming a catastrophe. (See *Libération*, Paris, 14 December 1990.)

Whatever may be the problems we face, we already know for sure that what was called 'communism' was only a criminal and sorry sham. We must correct our language.

The term 'national communism', applied by certain historians to the joyless regime built by Ho chi Minh; the title of Bac Ho (Uncle Ho — not just any uncle, but the father's senior brother — a revered title of tutelary prestige in traditional Confucian society) with which this individual persistently signed his pronouncements aimed at peasants and soldiers — such expressions which bend the mind in a direction contradicted by history remind us of the advice of Confucius to his disciples over 2,400 years ago, on the need to 'correct' mystifying terms (zheng ming).

Nowhere has the Marxist utopia — a world society, classless and therefore free of national antagonisms, that is, communism — been realised. Moreover its image has been tarnished by the Stalinist-totalitarian nationalism of 'Uncle Ho', with its oppression, its lies and its assassinations. It is a matter, in Maximilien Rubel's words, of a 'really non-existent' communism (Rubel, 1980), which tries to hide the new oppression of the workers and poor peasants with words of deceit.

18 December 1990

PORTRAITS OF SOME VIETNAMESE REVOLUTIONARIES

Ta thu Thau (1906-1945)

On 20 May 1939, three and a half months before the outbreak of the world war, Jules Brévié, the French Governor General of Indochina, sent a cable to the Minister for Colonies, Georges Mandel. Brévié devoted four pages to his bête noire: the Trotskyist Ta thu Thau, then 33 years old. He contrasted Thau with the Stalinist Nguyen van Tao, 'whose attitude in the event of war would be loyalist' in line with 'that adopted in France by the Communist Party' (the Laval-Stalin pact was not broken till August). The Trotskyists, 'under the aegis of Ta thu Thau' planned 'to take advantage of a possible war to win total liberation', warned Brévié. And 'as soon as Ta tu Thau is at liberty, the agitation resumes, working for moral, political and economic disruption.' Brévié urged the government to show no weakness in this matter.

Ta thu Thau, still young, had already lost his health at the hands of his French jailers. He had left prison half-paralysed in February 1939; he was to lose his life at the hands of the PCI's killers in 1945, ten months after finishing his last spell in captivity.

Thau lost his tubercular mother at the age of 11, and helped his father feed six mouths. After his elementary education he became an orderly in the Public Works; after secondary education he earned five piastres by giving private lessons to the son of a *notable*. At 14 years he passed an entrance exam for Chasseloup-Laubat College. At 17 he won a scholarship. He obtained his Higher Diploma just as the nationalist ferment among school students reached its height.

We lived through painful days of intellectual unrest. The atmosphere was supercharged by the extreme tension between the government and the native population. That tension grew incessantly. We spent our study hours reading banned newspapers, and our leisure hours holding secret meetings where our youthful enthusiasm was matched only by our ignorance . . . We were all drawn towards terrorism. We had only two thoughts: individual assassinations, and the creation in China of an army to regain our independence.

Later, on leaving school, I had a job which left me a lot of free time for 'plotting' . . . The trial of Phan boi Chau in 1925, the affair of Truong cao Dong, (a journalist expelled from Saigon), provided us with excellent material for agitation. Our forces crystallised from the beginning of 1926 in the Young Annam Party . . . In three days we recruited over a hundred members, not to mention sympathisers counted in thousands. (*La Vérité*, 18 April 1930.)

Ta thu Thau and his comrades marched in the funeral procession of the old idealist and reformist nationalist Phan chau Trinh, under banners proclaiming 'Long Live the Annamite revolution'. This funeral, and the arrest of the anarcho-romantic Nguyen an Ninh, provoked boycotts of schools — and even strikes in the Bank of Indochina and at the Arsenal. Many young people emigrated to France. It was Nguyen an Ninh who since 1923 had been confronting the colonial regime in his newspaper *La Cloche fêlée* (*The Cracked Bell*), urging youth to 'leave their fathers' houses', in order to escape the 'profound ignorance' in which they were kept by colonial obscurantism and prepare to build the 'Indochinese nation'. 'Oppression comes to us from France, but so does the spirit of freedom', he wrote.

At the age of 21, Ta thu Thau was in Paris at the Science Faculty. This opening to the wider world was to transform his mental outlook — but not all at once. First he was active in the Phuc viet (Annamite Independence Party), which he took in hand in 1928, after the return to Saigon of its founder Nguyen the Truyen. He wrote with Huynh van Phuong for the monthly *Résurrection*, seized by the police as soon as it appeared.

In January 1929, following a fight between the right-wing Jeunesses Patriotes of Pierre Taittinger[1] and Annamites influenced by the Annamite Independence Party, Ta thu Thau attacked *L'Humanité*, the French Communist Party newspaper, for reporting the incident in bad faith. He attacked the French Communist Party for its failure to intervene on behalf of the arrested Annamites. Alluding to the Annamite group of the French Communist Party, led by Nguyen van Tao, Thau attacked the 'paid hacks of the French Communist Party's Colonial Commission' for 'their counter-revolutionary faction work' among Annamite Independence Party members. Ta thu Thau ended one of his leaflets with a 'cry to the oppressed of the colonies: if you want a place in the sun, unite against imperialism, white or red.' (Here he used the word imperialism in its political sense, not as capitalist imperialism as defined by Rosa Luxemburg or as 'the last stage of capitalism' as defined by Lenin). In March 1929, Thau unsuccessfully defended the Annamite Independence Party before the tribunal of the Seine; it was dissolved.

From 20-30 July 1929, he participated in the Second Congress of the Anti-Imperialist League in Frankfurt. In his book *Dieux blancs, hommes jaunes* (1930), Luc Durtain describes him in the character Nguyen van Marx as 'a tall thin young man with a babyish look were it not for a determined mouth'. As he himself was to write, it was the end of his 'youthful folly'. A new dawn was breaking.

In left-wing circles in Paris Ta thu Thau met not only Félicien Challaye, Francis Jourdain and Daniel Guérin, but also Alfred Rosmer, who introduced him to the French Left Opposition (Trotskyist).[2] Thau read Marx, acquainted himself with the history of the previous 12 years of the USSR, and read Trotsky, who blamed Stalinist policy for the defeat of the Chinese revolution. He became convinced of a world view of the revolution, and of the idea that only the proletariat, by uniting internationally, could provide the motive force to bring a new world into being. This insight would guide his efforts at social analysis. For the rest of his life, neither arrests, prison, hard labour, nor physical and mental torture could make him deviate from the ideal of international communism.

After the Yen Bay insurrection of 1930, Ta thu Thau analysed the reasons for the defeat of the nationalist movement and outlined his ideas in relation to the Indochinese revolution in *La Vérité*, the organ of the Left Opposition (see Chapter 3, pages 18-20). For him the choice was no longer between independence and slavery but between nationalism and socialism — that is, between the coming to power of the educated petty bourgeoisie and the emancipation of the proletariat and the poor peasants. The Third International did not escape his criticism; after having 'led the Chinese revolution to slaughter', it sought to restore itself by adventurism, ('Third Period' policies), which was likely to be as ineffective and tragic as the preceding opportunism. The prediction was soon shown to be well-founded in the painful experience of the insurgent peasants.

Ta thu Thau was arrested during the Annamite student demonstrations in front of the Elysée of 22 May 1930, protesting at the numerous death sentences following Yen Bay. Together with 18 of his compatriots he was expelled from France on 30 May.

To earn his living, Thau began work as a teacher in private schools

— but was dismissed as a result of intervention by the Sûreté. His companion Nguyen thi Anh helped the little family survive by selling straw mats.

In Nghe an and Cochinchina, the crushing of the peasant movement of 1930-1931 generated within the ranks of the PCI a critical examination of the adventurism to which the Comintern's directives gave rise. Thau, Phan van Chanh and Huynh van Phuong found the·e a favourable situation in which to win new comrades. In November 1931, in agreement with Ho huu Tuong, they formed the Ta doi lap (Indochinese Left Opposition) with a theoretical review *Thang muoi*. But in April 1932, discussions on the feasibility or otherwise of entering the PCI to reform it, and also the exigencies of clandestine work, led the group to split. Thau formed the Dong duong cong san (Indochinese Communism) group and distributed an agitational paper *Vo san*.

Arrested together with 65 Trotskyists and sympathisers in August 1932, he was released under caution on 25 January 1933, but 15 comrades were sentenced to prison on 1 May.

He exposed the descent into hell produced by the pre-trial interrogations in a pamphlet, *Three Months at the Sûreté, rue Catinat*, in 1934. In it he denounced the systematic torturing of the political detainees.

Neither Thau nor any Trotskyist was a professional revolutionary. Each had to earn his crust at work. The discussions on the theoretical and practical problems of the revolution were often held in prison, where the old hands initiated newcomers in the thought of Marx, Lenin and Trotsky. In the Saigon Central Prison, Trotskyists and Stalinists shared cells numbers five, six and seven on the rue Filippini, bare cells where they slept on the ground on straw mats. After the hunger strike of 1936, the public prosecutor allowed them a blackboard in cells five and six and some concrete benches; there they were able to read Louis Céline's *Voyage au bout de la nuit*, André Malraux's *Le temps du mépris* and Victor Hugo's *Les Misérables*. Father Tricoire, the prison chaplain, lent them books on science and history. All they had to write on was the toilet paper their families sent them; the 'jail-boy', an ordinary prisoner, would sometimes slip them a precious pencil end when distributing the letter-cards they were allowed for correspondence.

As soon as he was freed, Thau was involved in the election campaign for the Saigon town council — the first attempt at legal agitation and the first united front between Trotskyists, Stalinists and nationalists. Having presented a workers' panel (so lao dong) for the election, the front, inspired by the senior figure of Nguyen an Ninh, published the paper *La Lutte* from 24 April 1933. The mandates of the two elected, the Stalinist Nguyen van Tao and the Trotskyist fellow-traveller Tran van Thach, were rescinded on 12 August — although Tao and Thach had been able to sit on the council while awaiting Hanoi's decision.

La Lutte ceased publication after the elections. Thau gave talks on dialectics to workers and students at the Mutual Education House, wrote for Phan van Hum's socio-literary review, Dong Nai, and translated Politzer's Principes élémentaires de philosophie into quoc ngu.

A second united front was formed in 1934. At the prompting of Nguyen an Ninh and Gabriel Péri, French Communist Party deputy, La Lutte resumed publication on 4 October, with the Trotskyists undertaking not to criticise the USSR in its pages and the Stalinists undertaking not to criticise Trotskyism. They entered the elections of March 1935 to the Colonial Council (unsuccessfully), and those of 12 May for the Saigon town council. Ta thu Thau was elected to the latter — and on 27 June was given a two-year suspended sentence for 'subversive activities via the press'. On 26 December he was arrested for the support he gave to the strike of Tilbury coach drivers but was released the following day. At the first trial of the paper La Lutte on 18 March 1935, he was fined 500 francs.

On 2 May 1935, the Laval-Stalin pact[3] shed a sinister light on the rightward turn of the Comintern and, in July-August, its Seventh Congress declared in favour of setting up popular fronts.[4] Since Thau was gagged by the terms of the La Lutte united front, the task of criticism was taken on by Ho huu Tuong and Lu sanh Hanh, dissident of the PCI since 1932, who in conditions of illegality launched the League of Internationalist Communists for the Construction of the Fourth International. On 3 May 1936 the coming to power of the Popular Front in France, even without an absolute majority in parliament, led to great illusions in Indochina.

A massive strike wave broke out in France. On 9 June 1936, Trotsky wrote: 'The French Revolution has begun'. The League of Internationalist Communists made a call for the formation of action committees and a general strike.

The core of the group was immediately locked up. Thau and La Lutte also called for the setting up of action committees — but with the sole aim of 'deciding the masses to make their wishes known and elect delegates to an Indochinese Congress', conceived as an attempt at a local Popular Front. It was intended that this Congress would pass on these wishes to a French Parliamentary Inquiry Commission planned by the Blum government, a commission that never arrived.

From September onwards, after the first Moscow trial, this moderate policy of Thau's was criticised by *Le Militant*, the first legal Trotskyist weekly launched by Ho huu Tuong. The Constitutionalist leaders, who together with *La Lutte* had called for this still-born Congress, withdrew from it. Thau, Ninh and Tao were arrested in September and October 1936. They were held under the regime for common criminals, although several long hunger strikes resulted in some improvements — exemption from wearing the penal blue uniform, blackboards and books. Political prisoner status was never won under the French colonial regime. The three militants were freed in November 1936, after 11 days on hunger strike.

Serious strikes broke out from 26 November 1936 onwards. The Blum-Moutet government had not yet adopted any measures to make the working conditions of the native population less inhuman. Thau uninhibitedly attacked the Popular Front, in *La Lutte* itself, for forgetting its promises of reforms in the colonies. The Stalinists immediately distanced themselves from him in an open letter of 17 December.

In April 1937 Thau and Tao collaborated for the last time, for the new municipal elections in Saigon. Both were elected. On Moscow's orders, transmitted via the French Communist Party, the Stalinists broke the united front at the end of May by launching a new paper *L'Avant-garde* in which they described the Trotskyists as 'twin brothers of fascism'.

Thau and Tao were then in jail and would only be let out on bail on 7 June.

On 11 July 1937, the International Secretariat of the Fourth International noted that the united front experience was now in the past and called for the Ta thu Thau and Ho huu Tuong tendencies to unite. *La Lutte* had continued to appear, but as a Trotskyist organ. Thau once more found himself in prison for having supported a strike, this time of the railwayworkers — and on 28 August replied in *La Lutte* to Nguyen an Ninh, who was accusing the Trotskyists of having 'given up all peaceful methods'. He reminded him that he and his comrades had opposed the 'infantile insurrectionism' of the Stalinists in 1930-1931, just as they were today fighting their descent into 'the worst opportunism', and he continued:

> We recognise the right of the workers' state to conclude military pacts with no matter who, in order to defend itself. But we do not recognise the Stalinist bureaucracy's right to determine the politics of the world proletariat in order to suit the needs of Soviet diplomacy. Franco-Soviet

Treaty? Possible. But let Stalin not declare that he approves of French militarism. (*La Lutte*, 29 August 1937).

Thau left prison paralysed. He had started a new hunger strike on 30 August 1937, and had resisted force-feeding on either 5 or 6 September. He was left in his cell without being visited for two days, and then left unconscious as a result of an injection. When he recovered consciousness he was partially paralysed down his right side. (See letter from his lawyer, M. Loyes, to Daniel Guérin, *Révolution prolétarienne*, 25 February 1938.)

On 17 September 1937, Ta thu Thau was carried before the Saigon tribunal on a stretcher. On 11 November he was sentenced to two years in prison; his residence ban was extended to ten years. On 18 January 1938, Thau wrote to Daniel Guérin from the Saigon Central Prison:

> I am still paralysed. . . . If, in view of my state of health, the Colonial Minister were to free me conditionally, I request to go to France where I might have the time to recover with the doctors there . . .

But nothing of the sort happened. He was not freed until 16 February 1939, on the eve of Annamite New Year (Tet). Still under a residence ban, he worked on the publication of *Tranh dau*, the name under which the former *La Lutte* appeared in quoc ngu from October 1938. The Fourth International had just been founded in Paris, in September 1938, and Thau appealed to his comrades in a special Tet issue of the paper to unite in a Fourth Internationalist Party.

In April 1939, Thau was elected to the Colonial Council, along with his two comrades Tran van Thach and Phan van Hum. They ceaselessly opposed the Stalinist support of French military forces and denounced the 'Defence of France in Indochina', the war loans and taxes, and the resultant lowering of living standards.

'The recent campaign of Ta thu Thau and his supporters necessitates . . . an urgent clampdown, in order to safeguard French authority in the country', Governor General Brévié cabled to Paris on 20 May 1939. At the same time, Nguyen ai Quoc (Ho chi Minh), from his Chinese abode, was vowing the death of the Trotskyists in his three letters to his 'beloved comrades' in Hanoi.

On 23 August 1939, Ta thu Thau left for Siam (Thailand), Governor Brévié having found an opportunity to get rid of him by authorising him to leave the country to get medical care.

But events followed rapidly on each other; on 24 August Stalin held out his hand to Hitler; on 1 September Nazi troops entered Poland and, on 3 September, the British and French governments declared war on Germany. *Tranh dau* and Ta thu Thau's group, like all the 'communist' publications and organisations, were banned.

Thau was arrested in Singapore on 10 October 1939 and brought back to Saigon. On 16 April 1940, he was sentenced to five years' imprisonment, ten years of residence ban and ten years' loss of civil rights. It was the convict prison isle of Poulo Condore for him — until October 1944.

Once his sentence was served he was assigned forced residence in the town of Longxuyen. On 10 November 1944 he wrote to Madame Phuong Lan, a friend from his youth:

> Here I am, where, a quarter of a century ago, I was living without worries . . . Twenty four years have passed . . . the young boy with the broken wings returns. . . . While on the island (Poulo Condore) . . . I was able to learn some poems and all of the *Kim Van Kieu*[5] . . . I would like to reread it to be sure of really understanding its meaning.

He had been out of touch for a long time and tried to familiarise himself with the situation. Under the pretext of seeking medical care he obtained authorisation for a short visit to Saigon. An old acquaintance, Doctor Pham ngoc Thach — who had close relations with Iida, chief of the Japanese cultural service, but was also in secret contact with the Vietminh — got him to meet Ha huy Giap, whom he had known in the Annam Youth and whom the PCI had sent to Saigon to guide the Stalinists of the South towards the Vietminh political line.

Thau also met Ho van Nga, driving force in the National Party for the Independence of Vietnam, and Huynh phu So of the Hoa hao sect, who had moved into the Vietminh's sphere of influence desiring unity — although not without concern about the Stalinists' hegemonic intentions. It seemed to Thau that relying on the Western powers or the Japanese to bring about independence was problematic — and in any case provided no perspective of liberation for the workers and poor peasants. It was necessary to build a workers' party and fearlessly swim against the nationalist and Stalinist currents. This is what he discussed with the old comrades of *La Lutte* when they found each other again in Saigon after the coup of 9 March 1945.

At the end of April, Thau left secretly for the north. Famine was raging in Tonkin and North Annam. The daily paper *Saigon* of 14 May 1945 published his appeal for help:

The situation is so disastrous that I allow myself to beg my brothers of Cochinchina to eat only enough to live, so as to collect all they can and get it here immediately.

He was happy to find in the north worker supporters of the Trotskyist paper *Chien dau*, and to meet a large number of young people who had given up their studies to devote themselves to the political awakening of the poorest class, which they hoped to free from servitude. They were not afraid of freedom of discussion and decision. He participated with them in secret workers' meetings in the mining areas, at Namdinh, and as far north as Haiphong, and in secret peasants' assemblies in the Haiduong and Thaibinh regions. He dealt, with a confidence obviously still unshaken, with their disquiet about lies — spread by the Vietminh and echoed by Tran van Gioi, Hoa hao delegate in Tonkin — describing the Trotskyists as 'elements hostile to the interests of the workers'.

Once more the pace of history accelerated. Atomic bombs were dropped on Hiroshima and Nagasaki on 6 and 9 August. Ho chi Minh called for a generalised insurrection on 10 August; Thau started his journey back to the south. At Hue, he parted company with his companion, the young writer Do ba The, in order to escape his shadowing by the Stalinists.

The commonly quoted versions of what followed vary as to the exact location of his arrest — but all agree that it was in early September 1945 in Quang ngai, that the responsibility for it was the Vietminh's, and that the militia men ordered to execute Thau were afflicted by doubts, because he defended himself during his kangaroo court trial by justifying his life as a revolutionary.

When ordered to fire. the militia men lowered their rifles. After their third refusal the 'prosecuting attorney', Tu Ty, ended the drama by a revolver shot in Thau's back.

After the 1954 Geneva Agreement,[6] the nationalist journalist Ngo quang Huy, a friend of Thau's expelled from France with him in 1930, went to My khe, south of the 17th Parallel, in the plain of the weeping willows by the sea shore. There, the men who had been ordered to throw the dead into a common grave (a whole group of young sympathisers, including Ho dac Di), had secretly dug up Thau's body and made a tomb for 'this brother' (anh ay).

Had the assassination order come from Hanoi, or from the *de facto* government of Tran van Giau in Saigon (25 August-23 September)? The accounts allow for both possibilities, and even for the crime having been a local initiative. It was learned later that Ha ton Thang from the Sam son region, and the printer Luong duc Thiep of Dan phuong, who had greeted Ta thu Thau with enthusiasm, were 'destroyed like noxious weeds' (lam co) with their friends and families. All trace of the other young people mentioned was lost.

Daniel Guérin questioned Ho chi Minh about the assassination of Ta thu Thau during the latter's visit to Paris in 1946. He received this reply:

> He was a great patriot and we weep for him, but all those that do not follow the line I indicate will be broken. (Guérin, 1954, p. 22.)

One of the Saigon streets was still named after Thau when the troops from the north entered the city in 1975. Some ten years later it was renamed by the new administration, but the Saigonese still call it Duong Ta thu Thau.

Phan van Chanh (1906-1945)

Phan van Chanh was a native of Binh truoc, Bienhoa, and son of a well-off family. His father was secretary to the government. He completed his secondary education at Chasseloup-Laubat College, left for France on 25 September 1925 and registered with the Faculty of Medicine of Paris.

He collaborated on Tran van Thach's *Journal des Étudiants anna-mites*, was active in the Annamite Independence Party with Ta thu Thau and, with him, joined the Left Opposition (Trotskyist) in 1930. He was one of the 19 expelled from France on 30 May 1930 after protesting at the Yen Bay executions (see page 18).

In Saigon he taught in private schools and participated in the formation of the Ta doi lap (Indochinese Left Opposition). In 1932, with Huynh van Phuong, he attempted to awaken working-class consciousness by distributing pamphlets, including translations of the *Communist Manifesto* by Marx and Engels, and *Socialism, Utopian and Scientific* by Engels.

He was arrested on 8 August 1932, and given a four year suspended sentence on 1 May 1933. He belonged to the *La Lutte* group and remained with Ta thu Thau after the split of June 1937. He was a candidate of the *Tranh dau (La Lutte)* group in the Colonial Council elections of April 1939. On 13 July 1939 he was arrested, and on 16 March 1940 sentenced to three years' imprisonment, five years of residence ban and ten years' loss of civil rights. He was deported to Poulo Condore.

In 1945, Phan van Chanh was in the *Tranh dau* group, and was shot by Tran van Giau's men at Kien an, Thudaumot, in October.

Huynh van Phuong (1906-1945)

Huynh van Phuong, who came from a rich family from Mytho, left for France in 1927 after studying at the Chasseloup-Laubat College in Saigon. He studied law in Paris for three years, joined the Annamite Independence Party and wrote for its paper *La Résurrection*. At the end of 1929 he joined Ta thu Thau and Phan van Chanh in the Indochinese Left Opposition. He was the author of 'The development of Indochina and the Annamite bourgeoisie' (published in *Lutte des classes*, April 1930).

Expelled from France on 30 May 1930 at the same time as Thau, Huynh van Phuong was one of the founders of the Ta doi lap (Indochinese Left Opposition) and was in charge of its publications.

He was with the first *La Lutte* group in 1933, wrote for the review *Dong Nai*, and belonged to the second *La Lutte* group in 1934-1936.

However, in 1935, Phuong supported two Constitutionalist candidates for the Colonial Council — Duong van Giao in the bourgeois journal *Dong Thanh*, and Huynh ngoc Nhuan in a leaflet at Baclieu. From that time, Ta thu Thau considered him 'the black plague of the workers' movement'.

Phuong left Saigon in 1936 for Tonkin, where he completed his law studies, simultaneously collaborating with the paper *Travail* (*Labour*) which was similar to *La Lutte*. Then he worked with *Progrès social* (*Social Progress*), a short-lived near-Trotskyist paper. Ho huu Tuong publicly disavowed him and the Tia sang group of Trotskyists in the north condemned him as a centrist and considered him a traitor when he wrote a speech for the royalist Pham le Bong.

Phuong returned to Saigon at the end of 1939 and established himself as a barrister. He was not troubled during the repression at the beginning of the war; no doubt the colonial authorities considered he had fallen in line.

After the Japanese coup of March 1945, he was again left alone by the Saigon Sûreté led by captain Ichikawa (in Vietnamese, Nhut xuyen; see *Saigon*, 1 June 1945).

Around Phuong was formed the Groupe des Intellectuels (Intellectuals' Group) — in no way Trotskyist — which in August 1945 took part in Ho van Nga's National United Front. The latter put Phuong, along with Ho vinh Ky, in charge of the Cochinchina Sûreté. There Phuong discovered a file on the Saigon Stalinist leader, Tran van Giau, which detailed Giau's contacts with the French Sûreté, and made four photocopies of it. He kept one and passed the others to Ho vinh Ky, to Huynh phu So the 'mad monk' and to Duong van Giao, the Constitutionalist leader — who were all, like him, to be assassinated by Giau's killers (see Nguyen ky Nam, 1964, p. 31).

Even if the ex-Trotskyist Huynh van Phuong had worked with the Japanese Sûreté, can the responsibility really be placed on the Trotskyists, who put him out of their ranks in 1935? And was there any foundation whatsoever for the accusation of Tran van Giau that 'from 9 March, the Trotskyists controlled the Sûreté and the police'? (Tran van Giau, 1963, Vol 3, p. 296.) This affirmation has been repeated in a French doctoral thesis by B. Tasteyre (Tasteyre, 1978), and is also part of the perspective of Tasteyre's tutor, J. Chesneaux.

Huynh van Phuong was stabbed to death by one of Tran van Giau's henchmen at Cho dem, Cholon, to which the Vietminh government had retreated after 23 September 1945. According to doctor Ho ta Khanh, one of his fellow prisoners, the pharmacist Thai van Hiep from Dakao, Saigon, witnessed the assassination.

Tran van Thach (1903-1945)

Born in Cholon into a well-off family, Tran van Thach obtained his school leaving certificate at the Chasseloup-Laubat College in 1925. He was in France from May 1926, studying for a philosophy degree at Toulouse and then at Paris University.

On 15 March 1927 Thach founded the *Journal des Étudiants annamites*. He published in it, on 15 December, an article entitled 'A strange dream', a political prophecy in which he imagined Saigon in 1955 on the eve of independence, with a bourgeois party and its adversary, a workers' party.

He had one of his progressive bourgeois characters say: 'The best programme of action we can adopt is that which resolves both the social and the national problems.' In January 1928 he repudiated the conservative nationalists.

That same year he protested, in the bulletin of the Anti-Imperialist League, against the 'ill will of those that govern us, and whose unavowed intention is to mould us into ever submissive individuals . . .' He met Ta thu Thau in the Annamite Independence Party, took part in a protest meeting against the arrest of Nguyen an Ninh on 28 September 1928 and asserted, in the 2 December *Manifesto of the Annamite Students*, that the goal of studies abroad must be the liberation of their country.

In the *Journal des Étudiants annamites* of January 1929, Thach emphasised 'the importance of the union of intellectuals and workers'. In May he became president of the Association Mutuelle des Indochinois de Paris (Mutual Association of Indochinese in Paris) whose protests against repressions he took to the Ministry for Colonies.

He returned to Saigon in January 1930, to a country that was about to be deeply moved by the Yen Bay insurrection and the peasant movement, and then by the bloody suppression of 1930-1931. He earned his living as teacher of literature in private schools. He participated in the first *La Lutte* group, the legal attempt by the 'returnees from France' around Nguyen an Ninh to openly defy colonial rule in the Saigon municipal elections of April-May 1933 on a reformist programme of the right to strike and the eight-hour day. Thach and the Stalinist Nguyen van Tao were elected, but their election was soon annulled by the authorities.

In September 1934, Thach was among those who restarted the *La Lutte* group. He was re-elected to the Saigon Town Council with Ta thu Thau, Nguyen van Tao and Duong bach Mai. In *La Lutte* he wrote the satirical column 'Petits clous' ('Titbits'), of which this is an example:

Arnoux [the Sûreté chief of Indochina] has toothache
The attitude of policeman Kim before the judges has annoyed several of our colleagues. Here is a man savagely ill-treated on two occasions in front of several witnesses, and who does not even dare admit he was hit. Only while 'gesticulating' did the honourable M. Arnoux 'graze' his face! . . .

There is in this cowardice something so unbelievable it borders on ignorance. But the fear that lies behind the policeman's evidence is of the same sort as that of the performing animals of the Vietnam Circus forced to win their food by acrobatics contrary to their nature. . . . Two hundred francs fine for a boxing bout with a policeman in the course of his duty, that's really generous: Arnoux got off cheaply for reasons which convinced the judges.

I hope this will not be lost on M. Pages [the Governor of Indochina]. If, one day, he needs to justify the arrest of four workers' municipal councillors, he will say: 'What do you expect? Too much good food heated my blood and the heat got on my nerves.' (*La Lutte*, 21 January 1936.)

Thach belonged to the action committee of *La Lutte* during the Indochinese Congress movement. It seems that the first Moscow Trial definitely drove him away from Stalinism; from then on he was totally committed to Trotskyism.

Thach's election to the Saigon town council was invalidated on 2 February 1937: after that he devoted himself to trade union work which resulted, on 9 September, in a two-month prison sentence. In June he aligned himself with Ta thu Thau when the Stalinists split the *La Lutte* group.

He was on the list of Fourth Internationalist candidates of the *Tranh dau* (*La Lutte*) group in the elections to the Colonial Council of April 1939. He was elected along with Ta thu Thau and Phan van Hum, and the election invalidated in October when he was in jail.

On 16 April 1940 Thach was sentenced to four years' jail with ten years residence ban and loss of civil rights; he was deported to Poulo Condore. At the trial, reproached with agitating against the 'national defence' budget, he replied that his country was too poor to bear such a burden.

After being freed in 1944, Thach was assigned to forced residence at Cantho. He organised the Revolutionary Workers' Party with his *Tranh dau* comrades after the collapse of the French colonial administration. Then came the Japanese surrender. In Ta thu Thau's absence, Thach proposed 'joint action' (against the return of the colonialists) to the Communist Party, which had just set up its *de facto* government in Saigon on 24 August. On 23 September, Saigon rose against the reoccupation of the city by the French who had been rearmed by the British. The Tran van Giau government fled to organise resistance outside the city. After suffering heavy casualties on the Tan binh front, the militants of *La Lutte* withdrew to the Thu duc region where Tran van Thach was arrested by Giau's police.

He was executed by firing squad in the Vietminh maquis of Kien an, Thu dau mot, just before the arrival of British-Indian troops. He handed his watch to one of his captors, a former pupil, for him to pass on to his brother.

The doctor Madame Ho vinh Ky, a leader of the Vanguard Women, and her husband were executed in the same batch of about 30 people. 'Aim well at my heart!' she cried to the firing squad, the author was told by a witness.

Phan van Hum (1902-1945)

Phan van Hum was born on 9 April 1902 at An thanh, Thudaumot, the son of a Buddhist small landowner. In 1922 he obtained a diploma at Chasseloup-Laubat College. He was a teacher at Soc trang in 1923, was accepted into the School of Public Works of Hanoi in 1924, and obtained his diploma in 1925. He worked as a technical officer from 1926 to 1928.

He was forced to resign from his job and to reimburse his study fees. This was punishment for having repeatedly visited the old nationalist Phan boi Chau, at the time residing under police supervision, and for having harboured some women students who were on strike.

On his return to Saigon he became a friend and disciple of Nguyen an Ninh. He travelled the countryside by bicycle with him to awaken the peasants. After his arrest at Benluc on 28 September 1928, he exposed the prison regime and its tortures in a pamphlet, *Ngoi tu kham lon* (*In the Central Prison*). This work, which also undertook the defence of Nguyen an Ninh, who was accused of forming a 'secret society', was published in instalments in the newspaper *Than chung* and was received with enthusiasm by the young.

A fragment from one of Hum's poems — translated here from quoc ngu — expresses very well his state of mind at this time:

> Today's society is full of iniquity.
> How can we make you hear our plea,
> O blue sky?
> Those who build multi-storey houses live in rotting palm-leaf huts,
> Those who weave silk have no good clothes.
> The learned exploit the labour of the ignorant,
> The dolts reinforce the bands of the crafty ones.
> Let the people become aware of their misery
> And the tens of thousands of calamities will be overcome.

On 27 July 1929, Phan van Hum was given a four months suspended sentence, but obtained permission to travel to the metropolis and boarded ship for France on 3 September. Ninh had inspired him with beautiful verse: 'A vast new world awaits only the wanderers'. He was to spend four years in France.

In Toulouse he joined the Annamite students' Committee of Struggle against the repression which, in February 1930, hit the insurgents of Yen Bay. He went up to Paris to take part in the demonstration of 22

May in front of the Elysée and avoided arrest by fleeing to Belgium with Ho huu Tuong. There, with Tuong, he produced the one and only issue of *Tien quan* (*The Vanguard*) — with the motto 'No revolutionary movement without revolutionary theory (Lenin)' on the masthead — in preparation for an eventual congress of revolutionary Annamite emigrés.

On his return to Paris in July Hum was won over to the ideas of the Left Opposition and joined the Indochinese group of the Communist League. He was sacked from his job as lecturer in the Annamite language at the Toulouse lycée (grammar school) for carrying out nationalist propaganda. He returned to Paris and registered at the Sorbonne, where he studied from the end of 1930 until 1933 for a philosophy degree, without giving up his political activity. He was active in the French section of the Anti-Imperialist League and on the Indochinese Amnesty Committee.

On returning to Saigon on 21 July 1933, Hum met up again with Ta thu Thau and Ho huu Tuong. He was taken on as editor of the literary review *Dong Nai*, which was banned in January 1934, and as a teacher of Annamite literature at the Lycée Paul Doumer, from which post he was removed in June 1935 for having organised a strike of the teaching staff.

Hum was active in the *La Lutte* united front while still busy with philosophical work. He remained with Ta thu Thau in the *La Lutte* split of 1937 and wrote in *Tranh dau* (*La Lutte*), now the organ of the Fourth International. On 30 April 1939, Hum was elected to the Colonial Council of Indochina. Arrested on 28 June, he was sentenced on 13 October to five years' imprisonment and ten years' residence ban, for having assumed responsibility for *La Lutte*'s agitation against the war loan and taxes. It was customary that 'politicals' sentenced to more than three years were sent to the convict settlement of Poulo Condore, and Hum went there.

Once his time was served, Hum was placed under supervised forced residence at Tan uyen, Bien hoa. Stricken with beri beri during his imprisonment, he went to Saigon after the Japanese coup of 9 March 1945, and was taken care of by Doctor Ho ta Khanh. He rejoined the *La Lutte* group. On 10 September 1945, Hum was proposed for membership of the Provisional Executive Committee of the Nam Bo (the *de facto* Vietminh government) at the conference which had been called to broaden the Committee. He refused to join.

Phan van Hum was arrested at Bien hoa by Duong bach Mai's secret police in October 1945. He was massacred with other Annamite political prisoners at Song Long Son, 232 kilometres from Bien hoa on the Trans-Indochina line, between Phan thiet and Tour cham. It was later learned that Hum's body was tipped into the river.

Before being taken away for execution, Hum had a final altercation with Duong bach Mai, alongside whom he had conducted the same socialist struggle in the *La Lutte* group in the 1930s, and together with whom he had been deported to the Poulo Condore prison island in 1940. This conversation was related to T.N. Phieu, who now works as a doctor in Houston in the US, by the teacher Truong minh Hai, from Cu lao Pho, who was imprisoned with Hum in 1945 but survived.

'At Poulo Condore', Mai told Hum, 'you took the blows of the prison warders on your own back, to defend others. But now it is the revolution . . .'

Hum replied: 'If you want to kill me, kill me here and now. What's the point of sending me away?'

For the Stalinist Duong bach Mai, it was necessary that this Trotskyist revolutionary, whose popularity had grown ever since the appearance in 1929 of *Ngoi tu kham lon* (*In the Central Prison*), should disappear without trace.

Phan van Hum's principal works were: *Ngoi tu kham lon* (*In the Central Prison*) (Saigon, 1929); *Duong Linh, May duong to* (*Silken cords*, anthology of poems); *Sa da du tu* (*Journal of a Wanderer, impressions of travel and life in France*) published in Than chung; *Bien chung phap pho thong* (*Dialectics made easy*) (Saigon 1936); *Nguyen phi Hoanh, Tolstoy* (Saigon 1939); *Phat giao triet hoc* (*Buddhist philosophy*) (Hanoi 1942); *Vuong Duong minh, than the va hoc thuyet* (*Wang yang Ming, Life and Doctrine*) (Hanoi 1944).

Nguyen van So (1905-1945)

Born into a poor family at Cholon on 6 October 1905, Nguyen van So was a fervent disciple of Nguyen an Ninh. He was sent down from his Saigon school (the École normale) in 1926 for political agitation. He got himself a job as a mess-hand on the ships of the Extrême-Orient line, spent some time in Marseilles and returned to Saigon in 1928. He then worked in a print shop and in a private school.

He was a member of the *La Lutte* group and a candidate in the elections of 1933, 1935 and 1939. He was arrested in July 1937 for 'illegal association' (in a trade union committee), was imprisoned in the Saigon Central Prison (Maison Centrale) and went on hunger strike, and was acquitted on 9 September. Seriously ill with tuberculosis, he was once more arrested and sentenced on 10 November 1937 to one year's imprisonment and ten years' residential ban for 'subversive activities'.

He was again arrested in September 1939 and deported to Poulo Condore. An active member of the *Tranh dau* group in 1945, Nguyen van So was among those shot by the Vietminh in the maquis at Kien an, Thudaumot, in October.

Tran van Si (1907-1941)

Born on 20 October 1907 at Tan thanh dong, Giadinh, Tran van Si worked as a technician after studying in Hanoi. He then left for France on 22 July 1929.

In Paris with Nguyen van Linh, he was from 1931 the heart and soul of the group of Indochinese Left Communists which took on itself the task of 'correcting the errors of the Indochinese Communist Party in the same spirit as the Trotskyist Left Opposition in Russia'. He worked politically with Maurice Nadeau, in the Communist League cell in the 13th arrondissement of the city.

From February 1932, the group expounded the theses of the Left Opposition on the Indochinese revolution in a duplicated bulletin which soon adopted the title *Duoc vo san (Proletarian Torch)*, and was violently criticised by the Annamite colonial section of the French Communist Party.

In October 1933, finally convinced of the impossibility of being accepted as an opposition faction inside the Communist Party, the group explained to the International Secretariat of the Left Opposition its intention to build a new communist party. In 1935, Tran van Si was one of the organisers of the Indochinese section for the Fourth International. The group intervened in the anti-imperialist associations and demonstrations and sought to win over dissident Annamite members of the French Communist Party.

Having returned to Cochinchina on 13 September 1937, Si joined Ta thu Thau in the Trotskyist *La Lutte*. In April 1939 he was on the Fourth Internationalist list for the Colonial Council elections in April. He was arrested on 13 July 1939, for having been 'against the setting up of a National Defence fund, and having demanded that this money be used for socially useful projects'.

He was sentenced to three years on 16 April 1940, and died in Poulo Condore.

Ho huu Tuong (1910-1980)

Coming from a farmer's family, Ho huu Tuong was expelled from Cantho College in 1926, left for France and soon obtained his matriculation. He started his studies in mathematics at the University of Marseilles and completed them at Lyons. In May 1930 he met up with Ta thu Thau in Paris for the Annamite demonstrations against the death sentences pronounced on the Yen Bay insurgents. He escaped the arrests and fled to Belgium with Phan van Hum; there they published *Tien quan* (*The Vanguard*) and returned to Paris some time after Thau's deportation. Together with Nguyen van Linh, Tran van Si, La van Rot, Nguyen van Nhi, Nguyen van Nam and Nguyen van Cu, they constituted the Indochinese group of the Communist League (Opposition), which was led by Pierre Naville, Raymond Molinier and Pierre Frank.[7]

On 21 August 1930, Tuong passed on to Molinier some reports from Indochina; not absolutely reliable reports 'because of the conditions of extreme illegality', they stated that the Thanh nien group had split and that a Communist party had emerged from the unification of 'three communist and three nationalist groups'; numerous small 'communist' publications appeared. Tuong and his comrades drafted a Declaration of the Indochinese Oppositionists (see note 3 to Chapter 3), which was sent to Trotsky but was above all intended for their fellow countrymen and women who were going through deep political turmoil and peasant agitation.

Back in Cochinchina at the beginning of 1931, Tuong taught maths in private schools. In May he met Dao hung Long of the Lien minh cong san doan (Communist League) group, which had organised oppositionists inside the Indochinese Communist Party itself after the defeat of the Nghe Tinh soviets; Tuong won them over to the Left Opposition.

In August 1931, he and Dao hung Long started publishing a pocket-sized duplicated review, *Thang muoi* (*October*). In November 1931, all the oppositionists united in the Ta doi lap (Indochinese Left Opposition), with *Thang muoi* as its theoretical organ. While in April 1932 Ta thu Thau published the *Vo san* (*The Proletarian*), Tuong continued with *Thang muoi*.

On 21 November 1932, Tuong was arrested. On 1 May 1933, in the trial of the 21 Saigon Trotskyists, he was given a three-year suspended sentence for 'belonging to a secret society and subversive activities'. Nguyen hue Minh, his woman companion, and Dao hung Long were sentenced to three months and one year respectively.

He took part in the municipal election campaign of the *La Lutte* group (April-May 1933) in Saigon. He also had a foot in the second *La Lutte* group (1934-1937). But he was essentially an anti-Stalinist theoretician, 'guru' of the League of Internationalist Communists for the Construction of the Fourth International founded by Lu sanh Hanh in 1935. He edited the one issue of a review, *Thuong truc cach mang* (*Permanent revolution*), Indochina's first printed underground Trotskyist publication.

After the victory of the Popular Front, Tuong predicted in *Thuong truc cach mang* a powerful workers' movement in France and the formation of a left-wing government. A great wave of hope seized the workers and poor peasants of Indochina who were about to move in their turn. It was urgently necessary to build a party mustering in large numbers the conscious elements emerging from the real struggle; a party that would not be bureaucratically controlled by obedient professional revolutionaries trained in Moscow, but would be a true reflection of the proletariat of the towns and countryside; a party that would prepare the general strike, in step with the French proletariat, for it was impossible to conquer and to build socialism within national limits.

In September 1936, Tuong produced *Le Militant*, the first legal Trotskyist weekly. It denounced *La Lutte*'s collaboration with the bourgeois Constitutionalists, the permanent repression by the Popular Front and the bloody comedy of the first Moscow trial.[8] Tuong organised the illegal activists into the Bolshevik-Leninist Group for the Fourth International, which launched the no-less-illegal paper *Tho thuyen tranh dau* (*Workers' Fight*). After the first Moscow trial, he republished *Le Militant*, supported by an increasing number of sympathisers, and published Trotsky's 'The Decisive Stage' and Lenin's 'Testament'.[9]

In June 1937, after the Stalinists left *La Lutte*, Ta thu Thau regained his freedom to criticise and Tuong definitively suspended publication of *Le Militant*. Taking advantage of the relative freedom allowed by Daladier to the quoc ngu press, Ho huu Tuong and Dao hung Long launched the agitational paper *Thay tho* (*Employees and Workers*) in September 1938, and revived the theoretical review *Thang muoi* (*October*), of which five issues appeared, the last in March 1939.

In *Thang muoi*, Tuong, referring to Thau, criticised the 'four years of errors relating to the united front tactic':

The paper *La Lutte* was characterised during the period 1934-1938 by being on the platform of the Third International . . . It often published extracts of articles that had appeared in [the French Communist Party paper] *L'Humanité* . . . and no article was published based on the documents of the Fourth International. Moreover *La Lutte* published *in extenso* the resolution of the Seventh Congress of the Comintern without any comments. (*Thang muoi*, September 1938.)

In January 1939, Tuong published in *Thang muoi* the statutes of the Fourth International, explained the theory of permanent revolution and called on all comrades from the north to the south of the country to unite to build the party of the Fourth.

A new weekly *Tia sang* (*The Spark*) was started in January 1939, to assist the *Tranh dau* (*La Lutte*) group's campaign in the April 1939 colonial elections. Dao hung Long, Lu sanh Hanh, Nguyen van Nam and Trinh van Lau were involved with it. Ngo van Xuyet, working in Phnom Penh since the end of 1937, and who had organised there a group of Annamite De Tu (Fourth International) sympathisers, became its local correspondent in the Khmer capital.

Paradoxically, although Tuong had always criticised the 'strange' collaboration between Stalinists and Trotskyists, which he described as 'fire and water', the *Thang muoi* proposed in its March 1939 issue a common electoral panel with the Stalinist Nguyen van Tao and his friends of the *Dan chung* (*The People*) group. This, he said, was an application of the Bolshevik tactic of 'marching separately and striking together'. In sharp contrast, Ta thu Thau stood on a Fourth Internationalist list (So De Tu), radically opposed to the Stalinists — not only because of their 'democratic front' position (that is, 'defence of France in Indochina', and hands extended to the Constitutionalists), but also because of the barrier of blood and corpses erected by the three Moscow frame-up trials.

In June 1939, *Tia sang* was confiscated and its editors locked up for having campaigned — on similar lines to *Tranh dau* (*La Lutte*) — against war and against loans and taxes for the 'defence of Indochina'. Ho huu Tuong was arrested at the end of September 1939 and deported to Poulo Condore.

He broke with Trotskyism on his release in 1944, saying:

I am rejoining the path of the people and of my race (con duong dan toc). I believe that the idea of the emancipation of humanity by the proletariat was the greatest myth of the 19th century, and that of the revolutionary potential of the proletariat of Europe and North America the greatest myth of the 20th.

After the 9 March 1945 coup, Tuong travelled to the north via Hue. On 30 June, he was one of the 14 persons asked by Bao Dai to draft a constitution (see *Vietnam tan bao*, 7 July 1945). His signature was on a telegram of 23 August, addressed to Bao Dai by the Popular Revolutionary Committee of Tonkin, side by side with those of two prominent members of the Vietminh, Nguyen van Huyen and Nguyen Xien. It stated:

A provisional popular revolutionary government has been set up, presided over by the venerated Ho chi Minh. We beg your Majesty to abdicate immediately so as to unify the country and consolidate its independence.

After the partition of Vietnam in 1954, Tuong became adviser to the southern pirate Le van Vien, for a neutralist movement (neither pro-Russian nor pro-American). He was condemned to death by the dictator Ngo dinh Diem in 1957 and then deported to Poulo Condore. After Diem's fall he became a deputy under the military regime of Nguyen van Thieu.

In 1977, two years after the entry of the northern troops into Saigon, he was sent to a 're-education camp'. He was released on 26 June 1980 and died as he stepped over the threshold of his home.

His autobiographical work, *41 nam lam bao, Hoi ky (41 years of Journalism, Memoirs)* was published in Paris four years later.

Lu sanh Hanh (c.1912-1982)

Born in Ben tre into a well-to-do family, Lu sanh Hanh studied at Mytho College. In 1932, as an influential member of the Saigon Committee of the PCI, he was shaken by the arguments of the Left Opposition and tried to reorganise his party on a critical basis. He started the paper *Lao cong (The Worker)*. He was arrested on 9 October 1932 and sentenced to 15 months in prison. He pushed tip-wagons at the Cap Saint-Jacques (now Vung tau) quarries side by side with common-law prisoners — whom he brought out on strike. He was put in solitary confinement, went on hunger strike and was returned to Saigon Central Prison.

On his release Lu sanh Hanh decided 'to devote his life to revolutionary work', sold off his inheritance and became a travelling barber for the purposes of making propaganda. Then he got a job as a reporter on the constitutionalist *Duoc Nha Nam (Torch of Annam)*.

In July 1935 he secretly organised the League of Internationalist Communists for the Construction of the Fourth International, which was suppressed the following year when it called for the setting-up of action committees. On 31 August 1936, Hanh was sentenced to 18 months in prison. As soon as he was freed he immediately resumed his revolutionary activity, and in January 1939 was working on the *Tia sang* newspaper published by Ho huu Tuong and Dao hung Long.

Hanh escaped the arrests of September 1939 and found refuge in western Cochinchina. He returned to Saigon in August 1944 to secretly rebuild the League of Internationalist Communists. Its Manifesto of 24 March 1945 called on the workers and peasants to prepare themselves for the coming revolution under the banner of the Fourth International.

After the Japanese surrender of March 1945, the League — which had always worked underground — surfaced with its radical slogans opposed to those of the Stalinists; its people's committees, which constituted a dual power[10] with the *de facto* government of Tran van Giau, were disarmed on 14 September 1945. Hanh was incarcerated in Saigon Central Prison; on 22 September the British took control of the prison and Hanh escaped assassination.

He emigrated to France in 1947 and was active among the Vietnamese coolies who had been imported to work in the war factories. He wrote for *Quatrième Internationale*, the journal of the Fourth International, under the name of Lucien. One of his articles, 'Some Stages in the Revolution in South Vietnam', comprises Appendix 1 of this volume, pages 150-162. Lu sanh Hanh returned from Europe to his own country in 1954 to continue, but without success, the underground struggle against the native governments of the South and then against the Stalinist Hanoi government. He died of tuberculosis in Saigon on 2 November 1982.

Nguyen van Linh (1909-1951)

Born at Ben suc (Thu dau mot), Nguyen van Linh went to France in 1926 and was educated at the Lycée Michelet at Vanves and then at the Faculty of Letters at Paris. He was active with Tran van Si in the group of Indochinese Left Communists from 1931 onwards. At the Amsterdam World Anti-War Congress[11] he spoke, along with French Oppositionists, against deceiving the proletariat into believing that one can prevent war without having destroyed its base — capitalism.

Nguyen van Linh was in the Indochinese Mutual Aid Association and in the Social Studies Circle, founded in 1934. It was in these cultural and mutual aid associations, formed to bring together Vietnamese emigrés from Paris and to help with their problems, that he met people expelled from the French Communist Party. He criticised the Popular Front for its repression of the Indochinese Congress movement of 1936. He wrote in the *Quoc te IV* (*Fourth International*) bulletin, launched on 1 October 1937, denouncing the dictatorship of the party in power in the USSR over its proletariat; he attacked the French Communist Party which, since the Laval-Stalin pact, 'pressurised the Annamite masses to support the democratic imperialisms' and called for 'the maintenance of peace by all means in the three French possessions of North Africa'

On his return to Cochinchina at the beginning of the war, Nguyen van Linh taught at Cantho. He joined the League of Internationalist Communists in Saigon in August 1945, and undertook the political education of the workers' militia of the Go vap tramways.

On 9 July 1947, Linh wrote to Raymond Molinier and Yves Craipeau from Saigon: 'If my friends and I have survived the brutal Stalinist repression, it is only after having fought with all our strength and in order to continue the struggle'. In 1951, Linh, Liu khanh Thinh and a Chinese comrade, Liu Jialiang, fell into a Vietminh ambush. The maquis radio announced their execution, accusing them of having sold themselves to French imperialism.

Dao hung Long (1905-)

A native of Long tri (Rachgia), Dao hung Long joined the Thanh nien in 1926. He joined its communist wing in 1929, supported Ngo gia Tu in the split and became special delegate (dac uy) of the Indochinese Communist Party in West Cochinchina.

The defeat of the 1930-1931 peasant movement — the Nghe Tinh soviets and the jacqueries in Annam and Cochinchina — caused him to question the policies of the party. He condemned it for its adventurism, its worker-peasant character and its mainly petty-bourgeois intellectual and peasant leadership.

At the start of 1931, he organised the Communist League in Baclieu with a ban mao hiem (death-defiers' committee) which took on responsibility for raising funds. In May 1931, Long was won over to the Ta doi lap (Left Opposition) by Ho huu Tuong. Arrested on 24 October 1932, he was sentenced to one year's prison on 1 May 1933 and sent to hard labour in the Chaudoc quarries. He led the common-law prisoners in a refusal to work and then on a hunger strike;

this struggle was severely repressed and Long was sent back to Saigon Central Prison.

In 1934 Dao hung Long established himself as a sign-painter in Saigon. In 1936 he wrote the pamphlet *Methods of work of an Action Committee*. The following year he received a two months' prison sentence for work in the trade union movement, still prohibited under the Popular Front government. At the end of 1938 he launched the legal quoc ngu language paper *Thay tho (Employees and Workers)*. He was one of the editors of *Tia sang*, which appeared from January 1939, denouncing war and the loans and taxes for the 'defence of Indochina'. On 2 October 1939 he was sentenced to two years' jail and ten years' residence ban. During the war he was interned in the Talai and Bara camps and then deported to Madagascar from which he returned only in 1947.

He abandoned the class struggle and followed Ho huu Tuong along the road of neutralist nationalism.

Tran dinh Minh, alias Nguyen hai Au (1912-1946)

Tran dinh Minh was a poet and author of a novel in which the young heroine, poor, ugly and dumb, recovers her speech and her beauty when she is loved — no doubt a symbol of all the oppressed who will be born into a real life through the social revolution. He also wrote on economics: his works included *Kinh te hoc pho thong (Political Economy Made Easy)*, Hanoi 1944; and *Kinh te the gioi 1929-1934 (World Economy 1929-1934)*, Hanoi 1945.

Minh gave up teaching to become a typesetter in the Le van Tan printshop in Hanoi, from which issued the underground Trotskyist paper *Co do (Red Flag)* in 1944-1945. He joined the League of Internationalist Communists in Saigon in July 1945, was accepted into the workers' militia of the Go vap tramway workshops and elected to its leadership with Nguyen van Thuong and S. during the Saigon uprising. Tranh dinh Minh fell on 13 January 1946 on the My loi front, under the fire of native auxiliaries of the French army disguised as maquisards. The villagers of My tay made a tomb for him. (See Liu khanh Thinh, 1947.)

Edgar Ganofsky (1880-1943)

Edgar Ganofsky was a Frenchman born on the French colony of Réunion Island in the Indian Ocean. 'A teacher dismissed for political reasons, ever an opponent of authority (see his paper *La voix libre* (*Free Speech*) 1923-1932) this old Jacobin, a bit naive, libertarian to his finger tips. . .' (Hémery, 1975, p.71).

He lived as an Annamite in a miserable lodging in Dakao. Profoundly anti-colonialist, Ganofsky was the unpaid manager of *La Lutte* from its inception. He attacked Article 91 of the amended penal code, the legal basis of of all prosecutions of newspaper editors.

In 1936 he belonged to the *La Lutte* action committee of the Dakao quarter. In 1939 he was manager of the Trotskyist newspaper *Tia sang*, and was sentenced on 5 September to one year's imprisonment and five years' residential ban.

In June 1940 his sentence was increased to three years in prison and ten years' residential ban.

He died in miserable circumstances at Cantho, where he was in forced residence, in 1943.

Hinh thai Thong (c. 1910-1945)

A student in France, and then a lawyer based in Saigon, Hinh thai Thong was a Trotskyist militant of the *La Lutte* group, not well known. He helped to organise the reappearance of *La Lutte* in 1945, and was assassinated at Mytho by the Vietminh.

Le van Thu (1906-)

Le van Thu was one of the 19 Vietnamese students expelled from France in May 1930, after the demonstration at the Champs-Elysée against the death sentences imposed after the Yen Bay uprising (see p.18).

He was a founder member of the *La Lutte* group in April 1933 and a Trotskyist organiser in the trades unions in the period 1936-1939.

In 1945, Le van Thu escaped assassination by the Vietminh. In 1949 he wrote, and published in Saigon, *Hoi kin Nguyen an Ninh (The Nguyen an Ninh Secret Society)*.

Le van Vung (?-1945)

A Trotskyist, member of the *La Lutte* group, Le van Vung was shot by the Stalinists in September 1945, outside his home in the Dakao area of Saigon.

Ngo chinh Phen (c. 1912-)

A member of the League of Internationalist Communists from 1935, Ngo chinh Phen was sentenced to eight months' imprisonment in 1936. He organised in 1939-1940 the 'Internationalist Workers' group, which published together with the Bolshevik Leninist group the journal *Cach mang (Revolution)*, and disseminated anti-war leaflets at Thu dau mot.

By 1946, Ngo chinh Phen had been deported to Madagascar.

Nguyen thi Anh (c. 1910-)

Nguyen thi Anh went to Paris to study medicine, where she met Ta thu Thau and became his companion. She rejoined him in Saigon after his expulsion from France in 1930. She shared all the hardships of his liffe.

Nguyen thi Loi (c. 1910-45)

A militant of the *La Lutte* group, Nguyen thi Loi formed under the rule of the Popular Front an illegal union of teachers. He was struck down by the Stalinists at Can giuoc in Cholon in September 1945.

Nguyen van Cu, alias Capitaine (c.1910-)

A radio operator in the navy won to Trotskyism in Paris in 1930. Returning to Saigon in 1936, he became active in the October group led by Ho Huu Tuong and became manager of its newspaper *Le Militant*.

Le quang Luong, alias Bich Khe (?-1945).

A poet, Le quang Luong was the organiser in 1936-1937 of a Trotskyist group in Thu xa (Tu Nghia) in Quang Ngai province. He translated into Vietnamese *Retour de l'URSS (Return from the USSR)*, written by André Gide in 1936.

On Le quang Luong's death in 1945, the local people expressed their liking and respect for him by naming after him the main street from the bus station to the eastern exit from the town. That name, rue Bich Khe, never appeared on official maps of Quang Ngai.

Le quang Luong's grave lay abandoned and anonymous on a grass waste land — a fate he foresaw in his poem 'The Tomb':

Covered with wild, green grass, layers piled high,
On the tomb a crow stands in silence.

(Day co xanh xao may lop phu,
Tren mo con qua dung im hoi)

In 1991, Le quang Luong's family were refused authorisation to remove his remains to Thu Xa, his native village. The decision was made by Bon, a young bureaucrat on the village committee; the reason given, that the bones of the deceased, who died of tuberculosis, could pollute the village; besides, he was a Trotskyist and 'according to our old revolutionaries, Trotskyism is very reactionary' (see the investigation by the journalist Trang Dang, in *Lao dong*, journal of the Confédération Générale du Travail du Vietnam, 20 January 1994).

There you have the obscurantism into which the bureaucratic mind can fall.

Appendix 1

SOME STAGES OF THE REVOLUTION IN THE SOUTH OF VIETNAM

This account of the 1945 uprising is by Lu sanh Hanh, the leader of the League of Internationalist Communists. It was published in September 1947, in French, in *Quatrième Internationale*, the journal of the Fourth International, under the pseudonym Lucien. It was first published in English in *Workers Press*, 10 and 17 January 1987.

The war and the revolutionary crisis

At 9 a.m. on 16 August 1945, news of the final defeat of Japanese imperialism was announced throughout the countries of Indochina. The following day, the Japanese general staff announced that it was handing over civil administration to the indigenous peoples. According to the terms of the statement, Japanese imperialism surrendered all power to the legal governments of the various countries that constituted Indochina: Vietnam, Cambodia and Laos. These peoples, the statement added, were from now on independent, with the right to self-determination.

Several hours after this news had broken throughout Vietnam, from the north to the south, from country to country, from factory to street, from one family to another, a social storm arose with the power to overturn everything and smash anything.

Men and women of all ages, regardless of their political persuasion, poured into the streets in surging waves, shouting cries of hatred mingled with joy; together they swore to fight to the last drop of their blood for the complete liberation of their country.

On 19 August, the workers of the Ban Co district of Saigon were the first to move into action and set up the first people's committee in the south. Some went out into the streets armed with rifles they had stolen from the Japanese and hidden away for months. Others carried pistols of various and dubious origins. Those who had no firearms carried daggers or bamboo pikes. With their blue caps on their heads, and their weapons on their shoulders, they formed armed detachments, marching together through the streets, in groups of 50, 100 or 200.

They paraded in military formation, singing the revolutionary anthem, then shouting with a voice that pierced the sky: 'Rather death than slavery! Defend the people's power!'

On the morning of 20 August, throughout the Saigon-Cholon region, hundreds of Vanguard Youth Committees declared before their flag their willingness to die for freedom. Phu Nhuan, the largest working-class district in the city, elected its people's committee, proclaimed the complete abolition of the former regime, and declared that from then on, 10 a.m. on 20 August 1945, only this committee would be considered the legal power in the district. In the days that followed, the mass organisations of many social and political tendencies mushroomed, and it was impossible to keep track of their numerical strength and the extent of their activities.

From 19 August onwards, the word went around the capital that there were peasant uprisings in the provinces. Armed demonstrations and terrorist acts struck mortal fear into the bourgeoisie and the feudalists.

On 19 August, the peasants of Sadec province ransacked about ten magnificent villas belonging to their landlords, and burned down a large number of granaries full of rice.

Many dignitaries and officials were arrested by the peasants, and a number of them were shot on the spot. While members of the rural police were drowned by the revolutionary masses, former officials of the French and Japanese government, who had all been declared enemies of the people, saw all their possessions go up in flames. In the course of a few days in Long Xuyen, an entire rural province, 200 dignitaries and rural police were stabbed to death.

From the middle of August, the revolutionary peasants in central Vietnam began to drive out the royalist-imperialist mandarins, and seized control of the organs of local governments by armed force. During the same period, well-equipped armed detachments of peasants launched surprise attacks on Japanese military posts, captured arms and ammunition.

From the second week of August onwards, the landowners of north Vietnam suffered the same fate as their brothers in the south. In a number of villages, granaries, villas and land were confiscated 'arbitrarily' for the benefit of the people's committees.

Big landowners and former officials were brought before popular tribunals, where they were tried publicly by the villagers. Several hundred former faithful servants of France and the Japanese general staff were beheaded in a few days.

The reactionary parties and the
National United Front

Faced with the revolutionary situation in full upsurge throughout the country, the leaders of the bourgeois and feudalist parties, known as Cao dai-ists and Hoa hao-ists, or nationalists, were unable to find any force either on the right or left that could save their country, as they saw it, from the sword of the threatening revolution.

On 18 August, these groups of political nonentities called a joint meeting, at which they decided unanimously to set up a political front that became known as the National United Front. The day after reaching this political agreement, this bourgeois-feudalist bloc issued a joint declaration calling on the people to take part in a demonstration under its leadership, at 6 a.m. on 21 August in Saigon's Norodom Square, to celebrate national independence.

Who were these political parties?

The Cao dai party: in reality this was only a semi-political religious organisation, based on a motley collection of mystical ideas. Essentially its purpose was to assist the French government in slaughtering the revolutionary peasants who followed the Communist movement in Cochinchina in the period 1930-1941.

But when French imperialism signed its military and economic capitulation to Japanese militarism in 1941, the Cao dai party turned its back on its former French patron in order to play the role of political double agent for the Japanese general staff.

With the coup of 9 March 1945, by which Japanese militarism ousted the French colonial government, this party's position changed completely. While its leaders preached loyalty to the emperor of Japan, its followers rose in revolt throughout the country, trampling god and landed property underfoot.

The second religious sect, the Hoa hao party, which brought together more than a million poor and middle-class peasants, played a no less important role in support of the Japanese army. Hoa hao-ism differed from Cao dai-ism in that it sought to unite political urban workers and rural proletarians, but on the basis of a total rejection of the class struggle. What the former and the latter parties have in common is that they are both instruments in the service of foreign imperialism, and both violently opposed to social revolution.

The National Party for the Independence of Vietnam, the acknowledged instrument of the national bourgeoisie, was essentially composed of petty-bourgeois intellectuals (academics, engineers, journalists, lawyers and former French government officials) and was totally devoid of theoretical and political principles. It was really no more than a group of socially degenerate careerists and speculators. During the years of revolutionary upsurge, the leaders of this party did nothing to conceal their reactionary attitude, and always placed themselves in the camp of the imperialist bourgeoisie. Today these petty bourgeois take advantage of the absence of workers' parties in the political arena, and impose their bogus patriotic sentiments to confuse the revolutionary masses.

The party of the Fourth International and the events of 21 August 1945

From 1939 to 1944 no revolutionary communist voice was heard among the masses. Hundreds of militants of the two parties fighting under the banners of the Fourth International (the *La Lutte* group and the League of Internationalist Communists) had been deported, exiled or jailed. Quite a few had disappeared into prisons and concentration camps. But towards the end of 1944 the Trotskyist movement became active again. At first the League, reconstituted in Saigon in August 1944, brought together only a few dozen members, among them five founding members of the Trotskyist movement who had each experienced at least 12 years of revolutionary struggle. To this number were added a few experienced comrades sent by the section in the north.

After the Japanese coup of 9 March 1945, the League lost no time in issuing a manifesto calling on the revolutionary masses of Saigon to prepare politically for a revolution in the very near future:

> The imminent defeat of Japanese imperialism willl launch the Indochinese people on to the road of national liberation. The bourgeois and feudalists, who today are the cowardly servants of the Japanese general staff, will likewise serve the Allied imperialist states. The petty-bourgeois nationalists with their adventurism will also be incapable of leading the people to revolutionary victory.

Only the working class, fighting independently under the banner of the Fourth International, will be able to accomplish the tasks of leading the revolution. The Stalinists of the Third International have already abandoned the working class in order to rally wretchedly to the 'democratic' imperialists. They have betrayed the peasants and no longer mention the agrarian question. If today they march with the foreign capitalists, then in the coming period they will assist the indigenous exploiting classes to crush the revolutionary people.

Workers and Peasants! Gather under the banner of the party of the Fourth International! (Manifesto of 24 March 1945.)

At 6 a.m. on 21 August more than 300,000 men and women, grouped in columns, thronged Saigon's Norodom Boulevard. Banners and placards blossomed above this human sea.

The Cao dai-ist and Hoa hao-ist peasants formed a column 100,000 strong, with the monarchist banner at its head. In opposition to the reactionary nationalist parties, the League of Internationalist Communists boldly unfurled its huge flag of the Fourth International, three metres long and two metres wide.

Carried by the worker C., an old Bolshevik-Leninist, the flag was a proud beacon of revolutionary strength, and attracted the lively attention of hundreds of thousands of the enslaved people, who had been duped for so many years by the exploiters of their country.

Revolutionary slogans were inscribed in huge letters on a series of huge placards and banners that waved above our heads: 'Down with Imperialism! Long Live the World Revolution! Long Live the Workers' and Peasants' Front! People's Committees everywhere! For a People's Assembly! For the arming of the people! Nationalise the factories under Workers' Control! For a Workers' and Peasants' Government!'

Thousands of workers, who had been leaderless, dispersed and demoralised during the war years, had never lost their memory of the revolutionary movement. From the first moment when the flag of the Fourth International and the slogans of the revolutionary proletariat appeared, they spontaneously recovered their political consciousness and felt their revolutionary faith reviving.

They embraced each other for joy in the midst of the crowd, and they competed for the right to carry this or that placard or flag. Workers arrived in waves, greeting each other with the clenched fist salute, and declared themselves ready to fight with their vanguard party. Within a few hours, the workers who gathered under the leadership of a few dozen Trotskyists numbered more than 30,000.

Terrified by the violence of the revolutionary masses, the bourgeois could only grit their teeth. They were politically paralysed, and obliged to leave the field clear for the activities of the Trotskyists. While the masses marched through the streets, the militants of the League tirelessly put forward their policies at open-air meetings.

For their part, the peasants, marching separately behind reactionary leaders, listened attentively to our speeches on the national and peasant problems. Disregarding the political discipline imposed by their parties, they enthusiastically applauded every time the flag of the Fourth International was carried past. Inspired by the Trotskyist slogan, workers and peasants looked to each other as friends.

The evolution of the balance of political forces after 21 August

After the military defeat of Japanese imperialism the bourgeois and feudalist parties had fallen into hopeless disarray, and had no idea how to put an end to the 'anarchist' terror. These political nonentities had tried to deceive the masses once again with the setting up of the National United Front, but when they had taken stock of the situation they felt more isolated than ever.

Within a few days there emerged, in addition to these nationalist parties, about 50 other separate petty-bourgeois political groupings, each with its own headquarters and military leader. The bourgeois and petty bourgeois disagreed and were divided among themselves to the extent that the political unity of the ruling classes crumbled irretrievably. From only a few members at the beginning of 1945, the League of Internationalist Communists saw its forces increase by the end of the August of the same year to 200, each of whom played a definite part in the revolutionary mass organisations. After the success of 21 August, the Trotskyists greatly increased their political influence, and formed, in relation to the bourgeois parties, an important political force. It was a formidable revolutionary pole of attraction.

On 23 August the League unfurled its huge red flag outside its headquarters, thus legitimising its political power in the face of reaction. The League had its own printing shops and press, and every three hours its political directives were sent among the people in the form of communiqués.

In addition to its political preparations, the League was actively engaged in the formation of military cadres. This was considered the burning question of the hour, in relation to arming the people and carrying out the historical tasks of the party in the approaching decisive period.

The Vietminh coup d'état and the Stalinist reaction

During the war, the Indochinese Stalinists had become docile servants of the Allied imperialists. On 23 August, the leader of the southern Vietnamese Stalinists, Tran van Giau, notorious above all for his anti-Trotskyism, admitted cynically in the proclamation of the Vietminh front of which he was General Secretary: 'For five years we have fought at the side of the democratic allies . . .'

In fact, after the defeat of Japanese imperialism, the Vietminh (the Stalinist party in disguise) put themselves forward to the bourgeois nationalist parties as an authority sanctioned by the Allied imperialists.

For their part, however, the revolutionary masses saw in the Stalinist party a force capable of leading them on the road of anti-imperialist revolution. Under these historical conditions, the Stalinist party rose spontaneously above the social conflict and established a bonapartist dictatorship.

At a meeting of the National United Front on the evening of 22 August, Tran van Giau, with the support of the former head of the Japanese police, Huynh van Phuong, ordered the leaders of the self-styled pro-Japanese parties to relinquish completely their official positions in the administration, which were to devolve upon the Vietminh, the 'official representatives of the Allies'. 'Your role is now finished', concluded Tran van Giau, 'hand over to us!'

The leaders of the pro-Japanese parties bowed their heads in submission and affirmed their loyalty to the Vietminh front. A day later, the National United Front issued a statement proclaiming its own dissolution and the adherence of all the nationalist parties to the Vietminh front.

On 25 August at 5 a.m. all governmental posts were occupied by the leaders of the Vietminh front without the knowledge of the people. The transfer of power was carried out quietly, behind the backs of the whole population.

The Vietminh took power with the ruling classes and the whole of the state apparatus behind it. Nevertheless, 24 hours after the accession to power of the Vietminh, Tran van Giau cynically proclaimed that the 'revolution' carried out by his party was truly 'democratic' and that there had been 'no spilling of blood' (sic).

This was nothing but a lie: this was not a revolution at all, just a coup d'état carried out with the support of all the exploiting classes and behind the backs of the revolutionary masses.

The events of 25 August

The League of Internationalist Communists had marched with the masses on the demonstrations of 21 August organised by the bourgeois National United Front. It was impossible for the League not to take part in the demonstration of 25 August, even though it had been organised by the Vietminh who, from the moment they came to power, sought to gauge the depth of the likely political and moral reaction of the revolutionary masses.

All social classes participated in this huge demonstration. The number of demonstrators, who arrived from every corner of western Nam Bo, amounted to more than a million.

Compared with the first demonstration, the political complexion of the second was expressed with much greater clarity and in much greater depth. There must have been as many as 30 political organisations of various tendencies that turned up in full strength. Of these the Stalinist Vietminh and the communists of the Fourth International were the most significant.

The class struggle had reached such a pitch that even the police, the loyal instrument of the bourgeois state, had split into two opposing political camps. The first, led by the two former chiefs of the Japanese police, Huynh van Phuong and Ho vinh Ky, marched under the banner of the Fourth International; they called themselves 'assault police'.[1] The second, more numerous, camp, influenced by the Stalinists, gathered under the banner of the Vietminh.

The number of workers marching with the League was reduced to 2,000 on this occasion, as opposed to 30,000 on 21 August. This was not accidental, as this time most workers felt obliged to march with their trade unions. In spite of its numerical weakness, the League still remained a political force to be reckoned with on the demonstration. On the strength of its clear and truly revolutionary slogans it attracted to its ranks all the best elements of the working class. Hundreds and thousands of workers and peasants constantly and loudly applauded the slogans 'Land to the peasants! Factories to the workers!'

Faced with the stand taken by the League militants, the Stalinist leaders could only grit their teeth, and had no idea of what to do in the face of the increasing excitement of the revolutionary masses.

The Stalinist counter-revolution

Faithful to its revolutionary programme, the League remained politically independent of the Vietminh front, while constantly insisting on the necessity of pursuing the tactic of the anti-imperialist united front,[2] a tactic in accordance with which the League marched separately from, but fought together with, all popular organisations against foreign imperialism.

The League never stopped explaining in its leaflets and its press that the Vietminh was a form of bourgeois coalition in which the Stalinists played a key political role.

Whereas the Stalinists originally maintained in their propaganda that the democratic republic had already been established, we, the Internationalist Communists, told the masses that the revolution had not yet been made.

While the Stalinists shouted: 'All power to the Vietminh!', we replied: 'All power to the people's committees!'

Two days after this coup d'état, the Stalinist Minister of the Interior, Nguyen van Tao, threatened the Trotskyists in the following terms:

> Those who incite the peasants to seize landed property will be severely and mercilessly punished.
>
> We have not yet made the Communist revolution that will solve the agrarian problem.
>
> This government is only a democratic government. Therefore it is not up to it to carry out such a task. Our government, I repeat, is a bourgeois democratic government, even though the Communists are the ones actually in power.

The day after this leader of Vietnamese Stalinism had made this statement, the entire Stalinist press viciously attacked the Trotskyists, accusing them of trying to stir up trouble and provoke social unrest.

Day in and day out, Dr Pham ngoc Thach, a faithful lieutenant of Tran van Giau, and a whole band of bureaucratic lackeys of the Stalinist government, constantly insisted to the people, through the press and radio, that the national independence of Vietnam was only a matter of diplomatic negotiations with the Commission of the imperialist Allies.

'Those who incite the people to take up arms will be regarded as saboteurs and provocateurs, as enemies of national independence', said Tran van Giau on 1 September. 'Our democratic freedoms will be guaranteed by the democratic Allies.'

The events of 2 September

At noon on 1 September, the Nam Bo government propaganda commission drove around Saigon-Cholon calling on the population to take part in the ceremony in honour of the Allied Commission that was to arrive in Saigon on the evening of 2 September.

The members of the propaganda commission insisted again that the country's independence depended entirely on the will of the Allied Commission, which therefore meant, the government claimed, that the population had to observe perfect law and order.

The people took the government at its word.

At 4 p.m. the following day, more than 400,000 people — men and women, young and old — marched peacefully past Saigon Cathedral in massed columns, armed with bamboo pikes and waving placards and banners above their heads. Suddenly, from high up on the church, a burst of machine gun and pistol fire was shot into the peaceful and defenceless crowd. About 40 marchers were killed and about 150 were wounded.

Loud cries went up: 'The French are shooting!' Maddened with fury, the demonstrators forced the church doors, climbed to the roof and searched every nook and cranny that might hide their criminal enemies.

Facing the common enemy

The events of 2 September produced an unheard-of turmoil in the hearts of the people in Saigon. It had been proved that the government was incapable of defending the country, and even more so of leading it to real independence.

From then on it was rumoured around the city that French imperialism would probably be helped by the Allied forces to reconquer its colony soon, and slaughter the revolutionary people. It was a matter of life and death.

On 4 September the Central Committee of the League of Internationalist Communists made an urgent appeal to the people for the revolutionary defence of national independence. In particular it said, in the following clear Bolshevik terms:

> We, the international communists, have no illusions at all that the Vietminh government, with its policy of class collaboration, will be capable of fighting the imperialist invasion in the days to come.

Nevertheless, if the government declares itself prepared to defend national independence and to safeguard the people's liberties, we shall not hesitate to assist it and to support it with all physical means in the revolutionary struggle.

But to this end, we are entitled to repeat again that we shall strictly maintain the complete independence of our party in relation to the government and to all other parties, for it is on this political independence that the whole existence of a party calling itself Bolshevik-Leninist depends. (League statement of 4 September.)

The people's committees and the massacre of the Trotskyist militants

In the south of Vietnam (Nam Bo) more than 150 people's committees were set up in three weeks under the influence of the League. One hundred of those in Saigon-Cholon were mainly working-class.

A provisional Central Committee, the highest body of the people's committees, consisting at first of nine members and later of 15, had been formed after 21 August. Its independent headquarters were guarded by armed workers. That was where delegates of various political tendencies came to discuss and study the problems of the revolution.

On 26 August the delegates of the people of Saigon-Cholon, gathered together in general assembly, decided on their common programme which can be summed up as follows:

1. Recognising that the Indochinese revolution is an anti-imperialist revolution, we insist that the national bourgeoisie will be completely incapable of playing the role of revolutionary vanguard, and that only the popular alliance of industrial workers and rural toilers will be able to free the nation from the domination of foreign capitalists.

2. The people's committees are the most concrete expression of the alliance of the revolutionary classes. They therefore proclaim the necessity for bringing together the proletariat and the peasantry under the leadership of the people's committees.

3. In relation to the bourgeois government and all political parties, the people's committees will maintain complete political independence.

4. The people's committees recognise only the Central Committee, elected on the principle of democratic centralism, as their highest body.

5. The people's committees recognise that they alone are the real basis

of the power of the revolutionary people. Their highest authority will be the national assembly of delegates from all people's committees, which will take place in Saigon in the near future.

6. The people's committees insist on the necessity for creating a single revolutionary front against imperialism, but categorically denounce all acts, from whatever quarters, that seek to sabotage the freedom of action of the working class and the popular masses. (Resolution of the assembly of the popular delegates of the district [place name illegible in original].)

Conferences were organised regularly at the headquarters of the people's committees at which participants were able to express their political position with the greatest of freedom. The League of Internationalist Communists led the revolutionary masses through the people's committees. It was due to these that it succeeded to a large extent in politicising the most advanced layers of the revolutionary masses.

For the first time in the history of the Indochinese revolution the League, in spite of its numerical weakness, carried out a great historic task, namely, the setting up of people's committees, or soviets.

The defeat of Trotskyism in Indochina by the counter-revolutionary Stalinist bureaucracy will never wipe out the correctness of putting Trotsky's theory of permanent revolution into practice in Indochina.

Once the question of armed struggle against the imperialist invasion had been posed at the beginning of September, the people's committees played an extremely important role in making the political and material preparations. Hundreds of committee members came to the Central Committee with many valuable proposals, about which the bourgeois governmental and military leaders hardly ever found out anything.

The workers of Ban Co district and of Phu Nhuan proposed at the conference of 4 September to expropriate all imperialist enterprises and turn them into war factories. Others suggested that we should turn the Bank of Indochina building into a fortress that would be very resistant to bombardment by enemy ships in the ports. Many very important revolutionary proposals were put forward and studied.

The people's committee movement posed an increasing threat to the Stalinist government — which was also the target of constant criticism from the bourgeois parties who accused it of impotence in internal affairs, that is, in repressing the revolutionary masses.

On 6 September the government launched a vicious attack on the Trotskyists, accusing them of being responsible for unrest and provocations. The entire Stalinist press went into action against the Trotskyists in an attempt to divert the people from the imminent danger of imperialist invasion. On 7 September Tran van Giau gave the order to disarm all non-governmental organisations. The decree stated: 'Those who call the people to arms and above all to fight against the imperialists Allies will be considered provocateurs and saboteurs.'

On 10 September British troops disembarked at Saigon, while successive waves of French aircraft flew over the city. Faced with the approaching danger, the League put all its efforts into preparing the masses for taking up the imminent armed struggle, in spite of all the slanders and threats from the Stalinist government.

On 12 September, the people's committees and the League issued a joint statement openly denouncing the political treachery of the Stalinist government in its capitulation in the face of the threat from the British general staff. The turmoil of the masses grew every day.

At 4.30 p.m. on 14 September the Stalinist chief of police, Duong bach Mai, sent an armed detachment to surround the headquarters of the popular committees when the assembly was in full session.

We conducted ourselves as true revolutionary militants. We allowed ourselves to be arrested without violent resistance to the police, even though we outnumbered them and were all well-armed. They took away our machine guns and pistols, and ransacked our headquarters, smashing furniture, tearing up flags, stealing the typewriters and burning all our papers.

This was a defeat for Trotskyism in a twofold sense: physical extermination of the vanguard of the revolutionary proletariat, and the handing over of the people in Indochina to 'democratic' imperialism.

Having carried out this operation, Tran van Giau, with the agreement of the government in the north, ordered the systematic killing of all Trotskyist elements in the country. Tran van Thach, Ta thu Thau, Phan van Hum and dozens of other revolutionary militants were murdered in circumstances that, to this day, have not been properly established.

The two former chiefs of the Japanese police, the accomplices of Tran van Giau in the carrying out of the Vietminh coup d'état, were also killed, having been accused of Trotskyism. For sympathising with Trotskyism, the woman doctor Ho vinh Ky, a former member of the government, was shot together with the leaders of the *La Lutte* group by one of Tran van Giau's agents. Our three most dedicated comrades, Le Ngoc, a member of the Central Committee, Nguyen van Ky, an engineering worker and trade union leader, and Nguyen Huong, a young Trotskyist and fighter in the workers' militia, were murdered by a Stalinist police chief in July 1946.

Appendix 2

MY FIRST STEPS TOWARDS THE PERMANENT REVOLUTION

This is an account of the activity of the *La Lutte* group in September-October 1945, and its repression by the Stalinists. It was sent just after the events by a young member of the group to the International Secretariat of the Fourth International in Paris. He attempts to draw lessons from the defeat suffered by the working class and the Fourth International.

The *La Lutte* group's Central Committee, even after the assassination of its main leaders, was able to reorganise itself in 1946, and submitted its own report to the Fourth International (*La Lutte* group, April 1948). Both this, and the personal report published here, were kept in the Secretariat's files and not brought before Trotskyists in other countries for nearly 40 years.

'My First Steps Towards the Permanent Revolution' was first published in *Revolutionary History* (vol. 3, no. 2, Autumn 1990).

I was then 17 years old. Japanese imperialism had suffered defeat. The French had been stripped of power, put under guard and concentrated in various large towns. The old political leaders were returned from exile and the extermination camps. Saigon, my birthplace, was able to breathe freedom for the first time. That was the political situation in Saigon on the day I joined the Trotskyist group, *La Lutte*.

La Lutte, the newspaper for the defence of the working class, reappeared before the Saigon public after eight years' absence. In a few days its circulation climbed to dizzy heights. Three editions a day were not enough for the workers and the public[1]. The Stalinist organisations were, on the one hand, preoccupied with the question of taking power; on the other they had already been defeated by the Trotskyists in the election campaigns of 1936-1937. They no longer had time to work among the factory workers and labourers in the towns.

Since the first day of political agitation it seemed to me that the October group wanted to carry out extensive work among the workers, and it succeeded overwhelmingly. But this work was unfortunately only done on the basis of revolutionary instinct. Its leading cadre, moreover, severely affected by imperialist repression as well as by the treachery or defection of a certain leading member[2], was unable to regain its sense of direction. It then abandoned this work and resorted to an adventurist policy of dual power with the Stalinists.

As for the *La Lutte* group, its leadership was re-established and the same personnel reunited.[3]

In the midst of the struggle, in the midst of the rising, one fact had tormented me for a number of years: our leader Ta thu Thau left us to return to north Vietnam. The entire defeat was partly the result of his departure from the field of battle.

Officially, as far as we rank-and-file militants were concerned, Ta thu Thau had left on a mission to the north. However, according to his second in command, he intended to get to Chungking (via Yunnan).[4]

In accordance with the unanimous political orientation at that time, 'march separately, strike together', the remaining Central Committee carried on its work of agitation and propaganda, while placing itself under the control of the Vietminh front when it came to action. In addition, the Central Committee obtained permission from the Stalinists to set up a workers' self-defence militia (with the proviso that the military command was under government control). The government, moreover, already under the direction of the Vietminh front, took charge of material aid, arms and ammunition. Nothing could get through without the permission of the Stalinists. Carried away by their enthusiasm, and by the favourable political situation at the time, our comrades had forgotten all distrust of the Stalinists. From then on our comrades slowed down the work of setting up soviets in the city, of turning the factories into fortresses, and of preparing for a civil war. The militants of the October group only weakly criticised the *La Lutte* group.

The final days of the existence of the Vietminh front in Saigon were painful. Everybody, on our side and through the entire population, felt something dire was threatening us and lying in wait for us. It was too late for we Trotskyists to do anything in the city of Saigon.

23 September 1945. A violent seizure of power by French imperialism, assisted actively by the British army, and passively by the Japanese military police.

The Vietnamese government [that is, the Provisional Government set up by Tran van Giau and the Vietminh] immediately gave the order to evacuate Saigon and await further instructions: 'Let us keep calm'.

The Central Committee of *La Lutte* was completely dispersed for several days. Then, in the middle of the night, I was awoken by a comrade who passed on an instruction appointing me as an aide to a member of the Central Committee.[5] I was ordered to meet him 150 kilometres south-west of Saigon and conduct him safe and sound to our headquarters, which was 20 kilometres north of Saigon. What joy! I can still remember how, half an hour after getting this message, having kissed my mother goodbye and leaving her in my sister's care, I left on my bike at one o'clock in the morning and pedalled non-stop to carry out my mission. Three days later we were at headquarters.

The 'General Staff' of the *La Lutte* group existed for about 12 days. It must be realised that we were far from really being that. The 'General Staff' existed in name only. The abrupt dispersal of our comrades led us, in fact, to total disaster: we only had 30 soldiers to the right and left of us, along with different organisations in a state of dissolution. As far as the city workers were concerned, they had either obeyed the evacuation order or were following the regular regiments of the government.

Among the Central Committee members present at headquarters were:

1. Tran van Thach, a lawyer and former editor of the paper *La Lutte*.

2. Phan van Hum, author and philosopher.

3. Phan van Chanh, a university lecturer.

4. Ung Hoa, the group's general secretary.

5. Nguyen thi Loi, a schoolteacher.

6. Nguyen van So.[6]

7. Le van Thu, a journalist.

These were seven of the 11 members of the Central Committee of *La Lutte*. We were very well-placed from the point of view of military strategy. We enjoyed sympathy and deep respect as regards the civilian population. They looked upon us as serious people, as revolutionaries who were willing to sacrifice themselves to build something better.[7]

In the remaining paragraphs I shall go over the entire meticulous preparation of the Stalinists for the extermination of the Trotskyists. As I see it, it was a conscious undertaking on the part of the Stalinists. For two weeks before 23 September, everywhere, in every village, on the official notice boards, could be found articles drawing attention to the secret preparations of a 'certain organisation' to sabotage the peace and the independence of the country. This was a blow aimed at the Trotskyists. So our comrades could easily determine the atmosphere among the public that surrounded us at that time.

I have forgotten to tell you until now that Saigon under the Vietminh government had four military districts: the first was controlled by the Stalinists and the other three by nationalist forces and by forces close to the Trotskyists.

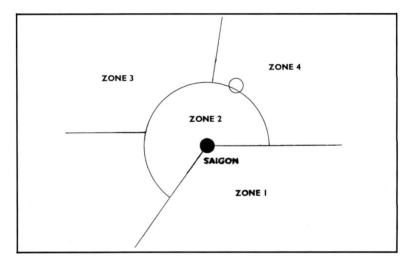

Here is a diagram that will enable you to follow the tactics of the Stalinists in action. Zone 1 was under Stalinist control and was mainly peasant. Zone 2 was half peasant and half working class, and was under the control of the second and third divisions of the Vietnamese army. The majority of staff in command of the second zone were Trotskyists (former members of the *La Lutte* group). In addition, a number of principled agreements had been reached between Vu tam Anh, the commander of the second division, a former officer in the Japanese army, and the leaders of the *La Lutte* group.[8]

One further point: the headquarters of the *La Lutte* group had been set up on the border of the non-Stalinist and Stalinist zones. Zones 3 and 4 had no military divisions, but the apparatus of the GPU (the Stalinist secret police) was in Zone 3. The administrator of Zone 4 was a neutral intellectual. All approaches to, and negotiations with, the Vietminh were carried out through his mediation.

My stay at the headquarters was an unforgettable and historic memory for me. United in a common cause, we, who previously had belonged to different social layers, helped each other and worked hand-in-hand under fire from our enemies. Day and night, in the sun and rain, through vicious jungles and vast rubber plantations, we soldiers of the proletarian general staff tirelessly carried out military manoeuvres. We used the techniques of guerrilla warfare. We were under the command of a former NCO in the French army. We had hardly anything in the way of weapons. Some reliable comrades were assigned the tasks of, on the one hand, buying or acquiring arms by our own means and, on the other, of negotiating with the Vietminh government.

While I am on this subject: as a soldier, I did not know anything of the various negotiations between our General Staff and the Vietminh leaders. Nevertheless, on several occasions our comrade Phan van Chanh was summoned by the Stalinist representatives. And on one occasion, four days before the arrest of our comrades, a Stalinist military and political commission came right into our headquarters — whether to negotiate or to look us over, I don't know which. As for the surrounding civilian population, they were very impressed by our ideals and actions. Every day they brought us firewood, rice and various foodstuffs free of charge.

Three days before our headquarters was disbanded, we received a number of items of disturbing news:

1. A French cruiser, the 'Richelieu', had disembarked Leclerc's troops onto our territory.

2. The second division of the Vietnamese army, on which we had placed all our hopes, had suffered reverses and had had to withdraw. At the front, the Allied airborne troops and those of Leclerc (the armoured division in particular) were on the rampage. In the rear, in Zones 3 and 4, the soldiers of the second division had been discharged by the Stalinist forces, who had incited the entire population against this division — a division commanded by a traitor.

3. Our comrade Phan van Chanh, asked to go to the Vietnamese police, gave himself up and was arrested on the spot. We have had no news from him since then. Even his wife — who was arrested at the same time and was afterwards released — has not been able to find out whether her husband is still alive.

From then onwards we witnessed the complete dispersal and disappearance of our comrades. Our General Staff sent Nguyen thi Loi on a mission in Zone 1, and then he disappeared.

Our General Staff (I do not know whether it was an order on behalf of the Vietminh government or by its own decision) informed and advised us to get ready to leave for the front in the course of the week. Each of us had to leave our dirty linen in the care of a reliable comrade, and we were able to obtain 24 hours' leave. As I was still a soldier, I was much intrigued by all of this; it meant leaving the front under arms.

One day before the entire headquarters was arrested, more and more alarming decisions enabled us to foresee certain disaster. And on the basis of all this, I insist that our leaders knew and were aware of the crime the Stalinists had in store for them.

Comrade Phan van Hum left the headquarters to go 20 kilometres to the north-east to prepare a camp, so that our soldiers could find refuge there after the 'final battle'. He left, and then disappeared.

On the final night comrade Tran van Thach was the only Central Committee member to remain at the headquarters. We soldiers received the order to form a double guard and search everybody who passed in front of the headquarters.

At 5.30 a.m. ten *gardes mobiles* arrived, under the command of the Stalinist police commissioner of the district, to take away comrade Tran van Thach, to search the entire building and to collect everything together. Then, for the first time in my life, I witnessed at first hand the slanders and actions of the Stalinists (both at once). Brandishing his revolver, the commissioner gave the soldiers a long lecture.

As for comrade Nguyen van So, he too was arrested a few days later in equally stormy circumstances (according to eye-witness accounts). Then he disappeared.

Of the seven comrades present at the headquarters, five had been murdered, and only two were able to escape.

One of them, Ung Hoa, has, I think, allied with Bao Dai during recent times, since he is related to the royal family.

As for the last of them, Le van Thu, he still remains in Saigon, sending money to *La Verité* [the French Trotskyist newspaper] from time to time.

'Forget!' 'Do Not forget!' 'Only conscience knows it!' 'And future deeds will respond to it!'

Comrade P.

Appendix 3

THESES

The following Theses were adopted by the Provisional Central Committee of the League of Internationalist Communists, which Lu sanh Hanh tried to reconstruct in illegality in Vietnam, after the partition of the country in 1946 between Ho chi Minh's 'Democratic Republic' in the north and the renewed French colonial regime in the south.

The Theses, dated 8 July 1947, point to the lessons, in the League's eyes, of the 1945 events, and outline its perspectives following them.

The League constituted itself as a section of the Fourth International and sent the Theses to the International Secretariat of the Fourth International.

Our position

1. August 1945, sounding the knell of Japanese domination, marked the birth of the Vietnamese Revolution.

It was born in the gap created by the disarray of the ruling Japanese military authorities and the inability of the Allies to get relief troops to the spot. The causes that gave birth to it are classic: the centuries-old slavery to which the Vietnamese people had been subjected by French imperialism, the misery and countless sufferings engendered by the last 'war to end wars' (two million dead during the 1945 famine in Tonkin),[1] the advance in the masses' political understanding, their awareness that French imperialism was inferior — a fact brought home by the military disasters it experienced when confronted by German imperialism, 'yellow' Japanese imperialism or the well-organised Vietminh.

2. The Vietnamese revolution could claim to encompass all classes and social layers, and all the political, economic, religious, social, philosophical and cultural organisations of the Vietnamese people. Saigon and Hanoi have witnessed enormous demonstrations of more

than a million, recalling the great revolutionary days in Paris, where all the banners were mixed together. Even if the worker and peasant population is very much the basis and inexhaustible reserve of the Vietnamese resistance, many of the bourgeoisie and landowners, up to and including the Emperor Bao Dai (citizen Vinh Thuy today), and a very great number of intellectuals, carried on a great struggle.

The Vietnamese Revolution is truly national and popular.

It has inaugurated the Vietnamese democratic republic with its own government, its own national assembly, its army and its finances.

3.(a) Dominated, however, by the 'bloc of classes' policy of the Indochinese Communist Party, the strongest and best organised of the parties that make up the Vietminh, the Vietnamese republican government defends primarily the class interest of the bourgeoisie and the landowners. The defence of private property (including the property of French imperialism), the defence of national integrity, a bourgeois parliament, finances and customs of an equally bourgeois type, together with an army, police and bureaucracy intended to guarantee private property, are all crowned with a policy of building an independent economy — obviously a bourgeois one — away from the grip of the world imperialist economy.

As for the layers of the petty bourgeoisie, the republic will reserve a host of careers for them — in parliament, in the administration, in the police, in the army, in commerce, in agriculture, in diplomacy, and so on.

For the mass of the poor peasantry, the Ta dien, there will be nothing, or practically nothing. Obviously the Dia to (tenant farming system) will be reformed, but private landed property remains sacred and inalienable.

As for the still weak working class, it was only granted a slight amount of labour legislation.

However, the Vietnamese bourgeoisie has turned out to be inherently impotent — an impotence from which the French imperialism of the great industrial combines, trading companies and large plantations of the Bank of Indochina never allowed it to break free. Just as in another way the interests of the native gentry are intimately linked with, and subordinated to, the interests of French imperialism, the bourgeois policy of the Vietnamese republic has been shown to be unworkable.

Economic, and consequently political, independence is no more than a hollow dream. Agrarian revolution would have been considered a crime. Thus neither of the two great tasks of the democratic revolution came to be resolved: the dream of the Stalinist strategists has evaporated, largely because of themselves. In fact, they have sabotaged independence and agrarian reform.

(b) Confronted by imperialism, they merely practised the grovelling policy of cowardly pacifists. At the news of the defeat of the Japanese, having straightaway seized power by a bold coup d'état in Tonkin, the Vietminh posed as democrats, boasting of their struggle on the side of the democratic Allies against Japanese militarism. They naively thought that the Sino-English imperialists, whom they had received with open arms, were going to grant them the independence promised by the Atlantic Charter.[2] Their illusions were soon dispelled when [the English] General Gracey opened the gates of Nam Bo (in Cochinchina) to the first troops of the puffed-up Leclerc, who in the meantime had been armed by Great Britain — at a cost of three billion francs — for the conquest of both Vietnam and Indochina.

Then the people — whom until then, the Stalinist leaders of the Vietminh had accustomed to bleat the slogan 'Hurrah Allied Forces' — were partly stirred up by revolutionary groupings, either extremist nationalists or International Communists. As if by instinct, the masses came to their senses and armed themselves spontaneously — some with sharpened bamboo sticks, some with hatchets, with machetes, with knives, and some with weapons stolen or seized from Japanese soldiers. They organised themselves rapidly into *popular militias* and *revolutionary people's committees*. The peasants began to take over the land and the workers the factories, mainly belonging to the French.

All these revolutionary measures were forbidden by the governmental committee of Nam Bo of Tran Van Giau, Nguyen Van Tao and Duong Bach Mai, all three of them ministers and leaders of the Indochinese Communist Party.

Arming the people! What a 'Trotskyist provocation' to the Allies! It was up to the popular militias to surrender all their weapons, including the sharpened bamboo sticks, to the governmental committee — who would hand them back to the Japanese, since they had to render account for them to the British, who had entrusted them with the maintenance of law and order. *Revolutionary Committees!* Yet another 'Trotskyist provocation'! 'Only administrative committees are necessary'. *Land to the peasants! Factories to the workers!* Yet more 'Trotskyist provocations'!

Thus the Stalinist leaders had opposed all the popular initiatives that would have guaranteed national liberation and the agrarian revolution.

Their enemies are the defenders of the working people and of the armed revolutionary people; they are the supporters of the Fourth

International; they are those who, at least during the first period of the resistance — for defending the poor peasants — the Stalinist leaders imprisoned, assassinated and offered as victims on the altar of the democratic Allies as represented by Gracey.

The reasons why numerous militants of the Fourth International, as well as of the Hoa hao, were exterminated physically, and why it was necessary for the Stalinists to secure the liquidation of the Fourth International, are clear. This was the *sine qua non* [indispensible] condition of their maintaining power and of their flirtation with imperialism.

(c) In spite of this attitude, or because of it, the Stalinists were driven from the capital by the first French troops. Their 'friend' Gracey lifted not a little finger to defend them, just as he had never allowed them to meet him, not even at the tradesmen's entrance. They gave up Saigon without firing a single bullet and left the people to itself, to the fury of the enemy . . . but also to its revolutionary militants.

Finding cadres within its own ranks, the people, angered by the flight of the Stalinist government, organised the resistance everywhere. It has lit up the bloody road to armed insurrection by a never-to-be-forgotten flame, that will yet astonish the world.

(d) Having recovered from their fright, our Stalinist ministers, trained as they were in the school of the Guomindang, then tried to regain the leadership of the movement of the insurrection, not without effecting the assassination of authentic revolutionary militants. But as always, they went from surrender to surrender.

First there was the suspension of hostilities in Nam Bo for the parleys with General Gracey that allowed the French reinforcements to arrive. Then there was the agreement of 6 March 1946,[3] which in exchange for the formal recognition of the Vietnamese Republic opened the gates of Tonkin to the troops of Leclerc. Finally came the *modus vivendi*, a booby trap that in spite of the warnings of the revolutionary opposition allowed the Moutet-D'Argenlieu-Leclerc trio to finalise its plans for the reconquest of Tonkin and Annam. The entire Stalinist policy has betrayed the cause of the bourgeois democratic revolution, and has continually played the game of imperialism.

4. Resistance — effective, angry and fiery — still continues at present with the most sophisticated guerrilla methods. The enemy, however, has re-occupied almost all vital and strategic centres. It is, nonetheless, exhausted, even by that. The permanent internal crisis in France (finance, food, supplies, interminable strikes, the threat of civil war), the financial incapacity of French imperialism to send and

maintain an expeditionary force of between 250,000 and 500,000 men that would be necessary for the complete reconquest of Vietnam, and the revolts of other French colonies, should and could have induced them to bargain with the Ho chi Minh government.

But here's the rub: he is obedient to Moscow, and clerico-republican French reaction, playing the tune of its yankee conductor, did not want any of it. For Vietnamese territory is coveted by Sino-American expansionism. Besides, it is likely to serve as a base for the future 'war to end wars'.

In Vietnam, while one faction of the bourgeoisie went back to its old French master, another faction feared its own ruin by an interminable policy of 'scorched earth' (houses and factories burnt down, rice-fields abandoned, trade ruined and communications cut), feared the measures of 'war communism' (confiscation of the harvest, of property and requisitions of all kinds). This faction of Nguyen hai Than, of Nguyen tuong Tam and Nguyen van Sam has turned to the ex-emperor Bao Dai to mediate for favours with the Americans.[4] These latter have systematically organised themselves, made a stand and regained their courage against the Stalinist policy under the name of the National United Front.

Making themselves the echo of a more gigantic struggle, between the US and the USSR, these two fronts have entered into open conflict, saturating western Cochinchina in blood. And so the Vietnamese drama continues, without any foreseeable way out for the moment.

What does, however, remain certain is that the Vietnamese working people and peasants, who did not struggle only in the end to remain inside the imperialist French Union, to allow itself to be still exploited and plundered, or to serve Sino-American interests, has shown itself to be satisfied neither by the Ho chi Minh set-up, nor by the set-up of Than Tam Sam (Nguyen hai Than, Nguyen tuong Tam and Nguyen van Sam).

The Viet Hong organisation in Tonkin is already being talked about as being the revolutionary wing of the resistance. Groups for resistance to the end are being born practically everywhere.

Negotiations could yet take place. Governmental combinations could halt the hostilities momentarily, though this does not appear probable.

But since nothing will be done to satisfy the deep aspirations of the people, at present organised and armed, the struggle will continue.

5. What has been the policy followed so far by the working-class political and trade union organisations of the metropolitan country as regards the Vietnamese revolution?

The Stalinist party, wishing to see the French tricolour flying over all its overseas territories, has betrayed the Leninist policy of the right of peoples to self-determination, up to and including the right of separation from the metropolitan country.

They have shown themselves to be accessories in this by their collaboration with the Bidault-Moutet and Ramadier-Moutet governments.[5] Abstention during the vote for military credits for Indochina does not excuse the betrayal of its war minister. The support it has given to the Ho chi Minh government has only been token. Will not, moreover, the prolongation of the war in Vietnam for certain aggravate the present crisis threatening the French finances (over 100 million francs per day is being gobbled up by the expedition to Vietnam), finally involving French imperialism with another Syria-Lebanon, at least? Its policy has in the end imprisoned Vietnam inside the French Union for the glory of a 'strong and happy' France, the France of Leclerc, of the Bank of Indochina, of the rubber planters, of water, of electricity, etc., etc. . . . it's well understood.

French imperial grandeur in danger could not find better defenders. Besides, isn't the Stalinist policy of class collaboration and Millerandism[6] a permanent betrayal of the socialist proletariat and the oppressed people?

The Socialist Party — which again, ten years after the Popular Front, has become the leading government party — has yet again revealed its thoroughly social-imperialist nature. Even the most experienced pen-pushers of [the French Socialist party daily newspaper] *Le Populaire* could not disagree with the fact that Bidault, Leclerc, D'Argenlieu, Moutet and its own Ramadier well and truly make up one and the same admirably balanced team. The truth is that the Socialist Party, characteristic as it is of the Fourth Republic, is parliamentarism, and is only there to make the Vietnamese pill palatable to the working people of France. History will one day tell us the amounts on the cheques that Moutet and Ramadier and sons have handled from Ganny, the planters and other sharks during their stay in Saigon. We must assign responsibility properly. But between them and us it is a question of war.

The Pivert-Rous tendency, the left wing of the Socialist Party, has indeed protested against the opportunism of their comrade ministers. But it only aimed at being able to replace them in order to realise a better policy of understanding imperialist interests. Isn't Dechezelles joining ranks with the Stalinists in recommending the inclusion of Vietnam within the French imperialist union, for an agreement with the Ho chi Minh government, may we add? What else could this 'French Union' be under the Fourth Republic, for ourselves and the working class, in the absence of a socialist proletariat revolution — if not a union of exploiters and exploited, dominated by imperialism?

As for the Confédération Générale du Travail [the French trade union confederation], its leadership, under the order of the Socialist Party and the Communist Party, has also failed in its duty of revolutionary support for colonial peoples in their struggle for liberation. Moreover, can we expect anything better from the bigwigs, Jouhaux, Racamond and Frachon?[7]

Faced with the Vietnamese revolution, all the great working-class organisations of France have either howled with the wolf or have shown themselves to be its accomplices.

The group of *La Revue Internationale*, pitifully, has only the attitude of a student amateur.

Only the Parti Communiste Internationaliste [French section of the Fourth International] has adopted a correct attitude of unconditional revolutionary support. But, in its organ at least, it does not seem to have sketched out perspectives for the future.

6. As far as we Internationalist Communists are concerned, we lay claim to the best tradition of Bolshevism on the national question. Forever basing ourselves on the principles of the permanent revolution, we think that the resolution of the national-democratic tasks in Vietnam — which are pressing down more sharply than ever — can only be accomplished by the resolution of the revolutionary socialist tasks. In other words, if for example we remain within the limits of the French empire, the true national liberation of Vietnam, as well as the agrarian revolution, can only be accomplished borne on the wings of the proletariat socialist revolution in France (or in another advanced country), which will sweep along in its wake of socialist liberation all the oppressed peoples in order to transform their national democratic revolution into a socialist revolution, with the aim of building a *Union of French Soviet Socialist Republics.*

To the imperialist slogans of the French Union, we therefore counterpose that of *the Union of French Socialist Republics.*

If the Vietnamese revolution is stagnating, for the time being, it is due to the lack of socialist revolutionary upsurge in the advanced countries.

To those who believe that the national liberation of Vietnam can be obtained by negotiations with French imperialism, with or without the mediation of other imperialisms, we say: we will only obtain this liberation by a concerted struggle of the Vietnamese workers and peasant population with the revolutionary proletariat of the metropolitan country, hand-in-hand with the other oppressed peoples.

French imperialism can only emerge from the present crisis by trampling upon the oppressed peoples of Africa and Asia, and by the installation of a military or a fascist dictatorship. Faced with the tragic dilemma of *socialist revolution or military-fascist reaction*, our duty is not to hold back the Vietnamese resistance to achieve some kind of independence which suits the national bourgeoisie and imperialism, but to prolong the resistance — to accentuate the general crisis of France, to help the revolts of the Madagascans and the Moroccans. While awaiting the French revolutionary upsurge, we prepare for the transformation of the present revolution into a socialist revolution. *There is no other solution, except on this road.*

League of Internationalist Communists (Vietnamese Section)
Theses adopted by the Provisional Central Committee, 8 July 1947

FOOTNOTES

Chapter 2

1. The author here means 'official' Indochinese Communism, i.e., that of the Stalinists. The Trotskyist organisations, whose origin is covered in Chapter 3, also considered themselves communists.
2. This change of policy was that imposed by the Stalinist bureaucracy after the death of Lenin: the abandonment of the international revolutionary perspective of the Comintern's early years, the anti-Marxist policy of 'socialism in one country' and the alliances with bourgeois forces, firstly in China. It is suggested that readers unfamiliar with this history consult the Introduction (pages ix-xvii) where a brief outline is given.
3. The New Economic Policy (NEP) was adopted by the Russian communists at their Tenth Party Congress, in March 1921. It marked the end of the policy of war communism, introduced during the civil war, under which the free market was curtailed, grain requisitioning introduced, and military methods applied to the economy. Under the New Economic Policy the Russian communists made what they considered to be a necessary retreat: they encouraged a certain measure of private ownership, allowed peasants to dispose of their surplus produce locally, and granted some concessions to foreign capital to exploit mineral deposits etc. The Russian communists saw a limited amount of collaboration with 'the possessing classes' as an unavoidable necessity; the quotation here suggests that Ho chi Minh and his followers regarded such measures as a permanent strategy.
4. The 'Three People's Principles' — nationalism, democracy and the people's livelihood — were formulated in 1905 by Sun Yat-sen, the founder of the Guomindang, the Chinese bourgeois nationalist movement. They served as the ideological basis of the movement, which was borne to power after Sun's death, in the Chinese revolution of 1925-1927.
5. A brief outline of the course of the Chinese revolution of 1925-1927 is given in the Introduction (pages xii-xv).
6. The 'third period' was the name given to the policy of the Comintern

between 1928 and 1935. According to the schema drawn up by the Stalinists themselves, this was the final period of capitalism: the 'first period' had been 1918-1923 (capitalist crisis and revolutionary upsurge) and the 'second period' 1924-1928 (capitalist stabilisation). In reality, the Stalinists felt endangered by the consequences of their own opportunist line in the late 1920s (conservative economic policy at home; alliance with bourgeois forces abroad, leading to the setback in Britain in 1926 and the disaster in China), and attempted an ultra-left solution to the problem. In the USSR this led to the forced collectivisation of land; internationally it meant swinging from opportunist alliances with reformist leaders to condemning them as 'social fascists' and refusing any tactics aimed at uniting with workers under their leadership.

7. The Paris Commune was established by workers' organisations in 1871, the first attempt by the working class to take power. After 72 days it was suppressed with thousands of deaths.

8. Information in this section from AOM, 7, F55, 'Crime de la rue Barbier'.

9. The 'white terror' referred to, the French suppression of the Vietnamese peasant movement, is so called by the author after the anti-communist terror during the Russian civil war of 1919-1921.

10. 'Coolie' was the common term, used by the Chinese and Vietnamese as well as their imperialist rulers, for the lowest-paid workers on the big plantations. Unskilled and illiterate, they were paid the bare minimum for hard physical work. The word originates from the Chinese K'ou Li (hard strength).

11. A *notable* was a native unpaid member of the local administration — roughly the equivalent of a local or parish councillor. The *notables* were the lowest rung of the French colonial administration of Indochina. They helped collect taxes, saw to the upkeep of local customs etc.

Chapter 3

1. Taittinger's Jeunesses Patriotes (Patriotic Youth) were fascists, inspired by Mussolini. They emerged after the election of a Radical-Socialist coalition in 1924. They were lumpen thugs, dressed in blue raincoats and berets for their street provocations, downmarket compared to the Croix de Feu, which was predominantly made up of ex-servicemen, and the Action Directe of Charles Maurras which headed the attempted fascist coup of February 1934.

2. Jean-Jacques Rousseau (1712-1778), a philosopher of the French Enlightenment, saw the cause of inequality in private property and provided inspiration for radicals of the French revolution in his main work *Le contrat social* (*The Social Contract*). Charles Louis de Montesquieu (1689-1755), another Enlightenment thinker, directed a scathing criticism at official religion. The 'natural and inalienable rights of man and citizen' were declared by the French national assembly at the height of the French revolution in 1789 and became the watchword of revolutionary movements of subsequent generations.

3. The Mur des Fédérés (Federals' Wall) in the Père Lachaise cemetery at Ménilmontant, Paris, is a memorial to the at least 20,000 workers who died defending the Paris Commune of 1871. The wall stands at the site of some of the fiercest fighting between the Communards ('federals') and the government forces. From 1880 French socialists marched there to honour the Communards.

4. Roubaud's title page reads: 'Vietnam! Vietnam! Vietnam! Homeland of the South! Homeland of the South! At the Yen Bay guillotine I heard this cry 13 times, uttered by each of the condemned one after the other, two metres from the scaffold.' (Roubaud, 1931.)

5. The Declaration of the Indochinese Oppositionists is published in English (Pirani, 1987).

Chapter 4

1. For *notables*, see note 11 to Chapter 2.

Chapter 5

1. The German National Socialist (Nazi) party led by Adolf Hitler won mass support for the first time in the elections of September 1930, when it polled 6.4 million votes, compared to 4.5 million for the Communists. The Chancellor, Heinrich Brüning of the Catholic Centre party, was left without an overall parliamentary majority and ruled by decree. Trotsky and his supporters called for a workers' united front of the Communists and Social Democrats to defeat fascism, but Stalin, in line with the ultra-left idiocy of the 'third period' (see note 6 to Chapter 2) rejected this policy, condemning the Social Democrats as 'social fascists' and arguing that there was little difference between Brüning and Hitler.

2. The Anti-War Congress was called at Amsterdam on 27-28 August

1932 by the French novelists Romain Rolland and Henri Barbusse, both close collaborators with the Communist Party. The Congress sought to encourage intellectuals, in particular, to associate with the Party in an anti-war campaign without necessarily becoming members. The congress was run in a highly undemocratic manner, with Oppositionists booed down or simply denied the floor. Forbidden from submitting their own resolution, the Oppositionists voted against Barbusse's, which was passed by a majority of 2,000 to 6.

3. Capitalist Germany sank deeper into political crisis through 1932; two general elections gave the Nazis the largest vote, but no overall majority, and the Social-Democratic and Communist parties between them won a combined vote of a similar size. But working-class opposition to fascism was paralysed by the policy dictated to the Communist Party leaders from Moscow, in line with 'third period' ultra-leftism: to reject a united front with the Social Democratic workers against Hitler, simply condemning the Social Democrats as 'social fascists'.

From January 1933, when Hitler was appointed Chancellor, the Nazis took control of the state machine. Trades unions, and all political parties except the Nazis, were banned, parliament wound up and anti-Jewish pogroms made official. The workers' movement, the oldest and best-organised in the world, was suppressed without mounting its own defence and literally without a shot being fired. Trotsky laid the responsibility for the disaster on the Stalinists' policy. The German Communist Party was collapsing, 'internally rotting', he said, and from exile in Turkey he called in March 1933 for the formation of a new communist party in Germany. At a clandestine conference of the German Left Oppositionists in Leipzig in the same month, Trotsky's proposed turn was supported by a minority but rejected by a majority led by Bauer (real name Erwin Ackerknecht). Discussion began throughout the Left Opposition on the issue.

In April 1933 the Executive Committee of the Comintern met in Moscow and affirmed that the Moscow line had been 'absolutely correct' during and up to the Nazi victory. This refusal to learn from the defeat, and the fact that no opposition was raised to it throughout the Comintern, led Trotsky to declare in July that the struggle to reform the Comintern was over; the working class needed not only a new German party but a new, Fourth, International. That same month, Bauer visited Trotsky in Turkey before the latter left for France. On the 'new party', Trotsky convinced Bauer, who wrote to his comrades that — because 'the Comintern failed the test of the German events' — a new International was needed. (See Broué and Stobnicer, 1983). In November 1933 the International Left Opposition turned itself into the International Communist League, to prepare to found the Fourth International. Bauer left the movement in 1934 in opposition to the 'entryist' tactic used in France, but the German Trotskyists played a key part in the League's work, despite repression from the Nazis on one side and Stalinists on the other.

Chapter 6

1. Indochina's municipal councils and colonial councils were described thus in a pamphlet published by the Fourth International in 1947:

> The Radical A. Sarraut and the Socialist A. Varenne, former governors of Indochina, taking care to create a democratic facade to hide the regime of colonial barbarity, endowed Indochina with parliamentary caricatures such as the colonial councils and municipal councils. Take the example of Saigon which, compared to the other towns, is considered a 'land of liberty' in the country. Besides the 120,000 Annamite inhabitants, there are 5,000 French citizens. The [Saigon] municipal council has twice as many French councillors as Annamite ones, and in any case only those Annamites who are sufficiently rich may vote. . . . It was [right-wing first world war President of France Raymond] Poincaré himself, if the journalist Louis Roubaud is to be believed, who said that 'the native parliaments pompously called Houses of Representatives hardly exist except in form.' (Anh Van and Roussel, 1947, p. 28.)

2. This workers' commission of inquiry was constituted by International Red Aid (an organisation backed by the Comintern) and the Amnesty Committee set up by Francis Jourdain in protest at the repressions of 1931-1933 in Indochina. The commission, consisting of Péri, Jean Chaintron of International Red Aid and the trade union delegate Bruneau, worked in Saigon for a month from 18 February 1934.

3. The Moscow trials, which took place at the height of Stalin's terror, were notorious frame-ups — now universally discredited — in which many of Russia's foremost revolutionary leaders gave false 'confessions' and were then shot.

The defendants at the second trial (ending on 1 February 1937), referred to here, were Karl Radek, Yuri Pyatakov, Nikolai Muralov, Grigori Sokolnikov, Leonid Serebriakov and 12 others; Trotsky was the chief defendant *in absentia*. The accusations, read by Stalin's notorious police chief, Andrei Vyshinsky, were that the defendants had allied themselves with the Japanese and German fascists, worked for the military defeat of the USSR, organised a campaign of sabotage and assassinations, etc.

Radek and Sokolnikov were sentenced to ten years' imprisonment; other defendants were shot.

Six months earlier, in August 1936, Grigory Zinoviev, Lev Kamenev, Ivan Smirnov and 13 others were accused at the first Moscow trial of having conspired to kill Stalin's henchman Sergei Kirov in December 1934, and of conspiring with the German fascists to kill Stalin and others. The 16 defendants were shot. Trotsky and his son Leon Sedov were again tried *in absentia*.

At the third trial, in February-March 1938, Nikolai Bukharin and other supporters of his political line (Rykov and Tomsky) joined Oppositionists like Christian Rakovsky and faithful Stalinists (including Stalin's former police chief Henry Yagoda) in the dock.

4. Trotsky's article 'The Decisive Stage', written on 5 June 1936 (reprinted in Trotsky, 1974b, p. 123), dealt with the tasks of the French working class in the pre-revolutionary situation that had erupted. It culminates in a call for the establishment of factory-based action committees to organise and develop the mass strike movement.

Lenin's *Testament* was a letter, written during Lenin's last illness in December 1922, to the Congress of the Communist Party of the Soviet Union. It gave his view of how the Soviet leadership should proceed following his death. The letter not only dealt with two crucial questions over which Lenin was in conflict with Stalin's faction — the state bureaucracy and the nationalities — but also included a bitter attack on Stalin's leadership, and called for his removal from the position of CP General Secretary. It was suppressed by the Stalinists and published only by the Trotskyist Opposition.

It was made known to the Communist Party of the Soviet Union only in 1956 by Khrushchev and added to official versions of Lenin's *Collected Works* only after that (Lenin, *Collected Works*, Vol. 36, p. 593).

5. For the first Moscow trial, see note 3 to this chapter.

Chapter 7

1. The piastre was worth ten French francs in the money of the day. At that time there were 105 francs to the pound sterling.
2. For the colonial councils, see note 1 to Chapter 6.
3. These Statutes, which outline the organisational form of the Fourth International, are published in English as an Appendix to the International's programme, *The death agony of capitalism and the tasks of the Fourth International ('The transitional programme')*, New Park, London, 1980.
4. According to an American scholar: 'At the elections for the Colonial Council of Cochinchina on 30 April 1939, the three Trotskyists Ta thu Thau, Tran van Thach and Phan van Hum received 80 per cent of the votes, defeating three Constitutionalists, two Stalinists, and several independent representatives in the balloting.'
   The same author adds that Stalinist participation in these elections 'resulted in a crushing defeat and a subsequent split in the [Indochinese Communist] Party. Nguyen van Tao formed his own faction while Duong bach Mai maintained leadership in the official party.' (I. Milton Sacks, 'Marxism in Vietnam', in Trager, (ed.), 1960, p. 143.)
5. On 23 August 1939, as Hitler finalised his war preparations, the Stalin regime abandoned its loose alliance with France and Britain and struck a non-aggression pact with Nazi Germany. The pact, signed by the Soviet and German foreign ministers, Vyacheslav Molotov and Joachim von Ribbentrop, was accompanied by a 'secret additional protocol' which divided eastern Europe into 'spheres of influence': Lithuania and western Poland for Germany; Finland, Estonia, Latvia, eastern Poland and the Rumanian province of Bessarabia for the USSR. The pact was a surprise, not least, to the world's Communist Parties, who overnight had to abandon the 'anti-fascist Popular Fronts' for a line of 'opposition to imperialist war'.
6. This crucial discussion in the American Socialist Workers Party (Trotsky's main contributions to which are published in *In Defence of Marxism*), concerned the class nature of the Soviet state. From this, and from the question of what attitude the Fourth International should take to the USSR during the war, the discussion moved on to questions of Marxist method, and ended with Max Shachtman and his supporters splitting from the SWP.

Chapter 8

1. One of the sources of information for this section is the 'Notice on the activity of political intrigues in the indigenous milieux of Cochinchina in November-December 1940' (AOM, 7, F27).

2. The Vichy government was set up with the collapse of France in front of the German invasion of June 1940. It was led by Marshal Henri Pétain, who concluded an armistice with Hitler's Germany and collaborated closely with it, carrying out Nazi policies including the deportation of Jews for extermination in the gas chambers.

3. Japan bombed a US naval base at Pearl Harbour on 8 December 1941, destroying 14 ships and a large number of aircraft, as part of its war of expansion across the Pacific. The attack drew the US into the war on the Allied side.

   The Japanese reverses in the Pacific, referred to in the next paragraph, came mainly at the hands of the Americans. With Australian support, the US throughout 1942 retook from the Japanese a series of European imperial possessions in the Pacific and south-east Asia. At the same time came the German setback at Stalingrad, where a German army of 600,000 men besieged the city for months, but failed to take it from determined Soviet defenders and surrendered. From then on the Germans lost ground on the eastern Front.

4. The Eighth Route Army, incorporated into the Chinese Guomindang government's army in February 1937, was made up entirely of the forces controlled by the Chinese Communist Party. Until then these forces, under the name 'red army', had been in conflict with the nationalist Guomindang. But as war between Japan and China came nearer (it was finally declared in July 1937), the Chinese Communist Party leaders concluded an agreement with the Guomindang under which they stopped confiscations of landlords' land and brought their forces under central military control. As part of this agreement Chou En Lai, deputy to Mao Zedong, joined the Guomindang government in 1938. After Japan was defeated in 1945, the Guomindang broke the alliance and renewed its attacks on the Communist Party's forces.

5. Mao Zedong's catchphrase, 'political power grows out of the barrel of a gun', appeared in his 1938 article 'Problems of War and Strategy':

   Every Communist must grasp the truth, 'political power grows out

of the barrel of a gun' . . . having guns, we can create Party
organisations, as witness the powerful party organisation which the
Eighth Route Army has created in northern China. We can also
create cadres, create schools, create culture, create mass movement. Everything in Yenan has been created by having guns. All
things grow out of the barrel of a gun. (Mao, 1967, Vol. 2, p. 224.)

The Chinese Communist Party — effectively destroyed after the
Stalinist betrayal of the Chinese working class in 1927 (see Introduction, and Chapter 2) — was rebuilt by Mao, not as a communist
party struggling for workers' power, but as the ruling stratum of a
peasant army. (As is explained in Chapter 2, Ho chi Minh was
strongly influenced by this particular form of Stalinist degeneration.)
6. The 'Free French' were the majority of the French bourgeoisie, who
    sided with the Allies against Germany. In 1943 their leader, general
    Charles de Gaulle, established a base at Algiers after the Allied
    landings in north Africa. From there he issued the 'declaration to
    the peoples of Indochina' of 8 December 1943 which reaffirmed that
    France would continue to rule Indochina on the basis of a 'free and
    close association between France and the Indochinese peoples'.
    The purpose of the declaration was to establish French control over
    Vietnamese nationalist movements in the course of the Japanese
    occupation. While doing so, de Gaulle kept his options open and
    also sent an emissary, Francois de Langlade, to make contact with
    Admiral Decoux.

Chapter 9

1. The Comintern, a dead instrument of the Stalinist bureaucracy from
    the mid-1930s, was disbanded on 15 May 1943.
    Its staff and national leaders learned about the decision through
    announcements in the Russian press. Stalin said in an interview that
    this action 'exposes the lie . . . that "Moscow" allegedly intends to
    intervene in the life of other nations and to "Bolshevise" them'
    (quoted in Degras, Vol. III, p. 476). Churchill and Roosevelt
    welcomed the gesture, although they were privately sceptical about
    Stalin's intentions.

Chapter 10

1. The surrender of Germany in May 1945 was followed by an Allied

war leaders' conference at Potsdam, near Berlin in Germany, in July. Its main purpose was to agree on the various powers' 'spheres of influence', both in Europe and east Asia, in areas where Axis rule had collapsed and in many cases there was a danger of independent challenges for control by the working class. On 26 July, a declaration was issued by Truman, Churchill and Chiang Kai-shek from Potsdam, demanding Japanese surrender. This came a few days later, after the atomic bombing of Hiroshima and Nagasaki.

The decision that Indochina should be occupied by Chinese and British forces was a minor item on the Potsdam agenda. It worried de Gaulle and the 'Free French'; they pressed their allies for the 'right' to reclaim Indochina as an imperial possession, and this was soon granted. There are different accounts of exactly how this was agreed: it seems most likely that it was arranged in secret communications between France and Britain immediately after the Potsdam conference, although some observers claim the French return had already been planned at Potsdam (see for example Warbey, 1972, p. 52).

What is certain is that Britain, where the Labour Party came into government in the days preceding the Potsdam conference, co-operated with France's efforts to get its own troops back into Vietnam as quickly as possible, in return for an agreement that France would cede its claims on some of its former colonies in the Middle East. (See also note 6 to this chapter.)

2. The first congress of the Indochinese Communist Party (PCI) was held in clandestinity in Macao, the Portuguese enclave in China, on 27-31 March 1935.

3. The issue of the 'united front of anti-imperialist struggle', which divided the *La Lutte* group and the League of Internationalist Communists, has figured in many controversies among those claiming adherence to the Fourth International.

The formula of the 'anti-imperialist united front' was adopted at the Fourth Congress of the Comintern in 1922, in its *Theses on the Eastern Question* (Hessel, 1980, p. 409). These reiterated the need for independent working-class parties, but left open the question of the extent to which national bourgeois forces could play a progressive role.

Even before the victory of Stalinism, the 'anti-imperialist united front' formula was used by Zinoviev, who led the Comintern, to justify major strategic concessions to national bourgeois parties — for example, the direction to the Chinese Communists in 1923 to enter the Guomindang. In his writings on the lessons of the Chinese revolution of 1925-1927, Trotsky for the first time explicitly concluded that any 'revolutionary' potential for the national bourgeoisie should be ruled out categorically: 'all who support, or spread, or defend in relation to the past, the legend that the "national" bourgeoisie is able to lead the masses to a revolutionary struggle are traitors' (Trotsky, 1976, p. 404). Trotskyists who considered that the 'anti-imperialist united front' formula had been overtaken by history pointed to these lessons of the Chinese events. While the possibility of the national bourgeoisie persisting in its struggle against imperialism could not be ruled out in Lenin's time, they argued, the Chinese revolution had settled the question; therefore the 'anti-imperialist united front', which had only turned out to be a slogan for Zinoviev's mistakes and Stalin's crimes, was outdated; any tactical alliances with national bourgeois forces could only be temporary and transient; no overall strategy could assume such an alliance.

In Vietnam, the Stalinists described the Indochinese Congress of 1936, in which they sought the co-operation of the bourgeois Constitutionalist Party, as an 'anti-imperialist united front' (see Hémery, 1975, pp. 285-301).

In 1945, the author points out, the *La Lutte* group adopted its 'more restrained' attitude to the PCI, contemplated military co-operation within the Vietminh, and restricted its immediate demands to national independence and agrarian reform, in the name of a 'united anti-imperialist front'. The League of Internationalist Communists, which counterposed to the Vietminh the slogan of 'all power to the popular committees', also considered that they were 'pursuing the tactic of the anti-imperialist united front', as Lu sanh Hanh wrote afterwards (see Appendix I, page 158). While the *La Lutte* group saw this front as something more permanent and strategic, in which the Trotskyists limited their political programme, the League regarded it as an episodic tactic.

4. In its ultra-left 'third period' (see also note 6 to Chapter 2), the Comintern programme for the backward countries combined its slogan of a 'democratic dictatorship of the proletariat and peasantry' with 'immediate' propaganda for the creation of soviets — and as part of this, the expropriation of the landlords.

The sixth Comintern Congress declared in 1928 that the Communist Party must everywhere 'consistently and undeviatingly follow the line of seizure of state power, organisation of soviets as organs of insurrection, expropriation of the landlords and big property owners, expulsion of the foreign imperialists . . . (quoted in Isaacs, 1938, p. 383). This was the line followed by the PCI in the disastrous 1930-1931 peasant movement. Earlier, in the mid-1920s, when the Vietnamese Stalinists led the Thanh nien, the Comintern policy in the backward countries was of two rigidly-separated 'stages' of revolution, the first to be taken together with the national bourgeoisie, the second postponed indefinitely. The main result of this policy was the debacle in China. In this schema, the demand for expropriation of the landlords was not to be raised — and in line with it, the Communist Parties of China, Vietnam and other colonial countries repressed peasant demands for land, from 1933 onwards. While in 1945 it was the Trotskyists who led the peasant movement to expropriate the landlords and Nguyen van Tao who attacked them for doing so, the Stalinists and others nevertheless subsequently circulated the slander that the Vietnamese Trotskyists had 'under-estimated' or 'neglected' the peasantry!

5. For the Algiers declaration, see note 6 to Chapter 8.

6. The support for the re-imposition of French colonial rule was not, of course, a consequence of a personal decision by Gracey. In the background was secret diplomacy by the Allied powers — Britain, the US, France and Russia — and an understanding among them that Vietnam 'belonged' to France. Privy to this understanding were the British Labour leaders.

Robert Denton-Williams, an officer in the Indian Army who served under Gracey, gave an account of the events in Saigon to the Labour MP William Warbey in 1965. He somewhat implausibly denies any collusion between the British army and French colonists before 23 September, but says some interesting things about how it developed subsequently:

> This [the French offensive in Saigon on 23 September] was a political matter for which the British military were quite unprepared. There followed a week of negotiations between the Committee of the South [i.e. the Provisional Committee of Nam Bo] and Brigadier Taunton [Gracey's second-in-command] and his staff. General Gracey was away in SEAC headquarters. The Vietnamese would admit no compromise. They were determined on unambiguous political freedom in accordance with the Atlantic Charter, and the wartime speech of General de Gaulle at Brazzaville, when he offered post-war independence to Indochina.

... the Central Office of Information has given it out that because of 'unrest and terrorism', General Gracey had given orders to arm the French. Both parts of the statement were wholly untrue. There was at this time no unrest and no terrorism, and General Gracey did not give the order to arm the French. The order came from the Foreign Office through an FO official in Saigon, and it was delivered to the local British commander, Brigadier-General Taunton.

As many British and Indian officers in Saigon understood it, a deal had been done between Ernest Bevin, British Foreign Secretary, and Massigli of France. Under this secret agreement, the French were to be allowed to re-establish themselves in Indochina on the understanding that they would not attempt to return to Syria and the Lebanon. The Committee of the South, in the face of western perfidy, resolved to fight; and nightly attacks on Saigon began.

... October and November 1945 saw some fierce fighting, and the Vietminh suffered severe casualties. Finally the Saigon bridgehead was made secure, pending the arrival of General Leclerc and his Foreign Legion troops from Madagascar.

When General Leclerc arrived in November, his only supplies consisted of one ship full of red wine. The British duly fitted his troops out with lease-lend materials including vehicles and uniforms. Then Leclerc took over the 'pacification' of Cochinchina. (Warbey, 1972, pp. 49-50.)

7. This Confédération Générale du Travail (general workers' federation) was named after the French organisation with the same title, which was (and is) the French trade union federation dominated by the Communist Party.

8. After the agreement of 6 March 1946 between France and Ho chi Minh's government, that Vietnam would remain a French possession and a referendum would be held on uniting its three parts (see page 117), a conference was called in Fontainebleau, outside Paris, to conclude a more comprehensive settlement.
After the conference Ho signed an understanding with Marius Moutet, the minister for colonies, which provided for a separate solution for Cochinchina, thus abandoning even the nationalist principle of uniting Vietnam. This attempted compromise broke down mainly because the French colonials in Indochina, led by Admiral d'Argenlieu, demanded control over Indochina as a whole.

9. In 1945, a senior leader of the French Trotskyist party, David Rousset, took the position that the Stalinists were carrying out the

revolution in eastern Europe with the Red Armies and that the whole basis of the Fourth International — its fight against Stalinism — was thereby negated. Rousset, and Pierre Naville who declared agreement with him, left the movement in 1946 and within a year formed the Rassemblement Démocratique Revolutionnaire, which advocated an alliance with Gaullism. It is to this tendency that Nguyen van Linh's letter referred. Pierre Rimbert (real name Pietro Torielli) had left the Trotskyist organisation in 1933 but remained active and in 1948 also joined the Rassemblement, along with other ex-Trotskyists including Yvan Craipeau.

10. Peng Shuzhi, Chen Bilan and Liu Jialiang constituted the organisational centre of the Chinese Trotskyist party which faced systematic repression by the Mao Zedong regime and the British authorities in Hong Kong. They left Hong Kong for Saigon in the hope that it would prove a safer place to establish a centre. Chen Bilan later related how the invitation to a conference 'organised by Trotskyist elements inside the Vietminh' turned out to be a trap.

> When the conference came to an end, all the Vietnamese Trotskyists, and our comrade Liu Jialiang, who had been invited to attend, were arrested. Shortly afterwards, Liu Jialiang died in prison. As for the Vietnamese comrades, the report was that they were still alive at the time we left Vietnam but we have never heard what their final fate was. ('Looking Back Over My Years With Peng Shuzhi', in Peng, 1980, p. 43).

Peng Shuzhi and Chen Bilan then moved to Europe where Peng joined the International Secretariat of the Fourth International. It was led by Michel Pablo, who with the support of Ernest Mandel was evolving the theory that the Stalinists were in many countries being forced to take the revolutionary road, and that the Trotskyist parties should liquidate into them ('entryism of a special type'.) Apart from his writings analysing Mao's regime, Peng has also left an account of how, under Pablo, the pro-Stalinist policy of the leadership of the Fourth International led it to abandon the defence of Chinese and Vietnamese Trotskyists from repression. In 1953, the Fourth International split when the American, French and other Trotskyists belatedly took a stand against Pablo, and Peng then wrote to the American Trotskyist leader James P. Cannon detailing Pablo's treachery.

He described how Pablo had for four months suppressed a written appeal by Chinese Trotskyists for action against Mao's repression; how Pablo justified his refusal to take up the campaign on the grounds that 'compared to the achievements of Mao Zedong's revolution, the arrest of a few hundred Trotskyists is insignificant'; and how he asked Peng not to tell a group of Vietnamese comrades, who were about to return from France to carry out 'entryism of a special type' in the Vietminh, of the extent of Stalinist persecutions. (For the letter, see Socialist Workers Party Education Department, 1974, Part 3, Vol. III; and *Tasks of the Fourth International* no. 8, London, 1990).

Chapter 11

1. This characterisation of the conflict between the Stalinists and Trotskyists is one of this book's most important conclusions.

It should be added to the author's statement that 'this movement practically disappeared' that in 1989 a group of elderly Vietnamese comrades came into contact with the Workers International to Rebuild the Fourth International. One of these comrades wrote to *Workers Press*, the newspaper of the Workers Revolutionary Party in Britain:

> From 1954 to today, we have not existed as an organisation worthy of the name . . . Our comrades were separated, working individually or in little groups doing completely non-political work in the trades unions [this included holding the leadership of the railway workers' union in Saigon up to the arrival of the Vietminh in 1975] . . .
>
> After 1945, some comrades were dispersed, by reason of the material difficulties of living, but the majority continued to live in Saigon. But they were not practising serious revolutionary activity.
>
> From time to time, we met between ourselves as a small group, simply to exchange the latest news, to talk briefly of our convictions and our aims, to talk about the question of regroupment, reorganisation, etc., and how it would be done. . .
>
> If there were a little over 30 comrades in south Vietnam in 1945, that is, the veterans of the 1930s, there now remain less than 20. The youngest is 60, and physically all have been weakened by undernourishment, the absence of medical supplies and of other necessities of life, and therefore some have been placed in old people's homes where there have been places available. . . .
>
> All in all, our comrades, having emerged shaken from a half-century of war, of revolutions lost or betrayed, are in many cases

gripped by a bitter scepticism, caused by the preceding long period of crisis. . . . As so-called 'substitute ideas' for their remaining years, some have given themselves to studying again the old humanism inspired by Buddhism, Taoism, Confucianism, Christianity, etc. . . . Apart from national independence, the Stalinist regime has made none of the political, social, economic or cultural conquests which real, authentic socialism fights for. Thirty years of forced, premature agricultural collectivisation, poorly prepared and realised, has brought nothing but famine, alienation and the suffocation of individual personality . . .

All the people heap their worst curses on communism — identified and incarnate in their minds as Stalinism — without the least distinction between this and the real, true socialism, the nature and theory of which is completely beyond their comprehension. . . . The liberalisation and democratisation of the regime [i.e. 'reforms' of the Gorbachev type introduced from 1989 onwards] certainly favours the organisation of the working masses, in the form of unions, of independent mutual aid societies; in the first instance of their economic and social interests, at a later stage for their political and cultural interests.

To start again building independent organisations of the masses will not be possible, except in a relatively liberal and democratic political atmosphere.

And without such organisations, no struggle against the inertia of the whole nation can be mounted, no progress can be made here where all hope and faith in socialism is being lost; where people live in unbearable poverty and misery, having for so long been oppressed, trampled on and betrayed. (*Workers Press*, London, 6 April 1991.)

The author of the letter died in 1990, shortly after writing it.

Portraits of Some Vietnamese Revolutionaries

1. See Chapter 3, note 1.
2. Félicien Challaye, Francis Jourdain and the writer Daniel Guérin were anti-colonialists, inspirers of numerous actions in support of colonial liberation, and founders in 1933 of an Amnesty Committee for Vietnamese political prisoners. For Jourdain, Guérin and Alfred Rosmer, see Glossary.
3. The Laval-Stalin pact was a non-aggression pact between the right-wing French government and the ruling caste in the USSR.

4. In 1934-1935, Stalin's diplomacy changed tack and he attempted to make alliances with the 'democratic' capitalist powers against Nazi Germany; the first of these being the pact with France signed on 2 May 1935. In line with this, the Communist Parties were directed to abandon their ultra-left 'third period' policy, and to develop alliances not only with the reformist workers' parties but with the 'democratic' bourgeois parties. This policy of class-collaboration 'popular fronts' was formally adopted by the Comintern at its seventh congress in the summer of 1935. See page 43.

5. The Kim van Kieu was a popular 200-page love poem, by Nguyen du (1765-1812), a Vietnamese writer influenced by Confucius.

6. The agreement signed in Geneva in May 1954, after the defeat of France by Ho chi Minh's 'democratic republic', provided for a ceasefire, for the temporary division of Vietnam and for nationwide elections. The southern regime, supported by the US, broke the agreement, paving the way for the US war with Vietnam.

7. The Communist League was the name of the French Trotskyist party 1930-1934. For Naville, Molinier and Frank see Glossary.

8. The first Moscow Trial: see note 3 to Chapter 6.

9. Trotsky's article 'The Decisive Stage' and Lenin's *Testament*: see note 4 to Chapter 6.

10. Dual power is the term used by Marxists to describe a highly unstable, pre-revolutionary situation, in which the class struggle has intensified to a degree that opposing class forces have simultaneously established a degree of governmental control. A classic exposition of the term is given by Trotsky in his *History of the Russian Revolution*:

> It is not a constitutional, but a revolutionary, fact. It implies that a destruction of the social equilibrium has already split the state superstructure. It arises where the hostile classes are already each relying upon essentially incompatible governmental organisations — the one outlived, the other in process of formation — which jostle against each other at every step in the sphere of government. . . . By its very nature such a state of affairs cannot be stable. . . . The splitting of sovereignty foretells nothing less than a civil war . . . (Trotsky, 1977, pp. 224-5).

Appendix 1

1. Huynh van Phuong was a former Trotskyist, who had broken with

the movement ten years earlier. For details of his role in 1945 see *Portraits of Some Vietnamese Revolutionaries*, page 132.
2. On the anti-imperialist united front, see note 3 to Chapter 10.

Appendix 2

(All the footnotes to this Appendix, except no. 2, are by the original author of the report.)

1. It should be noted that the circulation did not exceed 15,000. Nonetheless, this was a considerable figure for a non-industrial city of 250,000 inhabitants.
2. This is a reference to Ho huu Tuong (see *Portraits of Some Vietnamese Revolutionaries*, pages 140-143).
3. If the *La Lutte* group allowed some important political issues to bypass it, that was the result of the weakness of our movement on the international level at that time, of the lack of contact between the various sections and particularly of contact with the International Secretariat. Our comrades were unable to keep up with international movements during their five years of deportation.
4. Two years afterwards, once I was able to survey the events as a whole, I came to the conclusion that at that time Ta thu Thau was all too aware that the Central Committee of the Communist Party in the north and that in the south were not acting in concert with each other. The operations conducted by Tran van Giau in Cochinchina from the start were not dictated by Ho chi Minh. It was through wanting to meet Ho chi Minh, in other words the entire action committee, that Ta thu Thau exposed himself to risk in this way.
5. He was engaged in a campaign to form a trade union among schoolteachers.
6. I do not know exactly what his profession was. He was a former student at the *école normale superieure*. He did not live at the headquarters, but about ten kilometres from there.
7. Here we see a blunder on the part of our leadership. The population accused us of nothing. It could, however, clearly see the formation of a state within a state. [The first few words of the handwritten French text are unclear: it appears to say 'Voilà la maladresse . . .'. Presumably the author believes the leadership underestimated the popular support they had — ed.]
8. On 22 September 1945, one day before the decision to evacuate the

city, on the order of the Stalinist leader Tran van Giau, the government decreed the disarming of all military divisions, and the issue of a warrant in particular for the arrest of Vu tam Anh, on a charge of embezzling funds. Now it seems to me that he insinuated himself into the ranks of the Japanese army in order to get out of the country, since he had relinquished his command to his aide-de-camp.

Appendix 3

1. The 1945 famine in Tonkin is estimated to have cost between one and two million lives. One of its direct causes was the economic policy of the Decoux administration (see page 72).
2. The Atlantic Charter was drawn up — specifically for public consumption — by Churchill and Roosevelt on a battleship in the north Atlantic in August 1941 before the US entered the war. It laid down vague 'principles' for a post-war settlement, speaking of 'the right of all peoples to choose the form of government under which they will live' and of the hope that 'sovereign rights and self-government may be restored to those from whom it has been forcibly removed.'
3. The agreement of 6 March 1946 between Ho chi Minh and France accepted a continued French presence in return for the promise (never kept) of a referendum on the future of Cochinchina. See page 117.
4. Nguyen hai Than, Nguyen tuong Tam and Nguyen van Sam were bourgeois nationalists who had collaborated variously with the Chinese and French (see, for example, page 74). In mid-1947 they were endeavouring to set up a government, headed by Bao Dai and backed by France, as a counter to the Hanoi government. In August 1947, shortly after the publication of these *Theses*, they set up a new 'National United Front' in Saigon and telegrammed Bao Dai asking him to come and head a government. It took until 1949 to convince him.
5. From October 1946, what was effectively a dictatorship by de Gaulle came to an end in France; the constitution of the Fourth Republic was approved and, amid turbulent class conflicts, government passed to a series of unstable coalitions, mostly with some measure of support from the Communist Party.
Paul Ramadier, the right-wing Socialist, headed one of these from January 1947; Georges Bidault of the conservative Mouvement

Républicain Populaire headed another from June that year.

6. Millerandism was the name given by socialists to class-collaboration and, specifically, collaboration in bourgeois governments. Alexandre Millerand (1859-1943) became in 1899 in France the first Socialist to accept a post in a bourgeois government.

7. Leon Jouhaux was a trade union bureaucrat, originally a syndicalist, then a social-patriot in the first world war; general secretary of the Confédération Générale du Travail 1909-1940. Benoit Frachon and Julien Racamond were Communist Party members who held high positions in the trade union bureaucracy.

GLOSSARY OF PEOPLE, ORGANISATIONS
AND PUBLICATIONS

Annamite Independence Party (Phuc Viet). Formed in January 1926 in Paris by the nationalist Nguyen the Truyen, who returned to Vietnam in April 1928, leaving Ta thu Thau and others in the leadership of the party. Forcibly dissolved by the French government in March 1929.

Anti-Imperialist League. Initiated by the Stalinists, it held its first congress in Brussels in February 1927, and its second (and last), at which Ta thu Thau spoke, in Frankfurt-on-Main in July 1929. The League was one of many projects supported financially by the Comintern through Willi Muenzenberg, a Stalinist official of the Communist Youth International.

Bao Dai (1913-). The last emperor of Annam, of the Nguyen dynasty, succeeded his father in 1925 but did not take the throne until 1932. During the war he 'ruled' under Japanese protection; in 1945 he went into exile; returned in 1949 to rule with the support of the French during their war with Ho chi Minh's 'Democratic Republic'. In 1955 he was ousted in a referendum by Ngo dinh Diem, his prime minister, and left for France.

Bidault, Georges. After leading the Gaullist national resistance council during German occupation (1943-1945), Bidault headed the Mouvement Républicain Populaire, a strong Catholic party. He held many ministerial positions in the Fourth Republic (1945-1958), and was prime minister in late 1946, during the Fontainebleau conference.

Blum, Léon (1872-1950). Leader of the French Socialist party and prime minister of the first Popular Front government in 1936. Blum joined the youth section of the Socialist party and became a parliamentary deputy in 1919; when the party split at Tours in 1920, with the left joining the Communist International, he emerged as the leader of the right. After the Popular Front period, and a brief second premiership in 1939, he was arrested by the Nazi-backed Vichy regime and defended himself in a famous trial.

Bolsheviks. The party which, under Lenin and Trotsky, led the Russian workers' revolution of November 1917. The Bolsheviks ('majority-ites') were the revolutionary wing of the Russian Social Democratic Labour Party; they worked separately from the reformist Mensheviks ('minority-ites') from 1906 and finally split with them in 1912.

Bolshevik Leninists of the Fourth International. A Trotskyist group formed briefly in June 1939 in Cochinchina, after the Trotskyist victory in the colonial council elections and the subsequent wave of arrests. It unified three illegal organisations — the Thudaumot group, the International Workers of Giadinh and the Communists for the Fourth International.

Bolshevik-Leninist Group for the Construction of the Fourth International. Formed as an illegal Trotskyist organising centre at the end of 1936 in Vietnam by Ho huu Tuong and his comrades in the October group.

Borodin, Mikhail Markovich (1884-1951). Representative of the Stalinist Comintern in China 1923-1927. Arrested in 1949, he died in a cell in Lubyanka prison, Moscow.

Brévié, Jules. French Governor General of Indochina, January 1937-August 1939.

Bukharin, Nikolai (1887-1938). A Bolshevik from 1906 and one of their foremost leaders in the revolutionary period; leader of the 'left' communists in 1918, he swung to the right and supported Stalin against the Trotskyist opposition. President of the Comintern 1926-1929; formed a Right Opposition to Stalin but capitulated in 1929; a victim of the 1938 Moscow trial.

Cao dai. A religious sect which appeared in 1925-1926, built by a section of the Cochinchinese bourgeoisie, claiming to synthesise Buddhism, Taoism and Confucianism and organisationally modelled on the Catholic church. It suffered repression by the French and joined the National United Front of August 1945.

Cédile, Jean. A representative of de Gaulle's Provisional Government of the French Republic, parachuted into Saigon in August 1945 by the British. Later became strong advocate of France's war aims in Indochina.

Chiang Kai-shek (1887-1975). Leader of the Chinese bourgeois nationalist movement, the Guomindang. A follower of Sun Yat-sen from 1913; military leader of the movement after Sun's death in 1925; orchestrated the bloody repression of workers and communists in the 1926-1927 revolution; after the victory of Mao Zedong in 1949 fled to Taiwan and established a nationalist regime there.

Churchill, Winston (1874-1965). British prime minister and war leader 1940-1945. A ruthless anti-communist (he coined the phrase 'iron curtain') and a hated enemy of British workers, who voted him out of office in 1945 by the biggest majority ever recorded in a British election.

Chu van Tan (circa 1908-). From the Tho ethnic minority of High Tonkin, which had a rebellious tradition; a leading light of the 1940 insurrection at Bac son (Langson); joined the Vietminh in June 1942. Minister of National Defence in Ho chi Minh's first government in 1945.

Comintern (also Communist International or Third International). Formed in Moscow in 1919 under Lenin and Trotsky's leadership, to unite the revolutionary socialists who broke with the Second International after its main parties supported their respective imperialist governments in the first world war.
In its early years, up to its Fourth Congress (1922), the Comintern was an authoritative international revolutionary leadership, but under Stalin became a tool of the Soviet bureaucracy (see Introduction).
The Comintern's annual congresses were replaced by show-piece events: after the Fifth Congress (1923) there was a five-year gap before the Sixth Congress (1928). At the Seventh Congress (1935), no word of criticism was spoken against Stalin's disastrous policies which had enabled Hitler to take power and crush the German workers; it was this that brought Trotsky — who until then had called his organisation a faction of the Comintern — to call for a new, Fourth International.

Communist League. The name of the French Trotskyist organisation 1930-1934.

Constitutionalist Party. Formed in 1923 by the landowner Bui quang Chieu and the journalist Nguyen phan Long, it represented the Vietnamese bourgeoisie. Demanded liberalisation and equality for Vietnamese officials under French rule and opposed demands for independence or social reforms; called for more powers for the Colonial Council, on which it won a majority in 1926. Its importance declined as the conflict between the French imperialists and the workers' movement grew.

Craipeau, Yvan (1911-) (real name Auger). Began his political activity in the Communist Youth, but was won to Trotskyism in 1930; entered the Socialist youth in the 'entryist' turn of 1934, was expelled in 1935, and remained a leading figure in the French section of the Fourth International through the second world war; left the Trotskyists in 1946.

Cuong De, prince (1882-1951). A rebel against French domination, he emigrated to Japan in 1906; sentenced to death in his absence in 1913, he remained in exile in Tokyo. Led the Phuc quoc (see below) in 1940-1945.

Dai Viet (Great Viet). Nationalist group founded by the novelist Nguyen truong Tam in northern Vietnam, under the Japanese occupation of 1940-1945. It continued activity after the war, with some of its members participating in the various imperialist-backed Saigon governments.

Dai viet quoc xa (National Socialist Great Viet). Nationalist group formed in northern Vietnam under the Japanese occupation of 1940-1945.

Daladier, Edouard (1884-1970). Radical prime minister of France 1933-1934. As prime minister again in 1938-1940, he signed the Munich pact with Hitler and in 1939 sanctioned the savage wave of repression in Indochina.

Dao hung Long. See Portraits of Some Vietnamese Revolutionaries, page 145.

d'Argenlieu, Admiral Georges Thierry (1884-1964). French high
commissioner to Indochina appointed in August 1945; the following
year he organised with French colonists to try to sabotage an
agreement between France and Ho chi Minh.

de Gaulle, Charles (1890-1970). Right-wing leader of the 'Free French'
resistance to the Nazis 1940-1945. From his base in Algeria, he made
steps towards contacting both Decoux, the Vichy-ite governor
general of Indochina, and various nationalist groups including the
Vietminh. Provisional president of France 1945-1946; returned to
the presidency in the political crisis of 1958.

Decoux, Admiral (1884-1963). French governor general of Indochina
under the Japanese occupation of 1940-1945, appointed by the
pro-Nazi government of Marshal Pétain. He drowned the Cochinchina peasant insurrection of 1940 in blood. To aid the Japanese war
economy, he established a monopoly over the collection of crops and
stockpiled rice — factors which contributed to the famine which
killed two million people in Tonkin and Annam in 1944-1945.

Dong duong cong san dang — see Parti Communiste Indochinois.

Dong minh hoi. A nationalist group, subsumed into the Viet cach when
the latter was formed in China in 1942.

Duong bach Mai (1905-1964). Returning from Comintern training in
Moscow, he participated in the Stalinist-Trotskyist *La Lutte* front
in 1935-1937. Organiser of the Stalinist secret police in Cochinchina
under Tran van Giau's government, he was directly responsible for
the massacre of the Trotskyists.

Duong van Giao (1894-1945). Lawyer and leader of the Constitutionalist Party in Saigon. Formed a 'Provisional Government of the
Republic of Vietnam' in September 1945; assassinated in the same
month on the orders of Tran van Giau's *de facto* government.

Fourth International. Formed by Trotsky and his supporters in 1938,
on the basis that the Stalinist Comintern had become the main
counter-revolutionary force in the workers' movement and that a
new revolutionary party was the primary need of the working class.
After the war, the tremendous pressure of Stalinism — of physical

repression on one hand and ideological pressure on the other — bore down on its leadership, which became increasingly inclined to politically look towards, and even liquidate into, the Stalinist parties. This was the chief cause of the split in the International in 1953, with the opponents of pro-Stalinist politics forming the International Committee of the Fourth International. After further splits and reunifications, groups emerging from the International Committee met in Budapest in 1989 to form a Workers International to Rebuild the Fourth International.

Frank, Pierre (1905-1984). One of the leading French Trotskyists in the 1930s. A chemist, Frank joined the Communist Party in 1925 and adhered to the Left Opposition from 1927; played a key role in the Trotskyists' work inside the Socialist Party in 1934-1935; expelled from the Trotskyist movement along with Raymond Molinier in 1936; in 1939-1940 he was first imprisoned for opposing the war and then exiled to Britain. After the war he became a leader of the United Secretariat of the Fourth International led by Ernest Mandel.

Ganofsky, Edgar. See Some Portraits of Vietnamese Revolutionaries, page 146.

Gitton, Marcel (1903-1941). Member of the French Communist Party's Central Committee, leader of its trade union work during the 'third period' and then of its colonial section; a specialist in attacks on Trotskyism. In 1937 signed the letter to the Vietnamese Stalinists instructing them to break up the La Lutte front; in 1939 quit the French Communist Party, and, accused of collaborating with the German fascists, he was executed by Communist Party partisans in 1941.

Godart, Justin. A Radical minister, he travelled to Indochina several times to represent the Popular Front government.

Guérin, Daniel (1904-1988). A print worker and member of the left wing of the French Socialists in the 1930s; left the party in 1938 with Marceau Pivert to form the Parti Socialiste d'Ouvrières et Paysans (Workers and Peasants Socialist Party) and lived in exile in Norway during the second world war. Author of several important political books (Negroes on the March, Fascism and Big Business, etc.), he remained active as a libertarian socialist after the war.

Guomindang. Chinese bourgeois nationalist party, founded by Sun Yat-sen in 1912. From the capture of Canton in 1917, fought against the feudal warlords for control of China; after Sun's death, the Guomindang established a strong government in Canton in 1925; ruthlessly put down workers' revolts in 1926-1927 and became the ruling party, establishing a nationalist government over all China in 1928. During the war against the Japanese (1937-1945), the Guomindang was allied with Mao Zedong's Red Army and supported the Vietminh. Mao broke this alliance in 1946 and went on to drive the Guomindang out of China, forming the 'people's republic' in 1949.

Ha huy Giap (1907-). Participated in the student agitation of 1925-1926 after the trial of Phan boi Chau, and was dismissed from high school; turned to communism 'all the more since the French forbid it'. Member of Young Annam and then the PCI; deported in 1933 to the Poulo Condore prison island, freed in 1936 under the Popular Front; imprisoned from 1937 until the Japanese coup of 9 March 1945. Served in the Hanoi government as Minister of National Education (1956-1963) and of Culture (1963-1976). Director of the Institute of History.

Hinh thai Thong. See Portraits of Some Vietnamese Revolutionaries, page 147.

Hitler, Adolf (1889-1945). Leader of the German Nazi (National Socialist) party which took power in 1933, crushed the workers' movement, organised the genocide of the Jewish population and whose policy of expansion resulted in the second world war.

Ho chi Minh (1890-1969) (real name Nguyen tat Thanh). Having joined the French Socialist party as a student in Paris, Ho sided with the communists when the party split at its Tours conference in 1920. Became the leading Vietnamese Stalinist; was sent to China by the Comintern in 1924 to work with Borodin; using the pseudonym Nguyen ai Quoc (Nguyen the patriot), set up the nationalist-'communist' Thanh nien; participated in the fiasco of the Canton 'commune' and then left for Moscow; in 1930 in Hong Kong organised the merger of the Thanh nien and two other groups to form the PCI. Living mostly in exile, he urged his followers in a letter from China in 1938 to 'politically exterminate' the Trotskyists, and in an interview with Daniel Guérin in 1946 justified their assassinations. During the war, aided by the Chinese Guomindang, Ho built up a guerrilla force which assimilated various nationalist organisations and became the Vietminh; marched into Hanoi in September 1945 to declare the 'Democratic Republic of Vietnam' of which he remained president until his death.

Ho huu Tuong. See Portraits of Some Vietnamese Revolutionaries, page 140.

Ho van Nga (1905-1945). One of the 19 expelled from France in 1930 after the demonstration against the death sentences at Yen Bay. A private teacher. Founder of the National Party for the Independence of Vietnam; assassinated by the Vietminh at Mytho.

Ho vinh Ky (?-1945). A woman doctor, married to Ho vinh Ky of the National Party for the Independence of Vietnam; founder of the Vanguard Women movement in July 1945; shot by the Vietminh, along with her husband, in October that year.

Hoa hao. A political-religious sect, founded in 1939 by Huynh phu So, which preached a renewed Buddhism made accessible to the poor. Won the following of hundreds of thousands of peasants in the west of Vietnam and in Cochinchina. Suppressed by the French government on account of its nationalism in 1940, the sect came under Japanese protection. In 1947, the faithful — whose leader had been assassinated by the Vietminh — rallied to French imperialism in its drive to reconquer Vietnam.

Hoang van Hoan (1905-1991). A native of Nghe An, emigrated to China in 1926; joined the Thanh nien of the future Ho chi Minh; ambassador of the Hanoi government to Peking 1950-1957; member of the National Assembly in Hanoi 1958-1973; ousted for opposition to the pro-Russian tendency of Le Duan in 1979, he took refuge in China.

Hoi kin Nguyen an Ninh (Nguyen an Ninh secret society). A clandestine peasant movement guided by Nguyen an Ninh's nationalism, active in 1928-1929.

Huynh phu So (1919-1947). Leader of the Hoa hao religious sect, assassinated by the Vietminh in 1947.

Huynh van Phuong. See Portraits of Some Vietnamese Revolutionaries, page 132.

Iida. Japanese cultural attaché, responsible for relations with the Saigon intelligentsia during the Japanese occupation of 1940-1945.

Indochinese Communist Party — see Parti Communiste Indochinois.

Indochinese Congress. Formed on the initiative of the *La Lutte* group in Vietnam in 1936, on the tide of workers' struggles which followed the election of the Popular Front government in France and with the support of hundreds of workers' action committees. In the name of the 'anti-imperialist united front' policy, the Constitutionalist Party members were invited to join; they did so demanding that workers' and peasants' delegates be limited to a quarter of the total; acceptance of this demand made the Congress virtually impotent. In September 1936 the action committees were suppressed by the French regime; the Congress was briefly revived in the 1937 strike wave under the name 'Central Committee for Demands'.

Indochinese Left Opposition (Dong duong cong san doi lap ta phai). Formed in 1929 in Paris as the Indochinese group of the International Left Opposition. It began activity in Vietnam after the deportation of its leaders by the French authorities in late 1930.

International Left Opposition. Formed by Trotsky and his supporters in April 1930, when the repression against the Trotskyists inside the USSR was reaching its height; although its members considered themselves a faction of the Comintern they were organised completely separately. Held its first congress in Paris in February 1933; later that year, when it decided to work to build a new, Fourth International, changed its name to the International Communist League.

Jourdain, Francis (1876-1958). Anarchist and anti-militarist who proclaimed his supported for the Russian revolution and was active in the workers' movement. Joined the Communist Party in 1946.

Khrushchev, Nikita (1894-1971). General secretary of the Communist Party of the Soviet Union and ruler of Russia 1953-1964, Khrushchev presided over a 'thaw' following the darkest days of Stalin's dictatorship. His secret speech to the 20th Congress of the party in February 1956 acknowledged the extreme excesses of Stalin's dictatorship, leading to a political 'thaw' inside the USSR and a deep crisis among Communist Party members internationally who had defended Stalin's record in the workers' movement.

La Lutte group. Formed in Saigon in 1933 as an alliance of Stalinists, Trotskyists and nationalists (see page 35), and known by the title of its paper *La Lutte*; in June 1936, the Stalinists, under instructions from the French Communist Party, and at the end of the day from Moscow, broke from the front (see page 49).
From June 1936, *La Lutte* was a Trotskyist paper and from November 1938 it was published in quoc ngu, under the title *Tranh dau*, which like *La Lutte* means *The Struggle*. Led by Ta thu Thau, it was a 'legal' group, concentrating firstly on participation in elections, publication of legal newspapers etc.; this was in contrast to the 'illegal' October group led by Ho huu Tuong, which gave primacy to building an underground organisation and producing illegal publications. Both groups adhered to the Fourth International.

Lao Nong group. Set up by the Stalinists in Paris in 1928, headed by Nguyen van Tao, to counter the influence of and/or infiltrate the Annamite Independence Party.

Laval, Pierre (1883-1945). French foreign minister 1934-1935, and prime minister 1935-1936. Laval devised France's non-aggression pact with the USSR in 1935 (the Stalin-Laval pact) which led the Vietnamese Stalinists to take an increasingly equivocal line towards the imperialist regime, and also the notorious Hoare-Laval pact to divide Abyssinia in 1936. Began his political career as a Socialist deputy during the first world war; broke with the Socialists to join the Radical party; ended up as the vice-premier of the pro-Nazi Vichy government; tried and shot after the war for collaborating with the Nazis.

Le quang Luong, alias Bich Khe. See Portraits of Some Vietnamese Revolutionaries, page 148.

Le van Thu. See Portraits of Some Vietnamese Revolutionaries, page 147.

Le van Vien, alias Bay Vien (1904-1970). A pirate chief from the hamlet of Binh Xuyen in Cholon. He and his men were signed up by Tran van Giau as police and bodyguards; later turned against the Vietminh, and would be awarded the Legion of Honour by the French in 1953.

Le van Vung. See Portraits of Some Vietnamese Revolutionaries, page 147.

League of Internationalist Communists for the Construction of the Fourth International. Founded in Saigon in 1934 by Lu sanh Hanh and Ho huu Tuong of the October group; the principal illegal Trotskyist organisation in Vietnam at the height of the movement's activity in the late 1930s. Broken up by repression in 1939, it was reconstituted as the League of Internationalist Communists by Lu sanh Hanh in 1945 and played a prominent part in that year's events.

Leclerc, General Jacques Philippe. French military commander in Indochina in 1945.

Left Opposition. Formed by Trotsky in 1923 to fight the bureaucratisation of the Communist Party of the Soviet Union under Stalin and the policy of 'socialism in one country'; suppressed by means of expulsions, imprisonment, exile and then shootings from 1926 onwards. See also International Left Opposition.

Lenin, Vladimir Ilyich (1871-1924). Leader of the Russian revolution and of the communist government it brought to power, until falling seriously ill in 1922. Organiser of the Russian Social Democrats from the late 1890s; pressed home the split with the Menshevik (reformist) wing of the party from 1903 and continued as the main theoretician and organiser of Bolshevism.

Ligue francaise contre l'oppression coloniale et l'impérialisme (French League Against Colonial Oppression and Imperialism). Protest organisation of French intellectuals, active in the 1920s and 1930s.

Li Jishen (1886-1959). A leading figure in the Guomindang; governor of Kwangtung during the Northern Expedition of 1926-1927; headed a rebellion against Chiang Kai-shek in 1933-1934 but remained as a military leader afterwards.

Lu sanh Hanh. See Portraits of Some Vietnamese Revolutionaries, page 143.

Mandel, Georges (1885-1944). French minister for the colonies in Daladier's second government (1938-1940).

Marx, Karl (1818-1883). German revolutionary thinker; the founder, together with Frederick Engels, of scientific socialism, which has since born the name Marxism.

Molinier, Raymond (1904-). A founder of the Communist League, the French Trotskyist organisation, in 1929. A close collaborator of Trotsky until 1935, when he was expelled for publishing his own newspaper independently of the party; went into exile in 1939 and lived in Argentina until he returned to Paris in the 1980s.

Molotov, Vyacheslav Mikhailovich (1890-1986). A Bolshevik from 1906; Stalin's chief spokesperson in the Comintern in 1928-1929; chair of the USSR's Council of People's Commissars 1930-1941; foreign minister 1938-1949; part of the triumvirate that headed the USSR immediately after Stalin's death; was pushed out of power with the accession of Khrushchev in 1956.

Moutet, Marius. Minister for the colonies in the French Popular Front government formed by Leon Blum in June 1936. Exemplified those 'socialists' who serve imperialism: having established a reputation as an opponent of colonial repression over 30 years, participating in the League for the Rights of Man, the Amnesty Committee for Indochina (1933) etc., as minister for the colonies he sanctioned the repression of the workers' movement of 1936-1937, insisting only that the repression be 'legal and legitimate'. Returned as minister for the colonies after the war, in the governments headed by the right-wing Socialist Paul Ramadier and the conservative Georges Bidault; in December 1945, after the Saigon rebellion had been drowned in blood, wrote an article calling for continued French occupation of Indochina in order to 'impart an honourable meaning to the word colonialism'.

National Party for the Independence of Vietnam. A nationalist group, one of the components of the short-lived National United Front in Cochinchina.

National United Front. Formed in Saigon on 14 August 1945 — after the surrender of Japan and the collapse of its authority in Vietnam — with the stated object of creating an independent Vietnamese state; supported by various nationalist groups, including the Vanguard Youth, Cao dai and Hoa hao; liquidated it into the Vietminh by its leaders on 23 August.

Naville, Pierre (1904-1993). Having been won to Trotskyism along with a group of surrealists around the paper *Clarté*, Naville was a founder of the Communist League in 1929 and one of its leaders through the 1930s; split with the majority of the French Trotskyists in 1934, as he was opposed to joining the Socialist party, reuniting with them in 1935; broke with Trotskyism after the war.

Ngo chinh Phen. See Portraits of Some Vietnamese Revolutionaries, page 147.

Ngo dinh Diem (1901-1963). President of South Vietnam from 1955 to his death. An anti-communist nationalist, born into a Catholic family at Hue, he returned to Vietnam from exile in 1954 to become prime minister under emperor Bao Dai, whom he ousted the following year in a referendum; rejected the formula agreed at the 1954 Geneva convention for all-Vietnamese elections and worked with the American imperialists; overthrown and murdered by his own generals in 1963.

Ngo gia Tu (1908-1935). Joined the Thanh nien in 1926, and formed its Tonkin committee; split in June 1929 and formed the first Indochinese Communist Party. Arrested in Saigon in May 1930 and deported to Poulo Condore in 1933. He escaped in 1935 but disappeared at sea.

Nguyen ai Quoc. See Ho chi Minh.

Nguyen an Ninh (1900-1943). Drawn to nationalism and anarchism in 1920 when he began studying law in Paris, he joined the Group of Annamite Patriots and the Intercolonial Union, published a pamphlet against the French domination of Indochina. Returned to Saigon in 1923 and was tried and convicted in 1926, an event which itself gave renewed impetus to nationalist feeling.

Nguyen hai Than, alias Nguyen cam Giang (1878-). Nationalist who emigrated to China in 1912; sentenced to death in his absence for 'terrorism' in 1913; president of the Viet cach, created in 1942 on the initiative of the Chinese general Zhang Fakui; returned to Tonkin in 1945 with Chinese troops, and left again in 1946 the same way. A rival of Ho chi Minh, he would participate in a sham 'national unity' in the latter's government.

Nguyen hoa Hiep (c. 1900-). Former student of the Whampoa military academy in Canton; imprisoned in 1928-1929 after the so-called affair of the Nguyen an Ninh Society; joined the VNQDD and in 1945 headed an armed group, independent of the Vietminh, to oppose reconquest by imperialism.

Nguyen the Truyen (1898-1969). Chemical engineer, a founder of the Annamite Independence Party in Paris 1926; worked politically together with Phan chau Trinh, Nguyen an Ninh, Nguyen ai Quoc and Phan van Truong in Paris in the 1920s and returned to Saigon in 1928.

Nguyen thi Anh. See Portraits of Some Vietnamese Revolutionaries, page 148.

Nguyen thi Loi. See Portraits of Some Vietnamese Revolutionaries, page 148.

Nguyen tuong Tam (alias Nhat Linh) (1905-1963). Writer and journalist, founder of the Dai Viet in 1939. Went into exile in China in 1942, and returned to Hanoi in 1945 with the Chinese army; represented the VNQDD in March 1946 in Ho chi Minh's second government; opposed to the Franco-Vietnamese agreement of 6 March 1946, he left the country with Chinese troops. He committed suicide in Saigon after being arrested by the Ngo dinh Diem regime.

Nguyen van Cu. See Portraits of Some Vietnamese Revolutionaries, page 148.

Nguyen van Linh. See Portraits of Some Vietnamese Revolutionaries, page 144.

Nguyen van So. See Portraits of Some Vietnamese Revolutionaries, page 138.

Nguyen van Tao (1908-1970). Stalinist, member of the colonial section of the French Communist Party from 1930; participated in the *La Lutte* front 1933-1937; commissar of the interior in Tran van Giau's government. Later, Ho chi Minh's minister of labour.

Nguyen van Thieu (1924-). An army colonel under the regime of Ngo dinh Diem (1956-1963), Thieu participated in its overthrow and, with the blessing of the US, became president of South Vietnam (1967-1975). On the fall of Saigon he fled to Formosa and then to Britain.

October group. Named after the theoretical journal *Thang Muoi (October)*, published between August 1931 and March 1932 in Saigon, and adopted as the official journal of the Indochinese Left Opposition. Ho huu Tuong and his closest collaborators continued to be known as the October group (although due to repression the names of their publications constantly changed); at the end of 1933 they formed, together with Lu sanh Hanh and others, the League of Internationalist Communists for the Construction of the Fourth International; in 1938 *Thang muoi* re-appeared briefly before being repressed again. For details of the October group's differences with the *La Lutte* group, see Ho huu Tuong's biography in Portraits of Some Vietnamese Revolutionaries (page 140).

Parti Communiste Indochinois (PCI) (Dong duong cong san dang). Founded in 1930 by Ho chi Minh, following Comintern instructions, at a congress in Hong Kong which united the Thanh nien and two other groups. Officially dissolved in November 1945 as a manoeuvre by Ho to make a new deal with the bourgeois nationalist parties; continued its activity and was refounded as the Lao Dong (Workers Party) in 1951.

Pasquier, Pierre. French governor general of Indochina 1928-1934.

PCI. See Parti Communiste Indochinois.

Péri, Gabriel (1902-1941). A leading figure in the French Communist Party; general secretary of its youth section in the 1920s; later editor of its paper *L'Humanité* and a parliamentary deputy — in which capacity he headed a commission to inquire into French repression in Indochina in 1934. Left the Communist Party in 1939; betrayed in 1941 to the Nazis, who shot him.

Pétain, Marshal Henri (1856-1951). Became French premier in June 1940 and immediately concluded a peace with Germany; set up a pro-Nazi government at Vichy which closely collaborated with the German Nazis and collapsed as the German armies retreated in 1944.

Pham ngoc Thach (1909-1968). Doctor of medicine, nationalist. Leader of the Vanguard Youth, which he took into the Vietminh at a crucial moment in August 1945 (see page 87); this helped Tran van Giau to form his *de facto* government, in which Thach served as commissar of foreign affairs. From the formation of Ho chi Minh's first government, a minister in Hanoi.

Pham van Dong (1906-). Member of Thanh nien and then the PCI. Ho chi Minh's Prime Minister from 1955, after the Geneva talks; at the end of the 1980s, when the highest strata of the bureaucracy were thrown into a ferocious internal struggle, he made the complaint that he had didn't have any power.

Phan boi Chau (1867-1940). Nationalist writer, who, together with prince Cuong De, aspired to use Japanese support in order to drive the French from Indochina and establish a constitutional monarchy. A founder of the League for Modernisation (Duy Tan); went into exile with Cuong De in 1905 and was condemned to death in his absence by the French in 1913; arrested in Shanghai in 1925 and returned to Hanoi; sentenced to hard labour for life; pardoned by governor Varenne, he lived in Hue under a compulsory residence order until his death.

Phan chau Trinh (1872-1926). A scholar, condemned to death at the time of the peasant demonstrations in Annam in 1908; deported to Poulo Condore; freed in 1911 after the intervention of the League for the Rights of Man in France; lived in exile in Paris from then until 1925; died in 1926 in Saigon, where his funeral turned into a popular anti-colonialist demonstration.

Phan hieu Kinh (1904-). Engineer, graduate of the Engineering School of Marseille; having escaped the general massacre of the Trotskyists by the Stalinists in 1945, from 1 December 1946 he republished *La Lutte*, which was banned after four issues.

Phan van Chanh. See Portraits of Some Vietnamese Revolutionaries, page 131.

Phan van Hum. See Portraits of Some Vietnamese Revolutionaries, page 136.

Phuc quoc (National Restoration). A monarchist nationalist organisation led by prince Cuong De, a descendant of the Vietnamese emperors.

Phuc viet. See Annamite Independence Party.

Ramadier, Paul. A French politician on the extreme right of the Socialist party; prime minister of the conservative-Socialist-Communist coalition formed in January 1947.|

Rassemblement Colonial (Assembly of the Colonised). Set up under the French Popular Front government of 1936 by immigrant workers from the French colonies in Paris, to protest at the continued imperialist oppression of their homelands.

Resistance Veterans. Formed in 1987 by veteran high-ranking commanders of the Vietminh, as a means of voicing the dissent of one section of the bureaucracy, as economic crisis and the disintegration of the ruling bureaucracy of the USSR threw the Vietnamese leadership into crisis.

Roosevelt, Franklin D. (1882-1945). President of the United States 1933-1945, a leader of the imperialist Allies.

Rosenthal, Gérard (1903-1992). Joined the Trotskyists in the 1920s together with Pierre Naville and his circle of surrealist artists, and worked as Trotsky's lawyer in France.

Rosmer, Alfred (1877-1964). A French revolutionary syndicalist who came to the fore of workers' movements against the first world war;

after the Russian revolution he joined the Comintern and was elected to its Executive Committee in 1920; expelled from the French Communist Party after supporting the Left Opposition in 1924; worked until 1930 on the Secretariat of the International Left Opposition, but withdrew on account of political differences; renewed a personal friendship with Trotsky in 1936.

Roubaud, Louis. French writer, member of the Amnesty Committee for Indochina (1933), the Rassemblement Colonial and other anti-colonialist organisations.

Sainteny, Jean. A former bank clerk in Hanoi, sent to negotiate with Ho chi Minh on de Gaulle's behalf in 1945.

Second International. Formed in 1889, after the collapse of the First International, by the large European socialist parties. Its history was one of rapid expansion in its first decade, as the workers' movement flowered, and of the degeneration of its leadership into reformism and pro-imperialism. The outbreak of the first world war in August 1914 destroyed the wordy 'internationalism' of the Second International; its main parties supported their respective imperialist government's war drive; its revolutionary wing broke to form the Third International in 1919.

Stalin, Joseph (1879-1953). General Secretary of the Communist Party of the Soviet Union from 1922 to his death and leader of the bureaucracy which took political power from the working class in the Soviet state and destroyed the Comintern as a revolutionary force, turning it into a reactionary tool of Soviet foreign policy.

Sun Yat-sen (1866-1925). Founder of the Chinese bourgeois nationalist party, the Guomindang; leader of the 1911 revolution.

Ta doi Lap. See Indochinese Left Opposition.

Ta thu Thau. See Portraits of Some Vietnamese Revolutionaries, page 122.

Tan Viet, or Tan Viet cach mang dang (Revolutionary Party of the New Viet). An underground nationalist movement formed in Annam in July 1925.

Thanh nien, or Thanh nien cach mang dong chi hoi (Association of Comrades of Revolutionary Youth). An underground nationalist movement formed in Canton in July 1925 on the initiative of Ho chi Minh and the Stalinists.

Thanh niem tien phong. See Vanguard Youth.

Third International. See Comintern.

Tia sang group. A Trotskyist group active in Tonkin in the late 1930s, closely linked to the October group which was based in Saigon. Named after its paper *Tia Sang (Spark)*.

Ton duc Thang (1888-1980). Born at Longxuyen; a sailor on a French warship, he was asked by his shipmates during a mutiny on the Black Sea in 1919 to hoist the red flag; back in Saigon as a worker, he joined the Thanh nien; deported to Poulo Condore after the Rue Barbier killing in December 1928 (see page 9); became president of the Vietnamese republic after the death of Ho chi Minh.

Tranh dau group. See *La Lutte* group.

Tran dinh Minh. See Portraits of Some Vietnamese Revolutionaries, page 146.

Tran trong Kim (1882-1953). Nationalist, teacher; formed a government — without any real power — under Bao Dai after the Japanese coup of 9 March 1945; resigned on 14 August 1945, the day before the Japanese capitulation.

Tran van Giau (1911-). A leading figure in the PCI in Cochinchina, organiser of the Stalinists' seizure of power in Saigon in August 1945 and one of the instigators of the repression of the Trotskyists in the weeks that followed.

Tran van Si. See Portraits of Some Vietnamese Revolutionaries, page 139.

Tran van Thach. See Portraits of Some Vietnamese Revolutionaries, page 133.

Trotsky, Leon (1879-1940). Leader, with Lenin, of the Russian revolution and the Bolshevik government; founder of the Red Army; led the struggle against the rise of the Stalinist bureaucracy within the USSR (from which he was expelled in 1929) and internationally; after the debacle which led to Hitler's victory in 1933, called for a new International, the Fourth, which was formed in 1938; killed by a Stalinist agent in August 1940.

Truman, Harry (1884-1972). President of the United States 1944-1952.

Truong boi Cong (circa 1880-). Vietnamese nationalist, exiled to China, former officer in the Guomindang army, he was a leading light in the political bureau of the Viet cach of Nguyen hai Than.

Truong Chinh (1907-1988). General secretary of the PCI from 1941. Responsible for dealing with the peasant revolt which erupted in response to the blind, brutal agrarian reform policy, in Nghe an in November 1956, which was suppressed with 16,000 shootings.

United Revolutionary Party of the Annamite people. One of the small nationalist groups which emerged with Japanese support in 1940-1945.

Vanguard Youth (Thanh niem tien phong). Headed by Doctor Pham ngoc Thach, formed under the Japanese occupation out of the remains of the pro-Vichy Youth and Sports organisation. The Vanguard Youth's defection to the Vietminh at a critical moment in August 1945 in Saigon smoothed the Stalinists' path to power in the city.

Viet cach. (Full name, Viet nam cach menh dong minh hoi; Vietnam Revolutionary League). A union of Vietnamese nationalist groups, formed in October 1942 in China at the behest of the Guomindang general, Zhang Fakui, with Nguyen hai Than as its figurehead. After returning to Vietnam with Chinese troops in 1945, its leaders participated in various of Ho chi Minh's so-called coalition governments.

Vietminh. Shortened name of the Viet nam doc lap dong minh hoi (Alliance for the Independence of Vietnam), the political-military organisation of the Parti Communiste Indochinois, founded in 1940 on the Chinese border. In co-operation with the Guomindang generals, the Vietminh mobilised a guerrilla force, with which Ho chi Minh was able to take power in August 1945. See pages 78-80.

Viet nam ai quoc (Patriotic Viet). Nationalist group formed with Japanese support in 1940-1945.

Viet nam cach manh dong minh hoi — see Viet cach.

Viet nam doc lap dong minh hoi — see Vietminh (the shortened name by which it became known).

Viet nam phuc quoc — See Phuc quoc.

Viet nam quoc dan dang or VNQDD (National Party of Vietnam). Nationalist movement, formed in Tonkin in December 1927. Instigated the Yen Bay revolt of February 1930 and was broken up by the bloody repression that followed it.

VNQDD. See Viet nam quoc dan dang.

Vo nguyen Giap (1911-). Central committee member of the PCI, minister of defence in Ho chi Minh's government from 1954. While the victory over French and American imperialism was attributed to him, the holocaust of millions of unknown combatants was forgotten.

Vu hong Khanh (circa 1900-). One of the leaders of the VNQDD; exiled to Yunnan after the Yen Bay putsch in 1930, he returned to Hanoi in September 1945 with the Chinese army. Vice-minister in the second government of Ho chi Minh, formed in March 1946, he signed the Franco-Vietnamese agreement of 6 March 1946 with Ho chi Minh; fled to China in June 1946 when Chinese troops were pulled out of Tonkin.

Young Annam. A short-lived group of young nationalist intellectuals, formed in Saigon in 1926, whose participants included Ta thu Thau, Ha huy Giap, Trinh hung Ngau and others.

Zhang Fakui (1896-) One of the Guomindang's foremost generals; commander of its Fourth Army during the 1926 Northern Expedition; led the suppression of the Nanchang uprising 1927; during the war he was military governor of Guangxi, in which capacity he prepared to move Guomindang troops into north Vietnam and was sought out as an ally by Ho chi Minh; retired to Hong Kong 1949.

BOOKS, JOURNALS AND ARTICLES
QUOTED IN THE TEXT

AOM is used throughout the text to refer to the French Archives Nationales, Section d'Outre Mer

BDIC is used to refer to the Bibliothèque Documentaire Internationale Contemporaine at Nanterre University, Paris

CHEAM is the Centre des Hautes Études sur l'Afrique et l'Asie modernes

Anh Van and Roussel, Jacqueline, *Mouvements Nationaux et Lutte de Classes au Vietnam* (Fourth International Publications, Paris, 1947). Published in English as *National movements and class struggle in Vietnam*, (New Park, London, 1987).

Bauchar, R., *Rafales sur l'Indochine* (Paris, 1946).

Ba Phuong Lang, *Nha cach mang Ta thu Thau 1906-45* (*The Revolutionary Ta thu Thau 1906-1945*) (Saigon, 1974).

Boudarel, Georges, *La bureaucratie au Vietnam* (*The bureaucracy in Vietnam*) (Paris, 1983).

Brandt, Conrad, Schwarz, Benjamin and Fairbank, John K, *A Documentary History of Chinese Communism*, (Harvard University Press, Cambridge, Mass., US, 1952).

Brocheux, Pierre et al., *L'Indochine francaise 1940-45: textes rassemblés par Paul Isoart*, (Presses Universitaires de France, Paris, 1982).

Broué, Pierre, and Stobnicer, Maurice, Contributions à l'histoire du trotskysme en Allemagne (*Les Cahiers du Centre d'Études et de Recherches sur les Mouvements Trotskyste et Révolutionnaires internationaux*, no. 29, June 1983).

Buttinger, Joseph, *Vietnam: A Dragon Embattled* (New York, 1967).

Chaffard, Georges, *Les deux guerres du Vietnam* (*The two Vietnam wars*) (Paris 1969).

Chesneaux, Jean, *Contribution à l'histoire de la nation vietnamienne* (*Contribution to the history of the Vietnamese Nation*) (Paris, 1955).

Chroniques Vietnamiennes, Paris, 1987-

Degras, Jane, ed., *The Communist International 1919-1943, Documents* (Oxford University Press, 1956-1971).

Devillers, Philippe, *Histoire du Vietnam de 1940 à 1952* (Paris, 1952).

Devillers, Philippe, *Paris-Saigon-Hanoi* (Paris, 1988).
Engels, Frederick, *The Peasant War in Germany* (Progress Publishers, Moscow, 1956).
Franchini, P., *Continental Saigon* (Paris, 1977).
Godart, Justin, *Rapport au ministre des Colonies* (*Report to the Minister for the Colonies*), 10 March 1937 (AOM, Papiers Moutet PA28).
Guérin, Daniel, *Au service des colonisés 1930-1953 (At the Service of the Colonised)* (Paris, 1954).
Ha huy Giap, article in *Dac san* (Saigon, August 1987).
Hémery, Daniel, *Révolutionnaires vietnamiens et pouvoir colonial en Indochine (Vietnamese revolutionaries and colonial power in Indochina)* (Maspero, Paris, 1975).
Hertrich, J. M., *Doc lap!* (Paris, 1946).
Hessel, Bertil, 'Introduction', *Theses, Resolutions and Manifestos of the First Four Congresses of the Third International* (Ink Links, London, 1980).
Hoang van Hoan, *Giot nuoc trong bien ca (A Drop of Water in the Ocean)* (Peking, 1986).
Huynh kim Khanh, *Vietnamese Communism 1925-1945* (Cornell University Press, Ithaca, US, 1982).
Isaacs, Harold, *The Tragedy of the Chinese Revolution* (Secker and Warburg, London, 1938).
Isoart, Paul, *L'Indochine francaise 1940-45* (Paris, 1982).
La Lutte Group, 'La Revolution d'aout 1945 et le group de "*La Lutte*" (Quatrième Internationale)' ('The August 1945 Revolution and the "*La Lutte*" group (Fourth International)'), Archives of the Unified Secretariat of the Fourth International, BDIC Fo 455 (April 1948).
La Lutte des Classes, ed. P. Naville (Paris, 1929-1935).
Lautréamont, *Les Chants de Maldoror* (G.F. Flammarion, Paris,1990).
Lenin, V.I., *Collected Works* (Progress Publishers, Moscow, 1973).
Liu khanh Thinh, *Doan cong binh Khang chien (The Workers' Militia in the resistance)*, (duplicated, Paris 1947).
Lu sanh Hanh, 'Quelques Étapes de la Révolution au Nam-bo du Vietnam' ('Some Stages of the Revolution in the South of Vietnam'), written under the pseudonym 'Lucien', *Quatrième Internationale* (Paris, September-October 1947). See Appendix 1, page 150.
Mao Zedong, *Selected Works* (English edn.) (Foreign Languages Press, Peking, 1967).
Nguyen ky Nam, *Hoi ky 1945-54 (Memoirs 1945-54)* (Saigon, 1964).
Pedrazzani, J. M., *La France en Indochine, de Catroux à Sainteny* (Paris, 1972).

Peng Shuzhi, *The Chinese Communist Party in Power* (Monad Press, New York, 1980).

Pirani, Simon, *Vietnam and Trotskyism* (Communist League, Australia, 1987).

Roubaud, Louis, *Vietnam* (Librairie Valois, Paris, 1931).

Rubel, Maximilien, 'Le socialisme réellement inexistant' ('Really non-existent socialism'), *Le Monde* (Paris, 17 September 1980).

Savani, A.M., *Le Caodaisme* (CHEAM, Paris, 1966).

Socialist Workers Party Education Department, *Towards a History of the Fourth International* (New York, 1974).

Tap chi cong san, 2, (Hanoi, 1983).

Tasteyre, B., *La Revolution d'aout 1945 en Cochinchine (The August 1945 Revolution in Cochinchina)* (Doctoral Thesis, Paris, 1978).

Trager, Frank (ed.), *Marxism in South East Asia: A Study of Four Countries* (Stanford University Press, Stanford, US, 1960).

Tran van Giau, *Giai cap cong nhan Viet nam (The working class of Vietnam)* (Hanoi, 1958).

Tran van Giau, article in *Tuoi tre* (Saigon, 27 October 1988).

Trotsky, Leon, *Diary in Exile* (London, 1958).

Trotsky, Leon, *The Permanent Revolution and Results and Prospects* (New Park, London, 1962).

Trotsky, Leon, *In Defence of Marxism* (New Park, London, 1971).

Trotsky, Leon, *Writings of Leon Trotsky 1930-31* (Pathfinder Press, New York, 1973).

Trotsky, Leon, *The Third International After Lenin* (New Park, London, 1974a).

Trotsky, Leon, *Whither France?* (London, New Park, 1974b).

Trotsky, Leon, *On China*, with introduction by Peng Shu-tse (Monad Press, New York, 1976).

Trotsky, Leon, *The History of the Russian Revolution* (Pluto Press, London, 1977).

Truong Chinh, *Chien tranh Thai binh duong va cach mang giai phong dan toc Dong duong (The war in the Pacific and the liberating revolution of the peoples of Indochina)* (1942).

Trung Chinh, 'Thu tim xem Ho Chu tich tiep thu chu nghia le nin va truyen ba vao Viet Nam nhu the nao' ('How President Ho assimilated Leninism and applied it in Vietnam'), in *Nghien cuu lich su (Historical Studies)* (Hanoi, 1970).

Van, N., 'Un procès de Moscou dans le maquis de Ho chi Minh', ('A Moscow Trial in Ho chi Minh's guerrilla movement') in the Archives of the United Secretariat of the Fourth International, BDIC, Fo 445.

Vietnam State Publishing House, *Cach mang thang tam (The August Revolution)* (Hanoi, 1960).

Vietnam State Publishing House, *Nhung su kien lich su Dang (Material relating to party history)* (Hanoi, 1976).

Vietnam State Publishing House, *Giai cap cong nhan Viet Nam thoi ky 1936-1939* (The working class in Vietnam in the 1936-1939 period), (Hanoi, 1979).

Viollis, A, *Indochine SOS*, (Paris, 1935).

Warbey, William, *Ho chi Minh and the Struggle for an Independent Vietnam* (Merlin Press, London, 1972).

Werner, Yane, *The Cao Dai, the Politics of a Vietnamese Syncretic Religious Movement* (Cornell University, 1976).

Index quốc ngữ
Vietnamese names and expressions used in the text

Chu văn Tấn

Dân chúng

Dân mới

Dân nguyện

Dân quyền

Doãn

Dương bạch Mai

Dương văn Giáo

Dương văn Tư

Dương văn Tương

Đả đảo đế quốc quan làng địa chủ chia đất cho dân cày nghèo

Đại Việt

Đại Việt quốc xã

Đan phượng

Đảng dân xã

Đảng thợ thuyền xã hội

Đoàn công binh kháng chiến

Đoàn kết giai cấp

Đoàn thể cộng sản quốc tế chủ nghĩa, phái tán thành đệ tứ quốc tế

Đoàn văn Trương

Đồ lương

Đông dương đại hội

Đông dương cộng sản đảng

Đông dương cộng sản đối lập tả phái

Đồng minh hội

Đồng nai

Đông phương

Đuốc Nhà nam

Đuốc vô sản

Đức hòa

Đức phổ

Đường kách mệnh

Gia định

Giai cấp công nhân Việt nam thời kỳ 1936-1939

Giọt nước trong biển cả

Hà huy Giáp

Hà huy Tập

Hà tĩnh

Hải dương

Hình thái Thông

Hoa Nam công tác đoàn

Hoa quân nhập Việt

Hòa đồng

Hòa hảo

Hoàng đôn Vân

Hoàng quang Gịu

Hoàng quốc Việt

Hoàng thế Công

Hoàng văn Hoan

Hóc môn

Hòn gay

Hồ hữu Tường

Hồ Quang

Hồ tá Khanh

Hồ tùng Mậu

Hồ văn Ngà

Hồ vĩnh Ký

Hội kín Nguyễn an Ninh

Hồn trẻ

Hồng Sơn

hộp quẹt Đệ tam

Huyện bộ

Huỳnh phú Sổ

Huỳnh phú Mậu

Huỳnh tấn Phát

INDEX

action committees (1936), 44-46, 47-49, 64,
135, 144; see also people's committees
Algiers Declaration, 81, 84, 103, 185
Amsterdam Congress Against Imperialist
War, 33, 144, 179-180
Anchorites, 94
An nam cong san dang, 12
Annam, 3, 48, 72; peasant movement of
1930-1931, 24; Tran trong Kim
government, 93
Annamite Independence Party, 14-15, 16,
123-124, 131, 132, 133, 197
Anti-Imperialist League, 124, 133, 137, 197
anti-imperialist united front, 100-101, 158,
186-187
Association Mutuelle des Indochinois de
Paris, 134, 144
Avant-Garde, L' (The Vanguard), 50-51, 127

Ba De, 90-91
*Bao cong nong (Workers and Peasants
Journal)*, 6
Bao Dai, 86, 88, 94, 143, 168, 197
Bidault, Georges, 174, 197
Blum, Léon, 42, 47, 50, 127, 197
Bo xuan Luat, 81
Bolshevik-Leninist Group for the
Construction of the Fourth
International, 45, 53, 141, 148, 198; see
also October group
Bolshevik-Leninists of the Fourth
International, 60, 61, 198
Bolsheviks, x, 76, 198
Bon se vich (Bolshevik), 11, 12
Borodin, Mikhail, 4, 198
Brévié, Jules, 46, 55, 122, 128, 198
Bui quang Chieu, 116
Bui Tin, 120
Bukharin, Nikolai, 9, 30, 198
Bua liem (Hammer and Sickle), 11
Bui dong, 34
Bui duy Tu, 60
Buttinger, Joseph, 1

Cach mang (Revolution), 60
*Cach mang thuong truc (Permanent
Revolution)*, 37
*Cahiers du bolchevisme (Bolshevik
Notebooks)*, 33
Cambodia, 48, 65, 72, 86
Cao dai, 73, 74, 86, 94, 104, 114, 152, 198
Cédile, Jean, 103, 112, 115, 199
Challaye, Felicien, 124, 192

China, 4; revolution of 1925-1927, ix,
xii-xv, 7, 18, 21, 29, 124; 'Canton
commune' (1927), xiv, 7-9, 77; second
world war, 92
Chennault, General, 84
Chesneaux, Jean, 1, 133
Chi Quy, 114
Chiang kai-Shek, xiii, 7, 65, 80, 199
Chien dau (Combat), 90, 130
Chinh tru tuan bao (Political Weekly), 57
Chu van Tan, 81, 84, 199
Churchill, Winston, 92, 199
Civil Servants Federation, 94, 96
Cloche fêlée, La (The Cracked Clock), 3, 15,
123
Co cong San (Communist Flag), 11
Co de (Red Flag), 146
Co giai phong (Banner of Liberation), 102
Cochinchina: Colonial Council elections
(1935), 36, 126; (1939), 57-59, 128, 131,
135, 137, 139, 183; peasant revolt
(1930-1931), 23; (1940) 65-71;
autonomous republic of (1945), 117-118
Cochinchinese Association of Annamite
Journalists, 53
Comintern (Communist International or
Third International), xi, xiii-xvi, 4, 5, 7,
9-10, 12, 18, 19, 21-22, 32, 36, 42, 43,
54, 59, 89, 124, 126, 142, 177, 180, 185,
187-188, 193, 199; 'third period', 7, 10,
13, 25, 65, 187; congresses: fifth, 4;
sixth, 9, 15, 25, 187; seventh, 43, 126,
142, 193; dissolution of, 90
Commission of Inquiry into Indochina
(1935), 43, 46
Committee for the Defence and Amnesty of
the Indochinese and Colonised Peoples,
see Amnesty Committee
Communist League (China), 118
Communist League (France), 16, 18, 20,
137, 140, 200
Communist League of Baclieu, 134
Communist Party, Chinese, xii-xiv, 4, 5, 7,
21, 29, 76, 79, 80, 184-185
Communist Party, French, 2, 13, 15, 18, 34
36, 42, 43, 49-50, 61, 83, 123, 127, 139,
145, 174-175
Communist Party, German, 33
Communist Party, Indochinese, see Parti
Communiste Indochinois
Communist Party, Vietnamese (1929), 12;
(1954-), 2, 4
Communist Party of the Soviet Union, xii, 7